PENGUIN BO
BEYOND LION

Gavin Young spent most of his you
Wales. He studied modern history at Oxford University and spent
two years with a shipping company in Basra, Iraq, before setting out
to live in wilder places – first, with the Marsh Arabs in southern
Iraq between the Tigris and Euphrates rivers, then with the
people of the plains and mountains of south-western Arabia. From
Tunis he joined the *Observer* as a foreign correspondent in 1960
and subsequently covered fifteen wars and revolutions throughout
the world. He has also been the *Observer* correspondent in Paris
and in New York.

Gavin Young's first book, *Return to the Marshes* (1977, Penguin
1989), describes his adventures in Iraq with the Marsh Arabs, who
inhabit the ancient land of Sumer and Babylonia, and was the basis
of a BBC film in 1979. His second book, *Iraq: Land of Two Rivers*,
an account of a journey through the historic landscape of
Mesopotamia, was published in 1980. Gavin Young then travelled
round the world by whatever waterborne transport he could find at
the time. The story of that extraordinary voyage was told in his
next two bestselling books, *Slow Boats to China* (1981, Penguin
1983) and *Slow Boats Home* (1985, Penguin 1986). *Worlds Apart*
(1987, Penguin 1988) is a collection of pieces, most of them written
for the *Observer*, that summon up more than twenty years of travel
and adventure in some of the world's most remote and exciting
places.

Gavin Young is a Fellow of the Royal Society of Literature.

BEYOND LION ROCK

The Story of Cathay Pacific Airways

Gavin Young

A great hill dominates Hong Kong's
Kai Tak Airport. The shifting light
seems to give it a life of its own and
the Chinese call it Lion Rock.

PENGUIN BOOKS

PENGUIN BOOKS

Published by the Penguin Group
27 Wrights Lane, London W8 5TZ, England
Viking Penguin Inc., 40 West 23rd Street, New York, New York 10010, USA
Penguin Books Australia Ltd, Ringwood, Victoria, Australia
Penguin Books Canada Ltd, 2801 John Street, Markham, Ontario, Canada L3R 1B4
Penguin Books (NZ) Ltd, 182–190 Wairau Road, Auckland 10, New Zealand

Penguin Books Ltd, Registered Offices: Harmondsworth, Middlesex, England

First published by Hutchinson Ltd, an imprint of Century Hutchinson Ltd, 1988
Published in Penguin Books 1990
1 3 5 7 9 10 8 6 4 2

Made and printed in Great Britain by
Richard Clay Ltd, Bungay, Suffolk

Contents

TO

JOCK SWIRE
ROY FARRELL
SYDNEY DE KANTZOW
'BETSY'
and all the others
who made Cathay Pacific what it is

Dear Dad.

Thanc for all the support throughout the years.

I hope you find this book as interesting as i did.

Love Jaz.

This air business is certainly terrifying and they talk the most fantastic figures.

'JOCK' SWIRE:
Letter from Hong Kong to London
just before buying Cathay Pacific
for £175,000

An aviator's life may be full of ups and downs, but the only hard thing about it is the ground.

C. KINGSFORD-SMITH
Australian aviation pioneer

The author [brings out] a paradoxical truth of considerable psychological importance: that man's happiness lies not in freedom but in acceptance of a duty.

ANDRÉ GIDE:
Preface to *Night Flight* (*Vol de Nuit*)
by Antoine de Saint-Exupéry

Acknowledgements

When the idea of writing this history was first put to me I had my doubts. I knew next to nothing about aviation, nothing at all about the technology of flying, and I was positively uninterested in the business aspects of the commercial airline world. So I must thank Michael Fiennes, a former director of John Swire & Sons, Cathay Pacific's parent company, who enabled me to spot what a wonderful *story* this was. With painstaking thoroughness he had put together, from the mass of paper records of the airline in the capacious cellars of Swires' offices in London and Hong Kong, a synopsis of Cathay's history from its beginning in the forties until now. It was a fairly bulky synopsis, but easily handled by any man of moderate strength, and the important thing about it was that it told me that here was a truly Splendid Yarn. Behind the careful, formal words of this or that chairman's report to directors at this or that Annual General Meeting down the years there were incidents and characters to enthral not only aviation fans but anyone who, like me, finds the blood pumping faster when he hears of tales of the East, pioneers, Biggles, buccaneers, Old China Hands, hair's-breadth escapes, and derring-do in the clouds.

Of course, behind all those magical things there was also a serious story – that of the birth and struggling adolescence of Cathay Pacific Airways; of its expansion from a small airline operating from a tiny pimple of land on the South China Sea, to a much acclaimed international carrier. Today Cathay Pacific is a very serious airline indeed. Yet it started as a freewheeling outfit in an age more swashbuckling than our own, and the tensions, disasters and triumphs that accompanied its transition add up to a wonderful adventure. It was Michael Fiennes, New College scholar, Cathay director and, in retirement, the Company's archivist, who pointed this out to me.

Many others helped me with this book and most are named in the text. To some I would like to give a special mention. First of all, my friends John and Adrian Swire opened the Cathay Pacific archives to me without reserve, and allowed me to read the private diaries of their remarkable father, Jock. Roy Farrell, the survivor of the two founders of Cathay Pacific, gave me unique insight into those early pioneering days, as did Angela, the widow of Farrell's co-founder, Sydney de Kantzow, and his sister Eve. Former Chairmen of Cathay, Duncan Bluck and John Browne, provided invaluable and detailed information about the airline's development. In Hong Kong, David Bell and his indefatigable Public Affairs team – Edwin Shum, Shirley Leung, Maisie Shun Wah and Anne Paylor – were indispensable in ways too numerous to mention. Mike Hardy, the Company's Director of Operations out at Hong Kong's Kai Tak Airport, and Stewart John, its heavyweight Engineering Director – an authentic genius, I call him – gave me all the help I asked for. And I was unfailingly assisted on my way by Swire's Taipan, Michael Miles, and Cathay's Deputy Chairman and Managing Director, Peter Sutch, a quicksilver personality who never seems to come to rest. I owe a considerable debt of gratitude to Edward Scott, Swire's Chairman in Australia and a Cathay Pacific Director, nephew of Jock's close friend and colleague John Scott, and grandson of the Senior's partner, James Henry Scott.

For knowledge of the pre-air days of the Swire's eastern empire, I am grateful for the existence of Charles Drage's book *Taikoo*. As for Air, I cannot thank ex-Captain 'Chic' Eather too warmly for lending me the records of his many years with Cathay, and in his book *Syd's Pirates*, I found much fascinating information. Former captains Dave Smith and Laurie King lent me their notes and cuttings; and they, with Chic Eather, figure a great deal in the text that follows. Mike McCook Weir and Peter Jerdan gave up much of their precious spare time to put me through the thrilling experience of the 747 simulator. The patient explanations of Richard Stirland make plain much legal and administrative detail that otherwise would have baffled my simple mind.

Of the two other names that deserve mention here, one is that of Jim Macdougall, possibly Sydney's most attractive citizen and, at about eighty years of age, one of its most sprightly. The other is that of Captain Martin Willing who, out of sheer love of them, has painstakingly assembled the intimate history of every aircraft ever flown by Cathay. I am also deeply indebted to Robert J. Serling's fascinating book, *The Electra Story*.

Finally, I want to acknowledge my considerable debt to Charlotte Havilland, who helped me to hack a way through the jungle of company archives. Gill Gibbins and Sheila Colton gave me much excellent advice; my indispensable sea anchor, Gritta Weil, brought things together as usual; and Roddy Bloomfield at Century Hutchinson proved once more to be among the noblest of editors. Despite this support, all the errors in this book, technical or otherwise, are my own.

APPROACH

Cathay Pacific Flight 250, non-stop from London to Hong Kong, somewhere over Asia – but where? I have missed Russia completely. It slithered past in the dark, I suppose, at about the time I was pretending to watch the movie. Later, somewhere between Kabul and the Hindu Kush, well before we reached the Indus south of Peshawar, I lost any desire to stay awake. Until now. A moment ago I lifted the window blind next to my seat and revealed – a miracle. Instead of dark, infinite night it is improbable brilliant day, the sky a shimmering porcelain-blue ocean permeated with gold dust through which the plane steadily plunges, a white, green and silver whale that seems alive as ships at sea are alive. Jonah-like in its belly, I can feel the great, ponderous cylindrical body tremble in the remorseless rush of air.

I am heading towards Hong Kong, idly making mental notes at the start of a new experience. This is an international airline with a difference. It emerged only recently and rather mysteriously out of the political turbulence of the Orient. One moment, one might almost say, it was a feeble little thing, boldly thrashing about with only limited success; the next, it was a dragon flapping great strong wings across the world. It was as dramatic as that. I am not an aviation expert – far from it – but at least I am aware that the Cathay Pacific story, although it covers slightly less than forty-five years, is as full of incident as any yarn in an adventure magazine. Springing from the shared vision of two wartime seat-of-the-pants fliers in the chill immensities of the eastern Himalayas, it leads on to air piracy, a midair bombing, the battle for the routes to fly and the capital for the aircraft to fly them – milestones in a small regional airline's struggle for bare survival before ultimate international success.

A day or two before this flight I met in London the British principals of Cathay Pacific and was surprised to discover they showed no sign of

1

schizophrenia. They might have done so. For while the airline is based in Hong Kong where it grew up, the British family Swire, with whose name Cathay Pacific is indelibly linked, has its headquarters thousands of miles away, half a dozen Jumbo jet lengths from Buckingham Palace. There, a small mountain of Cathay Pacific's yellowing records waited for me, and there will be a similar mountain confronting me in Hong Kong. A daunting prospect. For now, moving half awake across Asia at something like 550 miles an hour, I can only note my impressions of a Boeing 747, the greatest of all commercial jetliners, in flight. A Cathay 747, of course.

How long have we taken to get to – wherever we are? Flight CX250 took off from Gatwick yesterday evening in an English summer deluge that fell on us like an irritating farewell thump on the back. My watch, glinting in oriental sunlight, tells me it is 4.30 a.m. Resting my forehead against the window I see an infinite fleece of white cloud thousands of feet below. Hong Kong is evidently still remote in the golden haze. I fumble my headphones on and let sounds of Mozart creep in my ears. Time passes. . . .

On the flight deck, high up where the whale's blow-hole should be, Captain Mike McCook Weir, a grey-haired, stocky figure, deliberately adjusts his headset askew so that one earpiece covers a single ear, leaving the other ear free to pick up remarks, technical or flippant, from his First Officer or Flight Engineer. He flicks at a switch among the array before him, which even in the light still give out a faint glow like coral under sunlit water. Into the mike he says crisply: 'Kunming control. Cathay 250 position Kunming 54. Level 12,000 metres.' Kunming is the provincial capital of Yunnan, so we are a scimitar slicing a swift, clean arc over the broad body of China at about 39,000 feet.

A Chinese voice with a faint American tinge comes in. 'Cathay 250, this is Kunming control. Your position copied. Over.'

The big jet tilts to starboard, into the last leg of a 7,250-mile flight, a turn barely perceptible but for the changing slant of sunlight over the blanketed passengers huddled in the semi-dark cabin. Cocooned and tousled, they stir reluctantly. Speed and the night have made distance quite meaningless, but surely there is still time to kill. . . .

'Ladies and gentlemen. Sorry to wake you.' The Captain's voice fills the cabin. 'I thought you'd like to know we are approximately one hour and twenty minutes away from Hong Kong. The time in Hong Kong is 12.30 p.m. on a fine, clear day with a temperature of 20 degrees Celsius or 82 degrees Fahrenheit, and quite a strong northeasterly breeze. Thank you.' A click and Mozart is restored to me.

2

Nothing in his voice showed that Captain Mike had only just settled back into his seat after a four-hour nap in the bunk behind the flight deck. This long flight deserves, and gets, two crews. After the best part of nine hours on cockpit duty, the Australian relief pilot, ready for his share of sleep, made way for McCook Weir with a quick briefing. At the same time, Steve, McCook Weir's co-pilot, fresh from sleep himself, now hunched down in the pallid glow of the instrument panel, starts to check the computerized navigation systems. That done, he squints down from his window, hoping to spot familiar landmarks, the pointed hills of Yunnan and the muddy snake-coils of the Hong Shui He river, and is gratified to find them as usual seven miles below him.

Another hour to go. The map page in *Discovery*, the Cathay Pacific in-flight magazine, shows me what I've missed. Over the Channel in the evening haze to Holland and on to the darker Baltic. Night and Moscow; then, high across the sombre immensity of Russia, the invisible Volga, the Urals, our wing lights winked unheeded at hundreds of sleeping villages; over the Aral Sea, over the Golden Road to modern Samarkand along which the pilgrims' camel bells no longer beat. It's important to keep dead centre on this only air lane on the trans-Soviet route, to avoid reprimands or worse from touchy Russian air controllers with spy-planes on the brain. Still, like Moghul conquerors we winged past the rampart of the Hindu Kush into Kabul control's airspace, over the Khyber Pass, safely over Lahore, Kipling's City of Dreadful Night. Across India, the darkness began to lift. I saw nothing of all that. We were rushing towards the sunrise and, sleeping, I missed too the first pearl-pink touch of sun on the Himalayas, the appalling sweep of towering mountains – Annapurna, Everest, Kangchenjunga – where Kim thought, surely the gods must live.

I see from the chart that our route over Bengal severs the C of Calcutta, and in a flash a memory of the sixties returns – a dismal airport shimmering in wet heat among limp palms, and huge kite-hawks wheeling and tumbling over the windswept runway like scraps of dirty brown paper, a menace to aviation. At this height we are unlikely to hoover an eagle into an engine or dodge a feathered missile homing in through a windshield; not even a condor could survive up here. Perhaps it wouldn't matter much anyway. I read somewhere that Boeing tests the strength of its one-and-a-half-inch-thick windshields by catapulting 10lb hamburgers into them at 190mph. Why hamburgers? Why not a frozen TV dinner? In another test dozens of plucked and frozen chickens are rapid-fired at every Boeing's nose. That sounds more sensible: frozen chickens must be capable of greater damage than hamburgers, but even they simply bounced off, leaving hardly a dent.

A recent copy of Cathay Pacific's *Flight Safety Review* glimpsed in the London office carried a report covering bird-interference for the period of July to September 1985: 'Bird strikes: Shanghai 4. (One bird struck First Officer's windshield. Nil damage to aircraft.) Peking 1. (During landing First Officer noticed small bird – sparrow-type – pass down right side . . . evidence of strike. Nil damage.)' Not a sparrow-type falls . . . but nil damage. It is reassuring.

'Good morning, ladies and gentlemen, this is your Purser, Albert Templo' . . . an avuncular Hong Kong voice announces brunch. Between mouthfuls of coffee and bacon I stare vacantly at the bulkhead panel in front of me onto which the sun strikes like a spotlight.

Back in the capsule of the flight deck the Captain is talking, crisply articulate, to Canton. 'Guangzhou control, Cathay 250. 12,000 metres. Request descent clearance. Over.'

'Cathay 250, your position copied.' A staccato Chinese voice. 'Cleared when ready to de-scend to one zee-lo thousan' feet.'

'Cathay 250 cleared to descend. . . .'

My headset clicks, and the music (Elgar now) is interrupted by McCook Weir's voice:

'Ladies and gentlemen, the Captain again. We'll be starting our descent to Hong Kong some 120 miles away. The weather is fine and we shall be making our approach today to runway One Three . . . runway thirteen, west-to-east, sharp right – sharp, *sharp* right – at the Chequerboard.'

The strong, sinewy chords of Elgar's Cello Concerto return and with them my thoughts of high-flying collisions with birds. And collisions in general – for example, head-on ones with other aircraft. Not that that danger worries me in the least: nothing like that has ever happened in the history of Hong Kong's airport. Anywhere in the world, all a pilot and co-pilot can do is to keep a good look-out, the proof being that 'open-eyed' pilots averted collisions over the United States ninety times in 1983, and the same number of times in 1984. A jokey directive I once saw in an aviation magazine said:

> If you waste seconds
> deciding what to do . . .
> It is no longer necessary to
> take corrective action . . .
> because you are going to be straining yourself
> unnecessarily . . .
> and are going to die all
> tensed up. . . .

Alice Yip, my stewardess, returns to remove my tray and, with half-moon eyes sweetly smiling, lisps an invitation from the Captain to join the flight crew for the approach and landing. I follow her up the staircase to the upper deck in the 747's hump. 'Hello. Mind your head', McCook Weir says just in time as I duck through the cockpit door and squeeze into the jump seat behind his left shoulder.

'Everything in working order?' I ask him.

'Wonderful.'

'747 – the queen of the skies,' says Steve, the young, blond co-pilot, leaning back to shake my hand.

The Flight Engineer greets me too, helps me with my seat belt and hands me a headset. He jabs a finger upwards at the escape hatch in the roof, grinning, 'If anything goes wrong, follow me because I'll be the first out.'

The flight deck, a padded cell with a multitude of knobs and clock faces, is surprisingly small for such a large aircraft. One must move stooped, with sloth-like deliberation. Cocked up over the Boeing's nose, we are 40 or 50 feet in front of her engines and more than 200 feet from her tail, facing ahead expectantly like spectators isolated in a rather cramped box in a very avant-garde opera house. All is grey – the only colours are the pale blue of a plastic mug slotted into a holder at my elbow and holding half an inch of tea dregs, the dark blue of the plastic straps securing oxygen masks above our heads, and the yellow of the spongy, disc-like earpieces of our headsets. We might almost be in an operating theatre. The atmosphere is clinical, unflurried, the pilot's softest remarks distinctly audible, the occasional tram-like hiss when the Flight Engineer swings his seat back and forth on metal runners fixed in the floor quite startling. You realize there are people under your feet – a loudspeakered Jeeves-like voice comes boldly through the floor from the First Class cabin below – Albert Templo's, talking about duty-free regulations.

In the calm tones of a surgeon consulting his anaesthetist at the start of a routine operation, Mike McCook Weir confers with China. At first ground control's voice babbles something very like, 'Kee bas how wa-a-a-. . . .' Let's see how McCook Weir copes with *that*, I think with mildly malicious interest. But evidently the remark was not addressed to us because the same voice follows impeccably with 'Cathay 250, 12,000 metres.'

'Cathay 250, 12,000 metres,' McCook Weir quietly acknowledges, and then to me, 'The Chinese and Russians use metres. We use feet like everyone else. Makes it slightly complicated.' He reads off a handy printed card that converts metres to feet at a glance: '12,000 metres, that's 39,400 feet. Now we go down.'

We sink heavily and evenly like a submarine beginning a dive. Below us a familiar landscape is taking shape. Over Steve's head, I can just see the Pearl River surging down muddily from Canton, slowly broadening as it gathers in the even browner water of its eel-like tributaries. On my left, a darker mainland; red mud roads writhing like frantic serpents between terraced hills. Ahead, broken glimpses of open sea between shifting clouds.

A clear Hong Kong Chinese voice now, friendlier. 'Cathay 250, heading of 220 degrees and descend to 6,000 feet. Over.' Steve reads back the instruction, the aircraft dips once more, and McCook Weir calls for the approach checklist.

'Cabin signs.'

'On.'

'Inboard landing lights.'

'On.'

'Altimeters.'

'Set for landing. . . .'

And so on, until –

'Checklist complete.'

The Flight Engineer has made his final fuel check. We shall still have 4,070 gallons in our wing-tanks when we land at Hong Kong. Cheerful news, because that quantity would be enough for us to make one quick circuit in case of a missed approach, or to divert to Canton and if necessary to circle there in a holding pattern for half an hour. An unlikely thing to happen, it's true: despite the tricky monsoon season, Kai Tak is only closed by bad weather for an average of three days a year. And Cathay's pilots are coming into their home port, a place they know in all its moods.

The glossy pages of *Discovery* confirm the outlines of the history I am setting out to write.

> It all began on 24th September 1946, when Roy Farrell, an American entrepreneur and enthusiastic amateur pilot, and Sydney de Kantzow, an Australian wartime pilot who has been flying C-47s over the Hump – from Calcutta over Burma to Chungking – registered Cathay Pacific Airways in Hong Kong. Flying a single DC-3, they carried 3,000 passengers and 15,000 kilos of cargo between Australia and Asia. . . .

Two engines, propellers, bone-shaking vibrations, ear-shattering noise – there must have been pros as well as cons in flying in those distant days. Not *all* that distant, of course, although certainly closer to the era of Biggles and biplanes held together by wire and safety-pins than they are to our own. In their slow C-47s (and later their twenty-passenger civilian versions, the Dakota DC-3s), pioneers like Farrell and de Kantzow would have had plenty of time to enjoy the dawn over Kanchenjunga. Would they think of us with envy or contempt, cruising seven miles up with hundreds of passengers, air conditioning, in-flight concerts, movies, hot four-course meals with an elaborate wine list and all mod cons? Alice Yip could bring you a 'baby bassinet' (whatever that is) and a nappy-changing table. All this in forty years! Could the world really have changed so much and so fast?

A thought: Roy Farrell and Sydney de Kantzow would have had another surprise. This aircraft, exhausted in every rivet, one might think, by the long, non-stop flight from London, would have precisely one hour on the ground at Hong Kong before another long flight – ten and a half hours across the Pacific to Vancouver. That hour would not be one of peace and quiet. A small army of cleaners waited even now at Kai Tak to storm on board like crack troops. What would they do? Vacuum the carpets, wipe meal trays, empty ashtrays, brush seats, chuck out used pillows, blankets, magazines and bulging plastic bags of left-over food from the galleys – then leap nimbly out of the way of another army, this time one of caterers bearing food and liquor, fresh pillows and blankets – and possibly a few spare baby bassinets as well. There would be lavatories to be emptied, fresh water and 44,000 gallons of fuel to be loaded. Within any given period of twenty-four hours, the aircraft I am sitting in is often airborne for all of that time except for a mere ninety minutes.

Threatening clouds, looking deep and solid, rush at us – but they part and melt at a touch like the brick 'walls' in a funfair's ghost train, spattering a burst of rain which streams away *upwards* in the airflow and is gone. We burst into clear air again.

We are at the ultimate edge of Asia. Old Cathay ends here where the mouth of the Pearl River yawns at the South China Sea. Macao is a pimple half-lost in haze. Immediately below, across Deep Bay, the wakes of a couple of motorized junks and a hydrofoil unfurl like stretched lengths of silver thread. We pass the point of Castle Peak – in Hong Kong territory now – above green islands encircled by sandy beaches and three cargo vessels lying in a bay as if abandoned.

Six thousand feet. 'On top of Lantau now' – McCook Weir jabs a finger downwards at the long, high dragon's back of Hong Kong's largest island. Again the plane dips. The window next to me is hot to the touch. The whole flight deck is overheated. I am sweating on my face and feel a certain embarrassment. The cockpit is such a small space that body odours – even a sweat-soaked shirt – matter. I can understand why flight crews are urged not to eat garlic less than twelve hours before a flight – halitosis or flatulence! Baked beans are totally banned.

A message from the Kai Tak controllers.

'Cathay 250, turn right onto 360 degrees and reduce to 200 knots.' 230 miles an hour.

'Flap one.'

'. . . further right onto 030 degrees cleared for the approach . . . last aircraft reported moderate turbulence and sinking wind shear.'

Mike McCook Weir eases back the four thrust levers beside his right knee and the aircraft settles down once more, gently, like a fat man gingerly sinking into a low armchair.

'Better put on the "No Smoking" sign now.'

Our speed is falling back: 190mph now.

'Gear down.'

Open Sesame. Lights flash, warning us that the undercarriage doors are unlocked and opening beneath us. With a noise like a medium-sized boat running aground on shale, the 747 is giving birth to eighteen monstrous wheels. The nose wheel directly below the cockpit follows them with a rumble and a hiss.

Not far now. Here are visual signs of Hong Kong: the Caltex storage tanks; the boulders of Stonecutters Island nearby to the right; the gaunt chimney of the Lai Chai Kok incinerator; motor boats and police launches lassoing ships in the Western Anchorage with their wakes. To the left, the steep skyscrapers of financial Hong Kong rise from the waterfront and march grandly up to the Peak. And then – dead ahead – at last, the famous Chequerboard, a Kowloon landmark, red and white squares painted on a sheer hillside, a challenge and a warning for approaching aircraft that says: 'Turn away now – *now*! Or else. . . .' It's a tricky spot: so tricky in fact that you can't even trust to electronics. No electronic approach aid is allowed – is even possible. The final turn to the runway *must* be visual. You can see why. Big white strobe lights, visible even by day, signal the steep 47-degree swing to starboard that brings the aircraft in line with Runway 13, stretched out straight and dark and very narrow in the waters of Kowloon Bay.

Four hundred feet. Our starboard wing tilts down into the turn – reaching daringly towards the leprous rooftops of rotting tenement housing sprouting TV aerials and strung with lines of washing. I have stood on those slum roofs and watched the planes coming in one after the other, unbelievably close above me, just like the man I see now, holding a homing pigeon in his arms and gazing up quite undisturbed by the familiar sight of a green and white leviathan plunging down over his head. A group of boys playing football in a side street must hear the change in engine-note, but they too ignore us. A double-decker bus overtakes a lorry on the road bordering the airport's boundary fence.

McCook Weir says, '150 knots,' as if to himself, meaning 165 miles an hour. And to Steve, 'Good. I've got the aircraft.'

'One hundred feet' – from the Flight Engineer.

Our speed is falling with the descent and McCook Weir nudges the thrust levers forward. The aircraft's nose now points directly at the control tower – that is to counteract drift to starboard. It must be interesting for the controllers to watch us heading briskly their way.

'Thirty feet . . .'

The plane's nose rises slightly, still just left of the runway's centre line. 'Twenty feet . . .'

A shift of the right rudder, and at last our nose is on centre. 'Ten feet. . . .'

Thrust levers back to idle; control column back. Light as a 220-ton feather we plane gracefully over the threshold. Eighteen massive wheels hit the runway. The brakes bite. Nose-wheel down.

'Lovely . . . right-o. . . .'

The flight deck quivers with the sudden braking as Mike reaches forward his right hand for the reverse thrust levers, yanking them sharply back as far as they will go. We slow, and then the brakes relax and the quivering dies. He cancels reverse thrust, pushing the levers forward to normal, and Cathay 250 U-turns smoothly off the runway and down the taxiway towards the house-high neon advertisement near the boundary road and our unloading bay. Dingy white buildings and the hills roll slowly by outside. Bare-chested in baggy shorts, a middle-aged Chinese on a rusty barge moored in the water that laps the runway is washing himself from a bucket, not heeding us at all.

'Thirteen hours four minutes,' McCook Weir says. 'Nice eh?'

We have shrunk a hefty chunk of space into thirteen hours and accepted the miracle as boring routine. Nice? We have won a victory. One victory in a war of a million battles – but still a victory.

I hang up my headset, wondering if Sydney de Kantzow and Roy Farrell ever envisaged anything quite like this. But of course they couldn't have.

'Beautiful,' I reply, and add a saying familiar on airstrips throughout the war in Vietnam: 'So we walk away from another one.'

Someone on the flight deck laughs. 'Almost a shame to take the money.'

PART ONE
ROY AND SYD

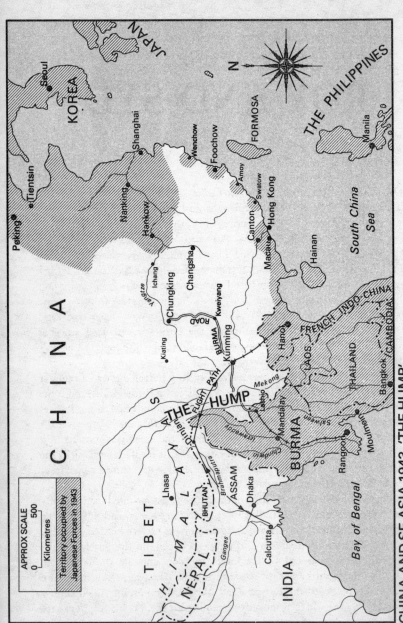

CHINA AND SE ASIA 1943, 'THE HUMP'

CHAPTER 1

One could toss a coin to determine Cathay Pacific's exact place of birth. There are two obvious choices. Shanghai in 1946 is one possibility – that is where Roy Farrell, the godfather of Cathay, began commercial air operations with his DC-3, 'Betsy' ('my baby' as he calls her), the pigmy ancestor of today's family of flying Titans. Hong Kong is the other – there Farrell's first handful of aircraft achieved adulthood as 'Cathay Pacific Airways', and there the airline first drew the attention of rich and important suitors. In a dilapidated Hong Kong painfully recuperating from Japanese occupation and the Second World War, Cathay was 'discovered' and launched to fame and fortune rather as Lana Turner was 'spotted' and shot to stardom from Schwab's drugstore in Hollywood – although in Cathay's case fortune did not come overnight.

Even so, the airline began as a gleam in Roy Farrell's eye in a remoter place and at an earlier time. The place was Dinjan in British India; and at the time, 1942, the Second World War had reached a point when circumstances were at their bleakest. Indeed, it might be said that one of the world's greatest international airlines emerged from the steamy confusion of a makeshift Assamese wartime airstrip rather as Life itself crawled out of the world's primeval swamps. Dinjan: who has heard of it? Yet for a while, from 1942, it achieved a certain fame.

That year, 1942, was the worst of times. The unstoppable Japanese army had rolled through Malaya, Singapore and Hong Kong, had pursued the British out of Burma and arrived at a gallop on the eastern borders of India, driving a wedge of mountain and jungle between, on the one hand, the demoralized British and Indian forces in India and, on the other, the Chinese Nationalists and their American allies. Moreover, on their way the Japanese had closed the Burma Road, the most important Allied supply route into China – in fact, the only remaining lifeline. For already Japanese forces, battling since 1937 with the ill-coordinated Nationalist Chinese units of Generalissimo Chiang Kai-shek, had occupied China's coastal cities and in a series of relentless offensives had pushed Chiang back into the remote upland regions of the country's centre and west. Japan was now poised to knock Nationalist China out of the war.

On the upper reaches of the Yangtze River at Chungking Chiang made an emergency capital. By now he urgently needed any help he could get from his allies. But with the Burma Road closed and the only other land supply route, from Hanoi to Kunming, sealed off by the surrender in 1941 of French Indo-China, how could help be delivered? Yet to deliver it became a priority for the Allied High Command. The reason for that was not simply altruistic love of Chiang Kai-shek. The fervent hope was that with the active support of China-based United States Air Force bombers and fighters under General Claire Chennault, Chiang's men would manage to tie down thousands of Japanese troops while the Americans' knockout effort against the Japanese fatherland got under way in the Pacific. 'Keep China in the war' – that was the cry in Washington and London. 'Keep the Japanese busy' was what that cry really meant. But to be kept in the war Chiang's China needed arms, ammunition, and an expensive spectrum of supplies from clothing to paper clips, or resistance to the Japanese might collapse. How on earth were these supplies to be delivered to the mountains of central China?

The Allied commanders saw only one possibility: by air from India – admittedly no ordinary route. This one would have to cross one of the world's natural wonders – the uncharted barrier of formidable mountains at the eastern end of the Himalayas, a region of soaring walls of dark or snow-covered rock that soon came to be known to the world as 'the Hump'. But was it feasible? At what times of the year could heavily laden piston-engined transports operate over it? At what height? What were the risks from Japanese fighters based in Burma? Could they operate at night? A swift reconnaissance led to a report, on the basis of which the planners in Washington and Chungking gave the go-ahead and the largest and most successful air transport operation of the war began, under the command of the irascible American commander-in-chief of the China–India–Burma theatre, Lieutenant-General Joseph Stilwell – 'Vinegar' by nickname, pure vinegar by nature.

At the Indian end of the Hump, British and Americans set up their headquarters in Calcutta, the largest port in eastern India, and looked for airfields. The Dinjan field was a mere pinprick on a general's wall map but it happened to be particularly well situated in Upper Assam for the launching of transports across the Hump. And it was already the operational base for two RAF squadrons. Dinjan it would be, and by the time Roy Farrell was posted there it had become a noisy, overcrowded home-from-home for aircraft and aircrews from both the American Army Air Corps' Transport Command (ATC) and the hybrid China National Aviation Company (CNAC).

CNAC is important to this story. It had been a Sino-American organization since 1933, when Pan American Airways acquired a 45 per cent share against the Chinese Government's 55 per cent. Prewar, Pan American had begun to fly passengers across the Pacific from San Francisco to Manila via Honolulu; later that route extended as far as Hong Kong, where CNAC's DC-2s and DC-3s, based in Shanghai, were waiting to shuttle Pan American's passengers into China. That link-up was a milestone in aviation pioneering, for in effect Pan American had built an air bridge spanning 8,000 miles of Pacific Ocean to join America to Asia.

The Second World War put paid to that. With the fall of Shanghai to the Japanese, CNAC's headquarters were moved perforce to Hong Kong, and when that fell, to Kunming. By 1942 Japanese soldiers were inside the borders of India, Japanese aircraft controlled the skies of Burma, administrative and organizational muddle and shortages of airstrips, supplies, roads and labour were the order of the day – but the men of CNAC rose to the occasion. Indeed, CNAC's pilots, engineers and radio operators became the human backbone of the Hump story. Roy Farrell and Sydney de Kantzow, an Australian, were only two of many experienced Pan American fliers to put on air force uniform. Engineers, air controllers and administrators did so too, and their experience made things work.

In the semi-chaos of Dinjan, Roy Farrell began to fly the aircraft that would shape his future. He and other young pilots, flying ten Douglas DC-3s (Dakotas) and three C-47s, the Dakota's military version, inaugurated the route to Kunming and Chungking – 550 miles to Kunming plus an additional 450 miles to Chungking on the Yangtze River. Another twenty-five aircraft in Calcutta completed the fleet. Dinjan airstrip took its name from a nearby tea plantation in the valley of the holy Brahmaputra River. A long way inland, it stood only 90 feet above sea level. To the north rose the Himalayas, the highest mountains in the world, a petrified tidal wave; to the east were the wild, razor-backed Naga Hill tracts where a tribal people, once head-hunters and only quite recently converted to Baptism by British and American missionaries, cultivated rice on precipitous hillsides to which their thatched huts clung like ticks to a dog's back. Beyond them were Japanese-occupied Burma, more mountains, more ravines, and – China.

Little backwoods Dinjan was far from ready for anything as considerable as the Hump operation, and the priority task of lengthening its runways and improving its primitive accommodation was hampered by the airfield's inaccessibility and by the fearful weather conditions that prevailed in Upper Assam for at least half the year. Between May and October there could be 200 inches of monsoon rain. Despite this, flying had to go on, and did so at considerable risk to aircraft and crews. Only when the water lay nine inches on the runway were operations suspended and the runway drained. At other times heavy fogs closed everything down.

The living conditions were poor and the food worse. The crews lived in dank huts half-hidden in tall grass. The first Americans to arrive were housed ten miles from the airfield, and each day faced the torture of a drive to the airstrip in ramshackle trucks over muddy roads and through a miasma of heat and dust. There was wildlife to contend with. Nights were shattered by the sudden trumpeting of inquisitive elephants. Screams of 'Cobra! Cobra!' halted operations as chalk-faced ground staff bolted from their DC-3s. Snakes took to the cool, dry metal floors of the Dakotas as men take to feather beds; coiled behind shady bulkheads, they had only to raise their sleepy heads to start a small stampede. As for mosquitoes, there were so many that it was rumoured that the devilish Japs were dropping them at night in camouflaged canisters.

Reminiscing years later in Dallas, Farrell told me, 'The things to avoid were malaria and dengue fever.'

'You got them?'

'Neither one. Although once, when I was drinking too much, I gave the grog up for six months.' He laughed. 'And then, of course, I got everything from leprosy down.'

As for the actual flying over the Hump – one wonders how for three years or so the Allied commanders could find enough men sufficiently bold or foolhardy to continue doing it. 'Praise the Lord and Pass the Ammunition' and 'Coming in on a Wing and a Prayer' were both Second World War hit songs from Tin Pan Alley, the lyrics of which would have sounded highly appropriate on the lips of the CNAC and ATC flyers (and probably did). One of them (not Farrell) wrote long afterwards, 'There was the army saying, "You don't find any atheists in infantry foxholes". We adapted to "You won't find any atheists in an airplane cockpit over the Hump". All pilots were fatalists. It couldn't happen to *them*.' Unfortunately, it happened to a great many.

As for the DC-3s and C-47 Skytrains, as someone said of the Model T Ford, they were 'hard-working, commonplace, heroic'. Their endurance

soon became a legend, and it remains one. Still in service after more than
fifty years – the first of them flew in December 1935 – the diminutive twin-
engined DC-3 is the most widely used transport plane ever built; 10,000 of
them left the assembly lines in the Second World War alone. The C-47 had
wider doors, a strengthened fuselage and undercarriage, and could carry two
jeeps or three aircraft engines or twenty-eight fully equipped men. It flew to
a normal maximum of 12,000 unpressurized feet; in the special conditions of
the Hump the American and British pilots habitually flew at 18,000 feet:
there was little choice if you wanted to avoid prowling Japanese Zeros
coming up at you from captured British airstrips in Burma.

As for the route itself, the Hump flight plan was simple and unvaried.
You wrapped up warm and took off from Dinjan; you turned east towards
the 10,000-foot Patkai Range; you climbed over the upper reaches of the
Chindwin River to the 14,000-foot Kumon Mountains; you bumped gamely
over three river valleys – the Irrawaddy, Salween and Mekong. And then, if
all was well, you faced your Becher's Brook: the 15,000–20,000-foot
Santung Range. The Santung was the real Hump.

It was a very bleak place to die in, and you could die in a number of ways.
Lack of pressurization was a serious drawback at Hump heights, but not a
fatal one: you felt sick and dopey, but you lived. If a Japanese Zero fighter
shot you down, of course you died. Engine failure in that wilderness would,
at best, land you among freezing mountain ridges and ice-choked fissures
which no one had mapped. There you froze to death unless by remote
chance some friendly local tribesmen, Nagas or Kachins, led you to their
huts and revived you with concoctions of stewed leaves and rice wine. Those
flyers who did bale out over the Hump and managed to walk out alive
eventually formed a club – the Walkers' Club. It was very small and very
exclusive.

The climate was the most successful killer of all. The absolute lack of
weather forecasting was a terrible hazard. In those days electronic systems
were primitive and the Hump weather was notorious. High-pressure masses
were forever rolling up across Burma to the eastern Himalayas, to
rendezvous there with violent blizzards sweeping down from the Gobi
Desert and Siberia. Crosswinds of up to 125mph were commonplace.
Several C-47s were flipped over by sudden down-draughts, which
sometimes literally tore cargoes out through the bottom of aircraft. Wings
were buckled and warped by severe icing, against which aircraft had little or
no protection. The overcast could extend up to 29,000 feet, and on so broad
a front that sometimes flights had to be made on instruments all the way
from Dinjan to Kunming. It was all right for a light-hearted Roy Farrell,

forty years later, cheerfully stirring his pint of iced tea in a Texan diner, to joke to me about driving his C-47 across the Hump without a glimpse of Mother Earth until he found his nose practically scraping the runway the other end, but what could it have been like to flog over those fearful mountains day after day – and often night after freezing night as well, because the CNAC crews decided to add night-flying over the Hump to their schedules? It was easier to lose the Japanese fighters in the dark.

Talking to Farrell in Dallas I said, 'You must have lost many friends.' 'Hell, yes. And, you know, now and again they went in a creepy way. One day, a guy, a friend called Cookie Cook, wanted my seat, the co-pilot's seat. We were going off to Chungking: four planes. "Sure," I said. Well, they got to Chungking. And it was overcast, see? What they didn't know was, at the airfield the people down there had moved the beacon. They'd moved it but no one had been told a thing. So what happened? The leading plane went down through the overcast, and soon a column of smoke came up. Why? Who knew? Then Cookie's plane went down through the cloud – well, hell, he thought he knew the place and no one had told him about that beacon. And so there was another column of smoke.' Roy paused to shake his head. 'As I said, Cookie had taken my place. That's how things happened.'

Random facts cast a lurid light on the terrible cost in casualties. During Hump operations between June and December 1943 there were 135 major accidents and 168 men were killed or posted missing. A single Hump storm cost ATC nine planes and thirty-one crewmen; one day, no fewer than thirty transport aircraft were obliged to circle Upper Assam for hours, unable to land for the dense fog. As time (and fuel) ran out, the men in the airfield's control tower had no alternative but to try to talk them down one by one, fearing the worst. Of the thirty, eighteen aircraft landed safely; seven crashed; and five planes ran out of fuel before they could get down and were abandoned in the air.

That's the kind of thing that happened in those days.

CHAPTER 2

Roy Farrell flew freight from Dinjan; Syd de Kantzow in Calcutta mostly flew people. An article in an Australian newspaper brashly entitled 'The Man Who Saved Chiang' described Syd's flying career as follows:

> Before going to China, Captain de Kantzow gained his commercial flying experience in Australia and in England. Later, as test pilot for the Bristol Aircraft Company, he flew Blenheim bombers to Greece. With the collapse of Greece, he returned to Britain and was immediately selected by the RAF Transport Command for the ferrying of much-needed bombers from America to Britain. . . . After a year of this work on the North Atlantic, he transferred to Pan American Airways to fly aircraft across the South Atlantic from Brazil to Africa. As Pan American Airways are part shareholders of the CNAC, de Kantzow later got his opportunity to fly in China. . . .

Australia. . . Britain. . . Greece. . . North Atlantic. . . South Atlantic. . . China – Syd de Kantzow had been well acquainted with responsibilities and risks by the time he first looked down on the Hump. It was Syd who had made the initial survey of the Hump supply route on which the decision to go ahead had been based. From time to time asked for specifically by name, he flew the Generalissimo and Madame Chiang, and 'Vinegar Joe' Stilwell and Major-General Orde Wingate, the eccentrically brilliant British Chindit commander, as well.

De Kantzow was undemonstrative by nature, yet he was one of those men people notice. He stood out partly because of his flying ability, partly because of his unusual accent – he was the only Australian flying the Hump – and, no doubt, partly because of his spick-and-span, movie star appearance. When the war was over he told an Australian journalist (who was understandably astonished to hear it) that flying the Hump had been a 'dull and monotonous job', but no doubt well before his three-and-a-half-year tour was up it had become so. True, the Hump was high, wide and dangerous enough for most men, but at one time de Kantzow and the other CNAC pilots were flying across it as much as three times a day. Never mind that you are squeezed into the tiny and very draughty cockpit of an aircraft given to falling thousands of feet without warning, only levelling out at the last possible minute and so abruptly you believe you can hear passengers and cargo dropping through the floor: boredom *will* set in.

One day, during the British retreat from Burma, de Kantzow was ordered to fly Chiang, Madame Chiang and Stilwell to Kunming, and soon after take-off sent a message to Chiang from the cockpit: he had just received an urgent call from a Chinese observation post that Japanese Zero fighters were after them.

'How many?' de Kantzow had asked.

'Fifteen,' said the voice from the ground. 'Oh, and they're just above you.'

When I discussed this moment many years later with Syd's elder sister, Eve, now eighty years old, in her little house in Sydney, she glanced fondly at a silver-framed portrait of her brother in CNAC uniform on a sideboard and said, 'Syd was a real daredevil, you know.' On this flight, the Australian daredevil saved the Generalissimo's life as well as his own. Throwing the DC-3 into a dive, Syd dropped through a mass of cloud heading into a tangle of mountain gorges where his camouflaged plane would be as good as invisible to the Zero pilots, deftly zigging and zagging through horrendous cliffs until the Japanese went home in disgust. Never mind that Madame Chiang was sick and his other passengers were half-dead with fear, he had saved them and the plane. 'He had nine lives, I think,' Eve said.

As a reward for this daredevilry, his widow Angela is inclined to believe, as well as for a number of hazardous air-drops of rice, salt and medicines he made to Chiang's soldiers cut off by the Japanese in Burma, Syd de Kantzow was awarded Nationalist China's Order of the Flying Cloud. It was one more decoration in a family that in its time had won quite a few.

Syd was born in 1914, 'on the day the HMAS *Sydney* sank the *Emden*,' Eve says. 'That was the reason for his first name. As for his second, the de Kantzows were Swedish, possibly of Polish origin. My nephew went to Sweden a few years ago and saw a family there called *von* Kantzow, they'd written to Syd in Hong Kong, having seen his name in some aviation lists.' According to Eve, a Charles Adolphus de Kantzow, married to a London girl called Emma Bosanquet, was Swedish ambassador to Portugal for many years until his death in 1867. This de Kantzow was a Chevalier Baron of St George in the Portuguese peerage and had a chestful of Swedish orders as well; one of his sons (Syd's great-uncle) served with considerable distinction in the Indian Army, surviving the Mutiny (but because of his almost foolhardy courage, only just) and ending up as a lieutenant-colonel.

There had been at least one literary de Kantzow. Eve interrupted our talk to bring me a neatly bound volume of poems published in 1906 with the title *Noctis Susurri* (Sighs of the Night) and written by Sydney de Kantzow's grandfather, Alfred, when he was a lieutenant in the 22nd Madras Native Infantry. One of them was called 'The Himalayas':

> Sheer this descent how many thousand feet
> From this my eyrie! It is legion lost;
> – The stifled passion of the torrent's beat –
> A labyrinth of rocks by ravines crossed . . . .

It is very far from Kipling or Swinburne, admittedly, but when I talked with Eve de Kantzow about just such things – sheer descents, ravines, the Hump – it seemed appropriate to Syd, the aviator grandson.

'Syd's friends died one after the other,' Eve said. And she added something of immense sadness: 'Old in the head, Syd was. Old for his age.'

We sipped weak whisky and water under Syd's framed portrait, under Eve's unsmiling brother with the handsome, quick-eyed face that was not quite Robert Taylor's, not quite Ronald Colman's. On the table between us we spread out old newspaper photographs of those dark, strenuous days of war – pictures of half-naked black GIs, shining with sweat, labouring in Calcutta docks; of elephants lifting ammunition crates with their trunks; of Hump pilots in sweat-stained khaki shirts and cowboy boots, arms round each other's shoulders, pinning on smiles for the cameraman from *Life* magazine. They were pictures of a time that seemed a very long way from this small house in the Sydney suburb of Vaucluse, with Chinese flower prints and an old Cathay Pacific calendar with a Thai dancer on its walls, and an old lady pouring me Red Label, clinking glasses, and turning the album's pages. Here on those pages were C-47s over Shangri-La – tiny, twin-engined aircraft that shifted 650 tons of arms, ammunition, spare parts, trucks and men across the roof of the world from Assam to China. Were the thousands of high-cheekboned scarecrows, like extras in a multi-million dollar Cecil B. de Mille production, really Chiang's coolies, levelling mountains to make airfields for the Americans? The pictures of General 'Vinegar Joe' Stilwell reminded me of a dyspeptic Grandma Moses, and General Claire Chennault, the American hero of the Flying Tigers, of a middle-aged John Wayne.

You could fit Roy Farrell into this game of 'match the film star' and label him James Stewart – except that, although he is tall and lean, Farrell is by no means laconic. Roy could be a shrewd but very genial Texan rancher rather than what he is – the son of the postmaster-general of a small town called Vernon that lies four hours' drive west of Dallas. Talking with Roy evoked the same sense of unreality I had felt with Syd's sister Eve. It was a long way from the cobras, mud and sticky heat of Dinjan to Farrell's air-conditioned room in the motel on the roaring Dallas–Fort Worth parkway.

Unlike Syd, Roy Farrell was not a veteran pilot when CNAC took him on in Burma. Far from it. According to a letter he wrote to me which he hoped would 'set the record straight', he had his first solo flight in his own Piper Cub at Singleton Field near Fort Worth on 7 January 1942, less than two years before he joined the Hump circus. He joked that 'The cockpit was very crowded. I had a bumblebee in there with me.' Despite the bumblebee, he was awarded his Commercial and Instructor's Licence on his twenty-sixth birthday, and later his ground school rating for instructing navigation and meteorology. 'I tried to get in with CNAC that summer, but to be hired as a pilot you had to have 1,400 hours of flying time of which 100 hours had to be in an aircraft of over 200mph. I had to do something about that. So I bought a 1929 Laird single engine, open-cockpit plane with a 220mph Jacobs engine in which I would get my hours of *heavy* time. A few months later I got my instrument rating from American Flyers in Forth Worth. So with that, Owen Johnson of Pan American Airways – he came through recruiting for CNAC – hired me. I left Miami for CNAC and the Far East on 7 October 1943.'

It had not been quite as orthodox as all that, however. A whimsical footnote to this honest testimony relates that on its second or third flight, the 1929 Laird blew a cylinder and for the next several months it sat totally immobile in its hangar because Roy could not find the spare parts. Nevertheless, he admits, as it were with a wink, 'The aircraft and engine dutifully had logged in their logbooks over 400 hours (a little over the necessary hundred hours) of flying.' How lucky! But we can see, as he intends us to, that Roy Farrell was certainly not an experienced flyer when he arrived in Dinjan to fly CNAC's DC-3s.

'The first look I got at the cockpit of a DC-3 (or C-47) lasted about twenty seconds – I sneaked in to a Braniff DC-3 on the ramp at Fort Worth. I was overwhelmed by all the instruments, gauges and switches. The second look I got was on the C-47 flight from Calcutta up to Dinjan. My third look was shortly after at the field at Dinjan and I was in the co-pilot's seat with Cliff Groh as captain.'

What followed might make a few scenes in a Woody Allen film. 'Cliff called for me to open cowl flaps when he started the engines. A Piper Cub doesn't have cowl flaps and I didn't know what he was talking about, so he reached over me and trailed the flaps. He ran the engines up and did a thorough cockpit check just as dark settled in, and he called for me to release the handle for raising the lever that lifted the landing gear. Again, Piper Cubs didn't have retractable landing gear so I didn't know what in hell he was talking about . . . .' Roy laughs at his amateurishness. 'At the end of my first trip to Chungking I heard one Chinese mechanic shout to another, "Whaddya know – he made it!" The second trip the same guy hollered, "Hey – he made it again!" – that shows you. Anyway, all co-pilots had to have thirty-two round trips to check out – to be passed – as senior pilot. I did them in time.' In all he made 523 trips over the Hump.

Farrell easily recalls the terrible coldness of the Hump. 'Freezing! No heaters. To make things worse, my beautiful fleece-lined jacket didn't meet with my pants.'

And how some people even found time for smuggling: 'One night I found gold bars and a few thou' dollars in US stashed in the C-47's bulkhead padding.

' "These yours?" I said to the co-pilot and the radio officer, both Chinese.

' "Oh, no, Captain. Not mine."

' "Good. Then they're all mine," I said and stuck them under my seat. 'Well, it was very cold, but oddly enough I could see the co-pilot streaming with sweat, the radio officer, too. So I said, "Look, boys. I know it's yours, all this. But listen, if anyone smuggles anything on *my* plane, *I* do. Please tell all your friends that. If not there'll be trouble. Plenty trouble." And I gave the loot back to 'em. We got on fine after that.'

Political bigwigs smuggled for much bigger stakes, as Syd de Kantzow found out when an engine caught fire as he was taking off from Chungking, obliging him to make a forced landing in the Yangtze River. Mail, diplomatic bags, all the cargo went to the river bed. Divers finally brought up a huge sum of waterlogged currency, currency Chiang Kai-shek's people were spiriting out of the country.

In that fevered time money itself became unreal. Pilots earning $2,000 a month with nowhere to spend it took to heavy gambling. A dangerous way to kill boredom.

'We'd play five dollars a point at gin rummy,' Farrell says. 'That's pretty damn high. In one game you could lose twenty thousand, fifty thousand dollars.' Imagine the whine of mosquitoes in a stifling hut, the heavy monsoon raindrops bouncing like bullets off the iron roof. 'Money had little meaning because you didn't know who'd come back from the missions next day and who wouldn't. After the war, the returning GIs and pilots went to the gambling houses at home and that's when they learned the value of money. The hard way.'

After a pause he said, 'See, those CNAC people weren't much good at anything but flying. Not much good at making a living.' He laughed. 'They were really the biggest bunch of renegades. . . .'

They were renegades at just the right place at just the right time. And two of them at least had their heads screwed on the right way. Roy Farrell in Dinjan and Syd de Kantzow in Calcutta were men who knew how to make a living.

'Guess where we came together?' Roy said.

I tried to guess. In Calcutta over curry at the Grand Hotel? At Dinjan in some airless Nissen hut, with a radio pulsing to Glenn Miller's Big Band, Artie Shaw's clarinet, the voices of Dick Haymes or the Andrews Sisters? There would have been pin-ups tacked to three-ply cupboard doors – Betty Grable in the famous tight sweater; Dorothy Lamour, Polynesian in her sarong; a pouting Lana Turner, very blonde under a strong studio light. . . .

'Tigers,' Roy said, grinning. 'Tiger-hunting, that's where we met. In Cooch Behar, an Indian state near Calcutta; Bayah, the maharajah, had a palace there. He was a great friend of Syd's. Tiger-hunting, golf, drinking: luxury. Bayah even gave us wine with rubies ground up in it. It's an aphrodisiac, the Indians say.'

'And was it?'

'Hell, I wouldn't know. Didn't need aphrodisiacs in those days!'

Eve de Kantzow had shown me photographs of those tiger-shoots. A caption to one of them read: 'Captain de Kantzow on the extreme left, the Maharajah of Cooch Behar (second from right), beside a team of trained hunting elephants and their "mahouts".' The maharajah wore his trilby cocked rakishly over one eye and a well-made safari jacket. Somebody else wore a pair of colonial, knee-length, bell-bottomed shorts. Syd wore a pith helmet.

'I had a very heavy gun – a cannon without wheels,' Roy said. 'It slammed me back eight steps and brought the tears to my eyes. . . .'

Tears in his eyes; visions of the future in his head. It was the China end of the Hump run that evoked the visions. They came to him in Chungking, a place that, because it was Chiang's temporary capital, was crammed with officials in limousines on one hand and people in sedan chairs on the other; soldiers in cheap uniforms and bewildered refugees with bare feet; a grossly overcrowded place of ostentatious riches and secret corruption, self-evident slums and degrading poverty. One ramshackle, rat-infested hotel, the Shu Teh Gunza, was run by a wizened Eurasian called Harris who touted for foreigners' custom, but the CNAC people stayed at the Standard Oil installation. For foreigners, life was cheap at twenty Chinese dollars to one American, but there wasn't much to do. There were prostitutes, of course. People went after them when they got bored with the poker, crap or bridge games.

Kunming was an altogether better place in Farrell's view. 'At 6,000 feet you had to wear several layers of clothes, of course. But, oh, what a lovely place in summer! Hell, you know if I were really picking a place to live – Calcutta in winter, Kunming in summer.'

Even then, even with victorious Japanese armies everywhere and no end to the war clearly in sight, Roy Farrell had liked the look of China as somewhere to do business. The entrepreneur in him made some calculations and came to that conclusion: the Far East would be the place for him when things returned to normal. He had read about a man years before and never forgotten him: an American businessman with his eyes open who had made a fortune immediately after the Spanish–American War by shipping sugar from Havana to New York. That was the sort of thing that appealed to Farrell. The Japanese were bound to be defeated sooner or later, and then there would be markets out here. No doubt of that. Look at China . . . its size . . . its population. . . . The thing would be to get in early. That's what the fellow in Havana had done.

Roy Farrell nursed his dream and waited patiently for the end of the war.

Quite independently, Syd de Kantzow was having similar thoughts, and unlike Roy Farrell he revealed them to the press.

'In his flight across the Pacific to the Philippines and Hong Kong,' an interviewer in the Australian magazine *Cavalcade* reported, 'Captain de Kantzow was very impressed with the efficiency of the organisation of the service and the flying equipment. He considers America has made tremendous advances in trans-ocean passenger flying.' Then, almost thrown away, came an interesting sentence: 'De Kantzow sees China as a vast undeveloped country and her many needs can be well supplied by Australia.'

Looking back across four decades, one can see that Cathay was even then a gleam not in one pair of eyes, but in two.

CHAPTER 3

The long-range Boeing 747s of today's Cathay Pacific fleet home into Kai Tak Airport over the rooftops of Kowloon on wings as broad as three-storeyed houses are high. Worlds apart in time, Farrell and de Kantzow used to fly into Hong Kong, bucking and skidding through the turbulence in overworked DC-3s – 'crates' was the affectionate word for them – that sometimes seemed unlikely to clear the enveloping hills. How did the two rough-riders of CNAC make the immense jump from unremembered sweaty Dinjan to the British Crown Colony of Hong Kong, the commercial hub of the Far East?

It is too late to ask Sydney de Kantzow; after surviving the perils of pioneer aviation, he died in a motor accident in 1957. But it is not too late to ask Roy Farrell. Farrell is, as always, a jauntily active man with a sharp eye for business, and an indefatigable talker who can make you see the old swashbuckling days from his wryly humorous point of view. Syd helped enormously, probably decisively, but even before Syd came Farrell's willpower had turned his own dream into reality. He launched a single aircraft in the air and watched it become a great airline. 'I wanted an empire' – that was the confession he made the first day we were together. Well, he mapped out an empire, even if in the end it was not to be his.

When I set out to find Farrell I knew he lived partly in Vernon, Texas and partly in San Carlos, Mexico. His grandfather, born in Hoboken, New Jersey, had worked as a foreman on the Union Pacific Railroad, and his second son Clint, Roy's father, had moved to Vernon in 1887. Clint was Vernon's postmaster under six Presidents and for more than twenty-eight years until his death in 1937; a bit of a businessman and a good golfer, too. Roy was born in Vernon in 1912. So he would be seventy-four years old, and I wondered if he would want to talk about the old days. I found his address at Cathay Pacific's headquarters in Hong Kong and we began to exchange letters. To my relief, he was friendly and sounded quite eager to reminisce. When I asked where we could meet he said, 'Come to Texas.' After a delay (his wife had recently had a stroke) I flew to America to talk to him.

'I arrive Tuesday, Roy,' I said on the line from New York. 'Dallas–Fort Worth Airport. 12.15 midday.'

A soft, cheerful Texan voice answered me. 'I'll meet you. Tall and bald. You may recognize me.'

'I'd know you anywhere.'

'Oh?'

'I've been looking at your picture. It'll be very good to see you.'

'You bet,' the Texan voice said.

The morning of my flight from New York was sunny and cold and my neighbour was a small man who slurped Diet-Cola and never said a word, so there was plenty of time to think about the man who would be meeting me. The photographs I'd seen were forty years old, but it should not be difficult, I thought, to recognize that long head, the slicked-back, fairish hair (it would be grey now, of course), the wide smile, the lean, wide-awake face. I had brought to New York what I think is the best photograph anyone ever took of Roy in the old days. It shows him looking out of the open pilot's window of Betsy, his first commercial and always favourite aircraft, broadly grinning, with a long, strong hand held serenely aloft. It was an appealing photograph that projected pride and good nature in equal measure – a forty-year-old photograph, but I was pretty sure I would know that laughing face any time, any place.

And so I did. The plane landed fast and swung towards airport buildings like a sand-red set of children's bricks. Farrell was waiting at the arrival gate. The face may have been seventy-four years old, but there was no mistaking it. He came forward, hand out, grinning the old grin, a tall, spare, balding, bespectacled man wearing a short-sleeved shirt open at the neck and casual slacks.

'So we do recognize each other.' He laughed and led me to a big maroon Oldsmobile in the airport's parking lot. We swung out onto a six-lane highway that stretched away across land flat as a board in both directions.

'I've booked you into La Quinta Motor Inn outside Dallas. That's where I'm staying,' Roy said.

He had come in from Vernon, a four-hour drive away, to do some business, to see his married children and to see me. His wife, Marjorie, was at their other home in San Carlos in Mexico. She was recuperating from the stroke he had written to me about, and he was still worried about her. Now and again during the next two days he would apologize and interrupt our conversation to telephone San Carlos, to soothe and reassure her, saying a gentle goodbye each time with, 'I love you, darlin'.' I thought: no doubting *this* man's good nature. 'Pappy' they had called him in the old days. I could see why.

We began to talk about his early life, and it was some time that first day that he said: 'I wanted an empire.' He said it sitting in his chair at the Motor Inn, a long finger tapping his bony knee abstractedly, as if he saw something very far away.

Outside La Quinta a non-stop flow of traffic belched its way past the neon signs, the untidy ribbon development and the expensive garden suburbs spreading out like a giant fan from the tight, unexpectedly small cluster of skyscrapers in downtown Dallas. Overhead, a twin-engined jet dropped down towards the Dallas–Fort Worth Airport.

'I wanted an empire. Yes, I did.'

An empire? Had that idea really churned in his head 20,000 feet above the peaks and ravines of Upper Burma as he peered around for Japanese Zeros and wished his fleece-lined jacket would meet his pants and keep out the cold? Apparently so. But young Farrell's vision had not been of the sort of empire of the skies that Cathay is today. Not then. For one thing, his original dream had been of ships, not planes. It is odd. In spite of all his flying over the Hump in C-47s and his confidence in those tough little aircraft, when Farrell returned to the United States in 1945, burning to get his hands on something to haul commodities across the 7,000 miles of the Pacific to the Far East and make a fortune, aircraft were not in his mind. Aircraft were too small. A ship: that was what he was after. Extraordinary? Well, a boat was what that entrepreneur had used to launch himself to success after the Spanish–American War.

'What I didn't know when I got back from the war,' Farrell was saying, 'was that there were no boats for sale. And had I been able to buy a boat I would have been unable to fill it with commodities. There *were* no commodities. The war was barely over and it was hard to buy even a dozen toothbrushes or a dozen lipsticks.' He laughed. 'Of course, it would be hard to fill a boat with lipsticks, toothbrushes and combs.'

A chance meeting put him on the right and – we can see it now – the obvious track. An old friend drinking with Farrell in the Revere Room of the Lexington Hotel, New York, hearing him moaning about the lack of ships, said, 'Pappy, why don't you buy an aeroplane? War surplus. They're available for purchase right now at Bush Field in Augusta, Georgia.'

Of course! In seconds Roy Farrell, the flier, had thrust ships out of his mind and was up and away to Bush Field, the only stop between his room in the Waldorf Astoria and that Georgia airfield a quick dash into a liquor store for a case of Black Label scotch whisky. Typically he thought: 'It might come in useful.'

Once his mind was on planes Roy knew exactly what he wanted. He closed his eyes, clenched his fists and prayed he would find a C-47 at Bush Field – one of the Douglas Dakotas, the old reliables, he had got to know so well in Assam and China. That was part of the dream. To go back to China in a C-47 would be a little like reliving old times with an old friend. At Bush Field he buttonholed a friendly sergeant and poured out his story. To his dismay, the sergeant, an important official in procurement, regretted that for the moment he was out of C-47s. Perhaps later. . . . If a C-47 came in, Roy implored him, would the sergeant call him – *urgent collect*? 'At the Waldorf Astoria Hotel, New York City.'

'Sure will, Mr Farrell.'

'I suppose you have a jeep?' Farrell wondered aloud. 'Where exactly . . .?'

Presently, when Roy Farrell had left for New York, the sergeant climbed into his jeep and drove off with the case of Black Label on the passenger seat beside him. The phone rang in the Waldorf two or three evenings later and a voice said, 'Captain Farrell, your C-47 will be landing tomorrow daybreak. Can you be here?'

'That's me you hear knocking on your door.' Roy was in a cab to Penn Station almost before the sergeant had rung off.

Sure enough, at Bush Field at daybreak, as Farrell watched, his palms wet with excitement, a C-47 touched down; she taxied up; her engines were chopped. A perky, good-natured little thing, he thought. In his euphoric state he could have sworn she winked at him when he walked up to her.

'I went aboard. I looked at her records. She had come out of Dismantling, Inspection and Repair, which was the most thorough going-over the Army Air Force could give to an aeroplane. I checked the instruments and the interior, then got out and kicked the tyres. I understood C-47s pretty well, and I knew – I just *knew* – I had found my plane.'

He had found Betsy.

There was a little formality to complete before he possessed her. He flew at once to Washington DC, bearing a cheque for $30,000 payable to the Foreign Liquidation Commission – and there for a moment he thought his world had come to an end. Eagerly pushing the cheque through the cashier's window, he heard the clerk's voice: 'Captain Farrell, this plane has already been sold to American Airlines.'

Farrell felt faint.

'I yelled, "No, it can't have been." The clerk assured me it had definitely been sold. No question. I said the rules specified the aircraft had to be inspected at Bush Field – *nowhere else* – and that no American Airlines representative had been at Bush Field the previous sun-up when she arrived there, so who but me *could* have bought her? "Makes no difference," the clerk said. "She's bought." '

Roy Farrell thought it made a big difference. ' "Can I use your phone?" I asked him. "Sure," he said. "Who are you calling?" I told him first I was going to call Congressman Ed Gossett who had lived at Vernon, our home town, for six years; and second, my friend Senator Tom Connally, who was Chairman of the Foreign Relations Committee. The clerk said, "Put the phone down. The plane's yours." '

Cock-a-hoop, Farrell hurried back to Betsy and flew her through a snowstorm to New York's La Guardia Field. There was much to be done. Betsy needed to be converted from a military to a civilian plane – from a C-47 to a DC-3 – and at La Guardia Farrell thought he had friends among Pan Am's mechanics. He begged them: would they do a rush job – for a favour? Sure, they would, his friends said. Oh, sure. Some friends. Days went by and poor Betsy, untouched by human hand, stood forlorn and lonely in the snow. In despair, Roy taxied her across to the maintenance apron of Pan-Am's rival, TWA. At TWA's No. 1 Hangar things did not look much better. A crew chief there laughed in a scornful manner and said, 'Look, bud, we're having so much trouble with these new Connies – these Constellations – we aren't about to spare a man to do any converting for *you*.' Horribly aware that China was a long, long way away, Roy decided it was time to show character. And a scene followed that would make an excellent climax to reel one of a film biography of Farrell. This is the chief actor's own account of it:

'I handed the head mechanic a hundred dollar bill, and at about four, at the end of the afternoon shift, I climbed onto the wing of a Constellation and a whole lot of mechanics were gathered below. I might have been "Vinegar Joe" Stilwell or Claire ("Flying Tigers") Chennault or Lord Mountbatten addressing the troops. You know, straight from the shoulder stuff. I told 'em exactly what I wanted. I told 'em I had bought a C-47 and was damned well going to fly it back to China to start an airline. There was a whole bunch of laughter. But they soon saw I was serious. And then any number of volunteers came forward and I told 'em I'd pay whatever bill they presented me – hey! eyebrows shot up at that. I added I thought they were good guys and would not overcharge. We exchanged grins. Yeah, grins. Within ten minutes my baby was in the hangar out of the cold and snow, and the mechanics were swarming all over her.'

While volunteer mechanics installed cabin tanks for the long haul to

China and removed heating equipment from the fuselage to give extra cargo weight, Farrell rushed about buying things to sell to the Chinese. Combs, lipsticks, a gross or two of toothbrushes. That didn't seem much, so he sped to a Fulton Street shop that specialized in buying used clothes from wealthy families and soon he had a plane-load of 'Lord Chesterfield' coats, tails, tuxedos, sports coats, suits, dressing gowns, smoking jackets. . . . The unsuspecting poor of China were about to find themselves perfectly dressed for the Kentucky Derby or dinner at the Waldorf. Never mind, Roy thought: the Chinese need clothes, any clothes, and clothes they will get.

Officially certified 'civilian', Betsy was swiftly packed to bursting with countless bales of morning coats and toothbrushes. Roy personally paid and thanked the cooperative TWA mechanics. One last problem remained. Who would fly Betsy to China? Roy could not fly all that way alone. He asked about and in no time had signed up Bob Russell, a young retired captain in the Army Air Force with much experience in C-47s ('or so his records showed'). A navigator? Up came a volunteer: Bill Geddes Brown. Now at last all was ready. Roy opened a bottle or two of champagne.

'All of a sudden it hit me,' he told me at La Quinta. 'Now, after thirteen years of dreaming of being the first to fly into a foreign country after the war with a cargo, I could see the possibility of actually *starting an airline*. After thirteen years, I realized I was ready to go. We got our spurs on and mounted our steed by crawling over all those bales of clothing in the fuselage. I taxied out, ran up the engines and called for take-off clearance. The tower called back and we were cleared. I released the brakes and started for the runway. We lifted off. . . .'

Roy paused and stared at me, his eyes wide, remembering something. 'Abreast of Philadelphia, Pennsylvania, I did a 90-degree turn to look back at New York. It shone as if it were fairyland.'

Miami, Puerto Rico, British Guiana, Brazil, across the South Atlantic to Ascension Island, Liberia – Pappy Farrell, Bob Russell, Bill Geddes Brown and Betsy flew gamely on to China, not without experiencing moments of interest. Approaching Belem in Brazil, Russell's presumed flying expertise had begun to display serious shortcomings and Farrell seized control of Betsy 'to prevent us ending as a pile of ashes'. It was the first and last time he'd ever had to do such a thing, and though he stayed in the team Russell never landed or took off one of Farrell's planes again. Over Libya they dropped down to 500 feet to get a look at the relics of the Desert War: hundreds of miles of crashed aircraft, burned-out tanks and half-tracks, shattered bunkers and Tripoli harbour blocked by sunken ships. Christmas Day in Cairo, then on to Abadan, Karachi, Agra. A New Year's Eve party in Calcutta, and next day Farrell was in Kunming once more – where his euphoria even survived a partial looting of Betsy by thieves who stole $5,000-worth of toffs' clothing. That left the final leg to Shanghai. But in Shanghai all air traffic was shut down; the airport had virtually no visibility. Was Betsy – were all of them – going to be written off at this moment of triumph?

'We had no fuel for an alternative field, if one had existed,' Farrell said. 'So we were going in, hell or high water, on the first pass. After all, I had landed in Assam in such ground fog that the first thing I would see was the runway at the tip of my nose. So now, over the tower on the correct heading, and a turn downwind. Gear and flaps down, at 90 miles an hour, I crossed over where the airport's boundary fence should have been.' Farrell's broadest grin. 'Lucky. First thing – a runway light out my left window. I was straddling the centre line. One half second either way – a total crack-up.'

The USAAF bedded down the three happy if exhausted Americans for the night. While Betsy slept on Lungwah Airfield, her oriental destiny assured, Roy Farrell lay with the bed-covers over his head, thinking: 'Suppose World War II hadn't come along, I would be in South America or some place, running an insurance business. But this is not South America, it's Shanghai, and – my God! – the first part of my plan is complete.'

Now he could start thinking seriously of that 'empire'.

SHANGHAI A CITY OF CHAOS.
OLD SHANGHAI GONE FOR EVER.

The headlines over two long features in an Australian weekly newspaper summed up a decidedly topsy-turvy postwar situation. The Shanghai into which Farrell had almost crash-landed was a chaotic city only recently given up by the defeated Japanese, and the Americans replacing them had moved in in a big and very noisy way.

'The Cathay and Palace Hotels, Broadway Mansions and Cathay Mansions out in French-town,' the Australian reported, 'are among the world's most luxurious buildings and apartment houses, and the Americans have them all.' He sounded bitter; had he been relegated to a doss-house? 'In them American officers live like kings.' Armies of cockroaches were doing the same: the city was once again a place of the ultra-rich and the devastatingly poor. Good food and drink was plentiful but fabulously dear. The hundred or more nightclubs ranged from honky-tonks to elaborate establishments with Chinese tumblers and White Russian girl dancers as the main attraction. The behaviour of the American Navy was 'scandalous' (the reporter let fly again) 'with American sailors from the warships lying out in the Whangpoo River brawling with Chinese nightly in the city's streets'. What is more, bribery was almost *de rigueur*. Still, like it or not, the reporter concluded, 'Shanghai was, and will still be, China's richest city, dominating as it has for a century the mouth of the mighty Yangtze and its valley. But from now on, with the abolition of the International Settlements and with them a 104-year-old direct foreign dominance over Shanghai's economic affairs, it will be a Chinese city, and it will probably take a decade to set in order again.' The guns of those foreign warships lying off the Bund would never again be called upon to protect the interests of European taipans ashore; they were there now by courtesy of the Chinese government – Chiang's government, for the moment. If anybody was losing sleep over the impending Communist victory, neither the reporter nor Roy Farrell seemed to meet them.

Roy himself was probably far too busy for political crystal-gazing. This young Texan-in-a-hurry soon found that his American passport was less than helpful. The China–America trade was already oversubscribed and he determined not to waste time with that. Where to turn? Australia? He made inquiries. It looked tempting. Wide open, too. He'd flown piece goods from America to Shanghai – why not piece goods from Sydney? In true bustling Farrell style, he buttonholed a friendly RAF squadron leader in the British Legation on Foochow Creek (the British were representing Australia in China) and soon had him hypnotized with his flamboyant account of life over the Hump, of how he'd adopted 'his baby' Betsy, and of the flight halfway around the world. Succumbing to Texan charm, the British airman nodded enthusiastically when Farrell spoke of using Betsy to fly Australian commodities to Shanghai; furthermore he promised to do all he could to arrange official landing permission for Betsy at the Australian end. Farrell floated down the British Legation's steps as if reborn.

Even so, anyone with his mind set on getting a new airline business off the ground in the corrupt world of post-war Shanghai had to face setbacks to shatter the strongest souls. You needed permits for everything: to stay, to go, to trade, to rent offices, and of course to fly – and you needed to find friendly officials to give them to you. Eight men out of ten might have given up – sighed, shed a tear for a lost dream, and headed home to sell encyclopedias door-to-door. Anything might have seemed preferable to the trekking round offices; the pleading with indifferent or hostile officials; the confrontations in freezing hotels and smoke-filled bars with idle or suspicious American majors, greedy Chinese colonels and evil-tempered generals of both countries who might offer invaluable help or invite you brutally to get lost. Farrell has never been, to put it mildly, unduly respectful of rank, and he needed all the tact he could summon to be civil to military men whose own financial ambitions were frequently tied to CNAC (now Farrell's rival), or whose officiousness was buttressed by contacts at the highest levels of government in Washington.

Luckily Roy Farrell had what it took. His relentless determination, his down-to-earth manner, his good-natured Texan smile (which can only be described as 'sunny'), made short work of the problem of operating from China. He naturally turned his partners' (and his own) easy way with a drink to advantage. Russell, Brown and Farrell could have drawn an extremely accurate map of Shanghai's bar circuit. 'And since,' as Farrell says, 'their clients normally were drinking a good bit, we learned a good bit about Shanghai.'

Within a mere day or two, Farrell and his partners began to settle in. First, where to live? It was mid-winter and unbelievably cold. All those American officers were said to occupy the best accommodation, yet Farrell somehow wangled a room in that imposing block called Cathay Mansions. Once upon a time Cathay Mansions had been grand, but the Japanese Army had changed that, even melting down the plumbing and heating systems to make bullets. Farrell bought six old-fashioned oil heaters that smelled and smoked abominably, and thanks to them – and an impressive intake of strong buttered rums at bedtime – the three partners usually managed to get enough sleep. As for an office, Brown and Russell warned Farrell he was foolish to want to rent one in a city like Shanghai without having any precise idea what the future was going to be. But Farrell had thought things out.

'You have to operate out of an *office*,' he argued. 'You can't go about building an airline or an empire without an *office*.'

Naturally he soon found one and left 'Ged' Brown in it to cope with the paperwork necessary to get a company properly licensed for business. Then he went after Australia. Striding hopefully up the steps of the British Legation, he shook hands again with the friendly squadron leader. He was not disappointed. With a few encouraging words, the squadron leader handed Farrell his landing permission for Darwin.

That permission was a licence to make big money and Farrell lost no time in simply gazing at it. In what seemed like a matter of seconds, with Russell beside him, he had clambered aboard Betsy once more and was winging south. As they went, Ged Brown threw open the office door at 25 rue du Consulat in Shanghai and introduced the world to the 'Roy Farrell Export-Import Company'.

CHAPTER 4

With the opening of the Shanghai office things began to move. Farrell and Russell, flying south, spent a single night in Canton and only a short time in the Peninsula Hotel, Hong Kong, which was then Kowloon's grandest but virtually empty in the aftermath of the Japanese occupation. Just time enough for Farrell to change his savings (some $30,000) into local currency and Australian pounds, then once more Betsy took to the air for the 4,000 miles via Darwin, where he wrangled a licence to land at Kingsford-Smith Airfield at Mascot, outside Sydney.

She arrived there on 4 February 1946. Farrell found delays to contend with at Sydney over landing permits, but eventually these were granted and with them the Roy Farrell Export-Import Company had won what he was after: the right to carry freight (but not paying passengers) between Australia and the Far East. The dream advanced. Again Farrell didn't waste a second. He and Russell ransacked Sydney for the woollen goods they needed for China. In no time they had opened their second office, in the Prudential Building, Martin Place, and recruited an Australian – a thirty-three-year-old ex-squadron leader and former accountant called Neil Buchanan – to help run it.

Then Farrell called a press conference.

It was another turning-point, for Roy was by nature a one-man public relations organization. Next morning every newspaper carried pictures of three cheerful young men in new suits and bright ties, grinning broadly. One caption read: 'A new air service, the only one of its kind, will begin to operate from Sydney to China tomorrow, when these three men set off in a Douglas Dakota aircraft, laden with Australian woollen knitwear and piece goods, which they will sell. They expect to arrive in Shanghai in three days' time. Left to right: Neil Buchanan (Aus), Roy Farrell (US) and R. S. Russell (US).' The *Sydney Morning Herald* gave details: 'Mr Farrell made 520 crossings over the hazardous Burma "Hump" route to China. Mr Russell won the American DFC air medal, a Presidential citation, and the Chinese Order of the Flying Cloud for air operations with the Chinese–American Air Force.' The accompanying story went on: 'This will be the first air shipment of Australian goods for China by the Roy Farrell Export-Import Co., three and a half tons of clothes – for the tattered of China.' The *Melbourne Herald* quoted Farrell as saying that on the return flights he hoped to bring back 'Chinese silks, fishing tackle and napery'.

Smiling, charming, expansive, he also revealed something of his vision of the future. 'We will continue to fly these needs into China until the sea routes are open again, and then, when we have established our markets, we will do most of our hauling by our own ships and fly in only urgently needed medical equipment and supplies.' So the ghosts of that long-dead entrepreneur of the Spanish–American War days and his long-dead ships still hovered.

On 28 February, Farrell and Russell set off for the first time from Sydney to Shanghai. A *Sunday Telegraph* journalist along for the trip enthusiastically reported at the end of it: 'Thirty-three hours flying time out from Sydney, Australia's first overseas air freight service delivered three-and-a-half tons of Australian goods for Shanghai – and sold them all in six hours!' The flight up to China covered a span of the recent Pacific War: Cloncurry, then bomb-battered, fly-blown Darwin; on to tropical Morotai in the Dutch Halamaheras, where jungle had recaptured an American wartime base save for a single red mud and gravel strip; to Leyte in the Philippines, then on to Manila (almost completely destroyed by American bombing) and thence to a Hong Kong still recovering from the shock of occupation, dilapidated but British once more, and desperate for trade.

'The American ex-Army fliers were offered high prices,' the *Sunday Telegraph* man wrote, 'to unload their freight at Manila and Hong Kong, but they had already contracted for Shanghai deliveries.' In Shanghai itself, he reported, there had so far been American and British deliveries of UN refugee relief aid and petrol, but little else. The market therefore seemed wide open for Farrell's woollens. 'Old traders are tipping that China will probably be divided into three main trading spheres – Russia will dominate Manchuria, America will control the rich Yangtze Valley with Shanghai and Hangkow as entry ports, while Britain will control the south through Hong Kong. . . .' In these predictions Mao Tse-tung was not mentioned. Although the proclamation that henceforth China would be known as the People's Republic was only three and a half years away, the wise 'old traders' of Shanghai had nothing to tell the *Sunday Telegraph* about a communist threat.

37

One photograph in particular of Roy Farrell taken at that time reflects his realization of the region's commercial possibilities. It is the one from which I recognized him at Dallas–Fort Worth Airport forty years later, the spirit of 'up, up and away' personified. And Betsy is shining brightly, no longer a drab little army work-horse anonymous behind her military number NC58093: a newly painted logo on her aluminium fuselage – a big circle enclosing the flags of Australia, America and Chiang's China with a kangaroo bounding in the top left-hand corner and a laughing green dragon bottom right – boasts of her new civilian identity. 'Bound for China,' the caption proclaimed. At that moment did Farrell remember the casual suggestion of the old friend in New York's Lexington Hotel – 'Pappy, why don't you buy an aeroplane?'. If so, those words must have seemed to him like something spoken in heaven.

Cash flowed in. The air cargoes of woollen goods from Australia sold out in Shanghai in no time. It was like throwing fish to hungry seals and, as Farrell pointed out to his suddenly prosperous partners, '$70,000 clear for seven or eight days' flying is not bad.' Indeed, in those days it was very big money – so big that after only a couple of deliveries it was possible to expand the organization. More aircraft, more managers – and more pilots to free Farrell and Russell to cope with burgeoning paperwork. When Millard Nasholds, another old American comrade-in-arms from CNAC days, asked Farrell if he could come in, Farrell said 'Sure', and put 'Nash' in charge of a rented staff house and a new branch office in Manila. The air shuttle of passengers (largely Chinese) between Manila and Hong Kong had become another money-spinner.

Then something of the greatest importance happened. Syd de Kantzow reappeared from Calcutta. It seems that even in the Hump days he had wanted to team up with Roy Farrell in some post-war aviation venture. As soon as he had heard of Roy's plans to sink money into a plane and fly her to the Far East, he had sent $10,000 of his own money from India to an absent-minded friend of Farrell's in New York, asking to buy a share in what he saw was an enterprise quite after his own heart. The friend, strangely, had forgotten to pass on the money to Farrell (he returned it later), but when Syd walked into the office in the rue du Consulat Farrell welcomed him with open arms. There and then he joined the partnership.

Farrell not only liked Syd; he admired him too. He was not alone, for Syd was as much respected in the Australian aviation world as he had been in Sino–American CNAC, and news of his new employment was greeted with excited interest Down Under. When he arrived in Darwin with Betsy his photograph was taken for the *Sydney Sun* of 17 April 1946 – the handsome, serious face with the slim moustache, as like Ronald Colman as ever. 'With a cargo of Chinese silk, Mr S. de Kantzow of the Roy Farrell Export Co.,' the newspaper informed its readers. Back in Shanghai, as if to celebrate his old friend's reappearance, Farrell bought a second C-47 (quickly named 'Nikki'). He also sent a message to Syd to do some recruiting, and so the company acquired its first Australian employees: John Wawn, known to his friends as 'Pinky', and Neville Hemsworth, both pilots and old friends of Syd; Vic Leslie, who had had much wartime experience in New Guinea and the Pacific as a first officer; and a radio officer, Lyell 'Mum' Louttit. These men were the first 'outsiders' to fly Betsy.

Although Farrell was soon able to augment this little fleet with two more DC-3s in 1946, and in the following year with yet two more, those pioneer postwar fliers had taken on a hard job. For 1947 was still a pretty ramshackle world to fly in. According to Farrell, 'Maps over Australia didn't exist, hardly. Sure, they showed rivers, lakes, etc., but for most of the year rivers and lakes didn't exist, and there was little if any trace of where they might have been.' It was often a case of taking off on a 1,000-mile flight and pointing the aeroplane in the general direction of where you wanted to go. When you began to get close, you turned on your radio and homed in on the airfield.

Neville Hemsworth was a Sydney man who had been with Qantas, flying six or eight passengers at a time in Liberators – old wartime four-engined bombers – between Ceylon and Australia. That had been a long, turbulent haul, but even he found the immense distances of the Sydney–Shanghai–Sydney route tough going. 'In those remote days,' he says, looking back, 'flying Betsy to Shanghai involved six hours from Sydney to Cloncurry, then, oh, I'd say twenty-four hours all told to Manila, and then another nine hours over Formosa to Shanghai. Thirty-three hours or more. Well, we were young then. We had no regulations about sleep. We dozed in the cockpit and just kept going hour after hour, just three of us – Wawn, myself and a radio officer. And that mountain of cargo sitting there behind us.'

I have squeezed my six-foot-three frame into Betsy's cockpit – an historic cockpit but so tiny that my knees would have been literally around my ears if they hadn't been immovably trapped by the control column. Thanks to this experiment I was able, as I listened to Neville Hemsworth, to speculate on what it might be like to fly for thirty-three hours on end in that tortured position. I said, 'You must have been dead at the end of each trip.'

'Buggered, yeah.'

Eric Kirkby, the astute Australian who came in to help in the Sydney office of which Russell was now in charge, remembers only too vividly a flight he took as a passenger to Hong Kong and back. 'Coffee in vacuum flasks. Packed sandwiches. Grog? Good Lord, no. And the heat! No air conditioning then. Morotai is bang on the Equator. Nothing there; no buildings; no shelter. Phew! You stood under the wings for shade, and stared at a few red-hot fuel drums. If anything, the field at Darwin was worse – notorious for its swarms of huge, black flies that covered you from head to foot like bees swarming.'

All this and the weather too; the north–south route crossed both the Equator and the typhoon belt. Luckily, Betsy (like all DC-3s and DC-4s) was exceptionally canny; she could ride a typhoon as a bird rides a gust of wind, and it was just as well she could. In those days of simple navigational aids, you didn't always know when to expect bad storms, and when they loomed up, as Neville Hemsworth explains, 'You couldn't afford to change course to go very far round them. If you diverted too far you could end up not knowing where you were.' Another hazard lay in Farrell's precious cargo. In really bad turbulence the crew would be seriously worried that all those tons of freight might shift and crush them. 'If it got very rough, we could only put the gear down so that going slower we'd rise and float with the weather. Going fast, we'd cut and bump right through it.'

In the book of reminiscences he called *Syd's Pirates*, Chic Eather, a young Australian who joined the company shortly after Hemsworth, described an occasion when survival depended on how quickly he and the crew could dump most of a very precious cargo. Heavy with freight, his DC-3 had lurched up so ponderously from the coral strip of Morotai, her wing-tips so perilously close to the fringe of coconut palms, that Eather suddenly wondered whether he had chosen the right employment. At 9,000 feet, he was even more appalled to hear the normally placid voice of the pilot, Pinky Wawn, yelling, 'Get back and start tossing out the cargo!' It seemed they had lost 3,000 feet and were going down fast – the port engine had packed up. Roy Farrell himself was aboard, Eather wrote, 'and as I pushed past him his face was white and strained. With his background of flying the Hump, this emergency would not have frightened him – but jettisoning his cargo of woollen merchandise . . .!' And the precious cargo was followed by two life rafts, two stretchers, sundry aircraft tools, safety belts, life belts and other small but expensive items. Snatched from the jaws of death, young Eather was beset with visions of puzzled inhabitants on the beautiful islands below fleeing a lethal hail of 180lb bales of woollens. What had they done to make the gods so angry?

Something more must be said now about Sydney de Kantzow, for his sudden reappearance at Farrell's side is crucial to the history of Cathay Pacific.

Peace had thrown him into a new and unfamiliar world. The pith helmet had gone; India, the Hump, tiger-shooting – all that must have seemed a long way behind him. When de Kantzow, a demobilized pilot with a determined expression, stood at dusty, fly-infested Darwin airfield next to a DC-3 loaded with Chinese silk-lined hats and pig bristles, he was in some ways a different man.

One important link with India remained. Syd was about to marry a beautiful English girl he had first met in Calcutta in 1943 – Angela, daughter of the British Resident in Patiala, John Duncan May, had been born in Multan, a city in that part of the Punjab which is now in Pakistan. They were married at the Anglican Cathedral in Shanghai shortly after Syd joined Roy Farrell, and the *China Press* made the event doubly memorable by attaching to the photograph it published of the happy couple on the cathedral steps a caption of bewildering inaccuracy. 'The marriage of Miss Angela Mary de Kantzow to Capt H. L. Woods. . . .'

Flying expertise coupled with a driving organizational ability were exactly what was needed in Farrell's outfit, and Syd's partnership with Roy was as fitting as that of Marks and Spencer or Laurel and Hardy. From now on, de Kantzow worked like the fanatic he could be to build up a flexible, if rough and ready, flying organization that was in effect the air transport wing of the Roy Farrell Export-Import Company. If Roy was the 'Pappy' (his universal nickname), Syd became the show's stern and exacting Nanny. All those still alive who flew with him talk with reverence of Syd's flying ability. Neville Hemsworth, whose good opinion is not thoughtlessly bestowed, speaks for many others: 'Syd was a very *smooth* pilot. I mean, you get "flyers" and you get "drivers". Syd was a "flyer".' Roy Farrell says simply, 'Syd was as good a pilot as I ever rode with.'

Because Roy himself was less interested in flying than in the buying and selling – in fact he soon stopped flying altogether – the two men complemented each other as perfectly as a good tennis doubles pair, and thus the pattern of the future began to assert itself. The new 'order of battle' was: first Bob Russell, then Eric Kirkby (a most competent ex-RAAF equipment officer) in the Sydney office; Farrell and 'Nash' in Manila; 'Ged' Brown in Shanghai; and Neil Buchanan in Hong Kong. Syd, the air 'supremo', flitted purposefully about, gnawed by visions of more and better planes and more pilots to fly them. Soon, because Hong Kong was at the geographical centre of things, he acquired an office of his own there – a room rented from P. J. Lobo & Co. at 4 Chater Road.

Business continued brisk but in a characteristically hit-and-miss fashion. As far as outside appearances went, Buchanan's office writing paper was pretty smart, carrying not only the Farrell company's address ('Prince's Building, Ice House Street, Hong Kong' and its cable address, 'Bronco') but the company logo that Betsy and the other planes already wore – the debonair kangaroo, the smiling dragon and the three flags. Beneath the logo the company proclaimed itself 'The first international Airmerchandising service in the world', and its prospectus that the interesting range of Australian products it 'airmerchandised' ran from men's worsteds and Scamp swimsuits, to plastic belts and picture frames. Nor did things stop there. Presently a most unusual advertisement appeared in Hong Kong's *South China Morning Post*.

OYSTERS!
SYDNEY ROCK OYSTERS
BY AIR

From Australia,
in 32 Hours

These very fine oysters,
well known in Hong Kong as a great delicacy,
have been brought, alive in the shell, to Hong Kong
from the Sydney Oyster Beds
in the same time as they reach the Sydney householder.

Yet another service from the

ROY FARRELL EXPORT–IMPORT CO., LTD.

Farrell's Sydney office still treasures a cable that Kirkby and Bob Russell received from Hong Kong: 'Strictly confidential Korea shipment netted over £60,000 sterling.' Kirkby still feels proud of it – for good reason. For those days it was a *very* big sum which puts Farrell's success into perspective, just as the 'Oysters by Air' idea demonstrates his flair for salesmanship. As for his partners, what they lacked in business experience they made up for with a simple exuberance that can be seen in the boisterous letters (often in longhand since they decided they should save money on secretaries) that flew back and forth between them. 'Have lined up a terrific cargo,' Buchanan wrote to Russell from Shanghai while on a visit to Ged

Brown. 'Some costume jewellery in the form of real silver bracelets, some leather fancy goods ... brocade Mandarin jackets.' Chinese Mandarin jackets for Sydney's élite – Why not? In another letter to Russell, Buchanan talked excitedly of the big money in dried fruit and radiator wire (whatever that is), signing off breezily, 'Keep your legs together, Yours sincerely, Neil B.' Another time, Russell seemed quite carried away by the thought of a consignment of blankets and '700 gross human hairnets at £2,000 selling price Australia'. Something of the haywire element of the whole venture comes into focus in a long, peppy letter from Roy Farrell himself during a recce of the China market. Typed in slapdash fashion on the (second-hand) Shanghai office Remington and addressed to 'Dear Bob and Syd', it reveals the warmth of Roy's easy-going character that was itself vital to the success of the enterprise. The letter reads, in part:

> Here is some of the latest 'gen' in Shanghai.
> 1. We have purchased another C-47, price $11,000. It has 2 good motors, full radio equipment, good instruments etc. . . .
> 2. Our Chinese (maintenance) crew is more on the ball than ever. . . .
> 4. Vickie is married. The reason I know is that Ged Brown says she hasn't called him the last few days so she must be married.
> 5. We have submitted a letter to UNRRA [United Nations Refugee Relief Agency] offering our willingness to charter a C-47 to them . . .
> 10. The sun refuses to shine . . .
> 11. Customs stopped us from going in or out. . . . But this afternoon decided to let us leave. Coming back is discussed in the next chapter . . .
> 13. Business here is still OK, but the market on woollens (women's) is beginning to fall off . . .
> 19. I think Ged Brown has worms . . .
> 20. Angie is missing Syd an awful lot.

It ends: 'Love and kisses, Roy.'

Syd had already rented office space in Chater Road, and the company also opened a passenger ticket office (it was a desk opening on to the lobby) at the Peninsula Hotel – visible signs of the mutually agreed division of powers in the Farrell–de Kantzow partnership.

The separation of the almost wholly American-owned Roy Farrell Export-Import Company from its aviation department was first foreshadowed in a most significant report from Neil Buchanan in Hong Kong. The report refers to a 'successful' meeting he had had with Mr A. J. R. Moss, Hong Kong's Director of Civil Aviation, 'over a cup of tea and a bottle of whisky'. The subject of the meeting was one of critical importance – namely, the immediate necessity for the company's air operations to be registered in British Hong Kong if they were to be allowed to continue using it as a base.

Buchanan wrote:

> As regards air ops. into and out of the Colony, that is very definitely on the up and up. . . . I have been given full approval for as many flights as we can make – *subject to British registration of aircraft, the only basis on which we would be allowed to operate*. When Betsy is due for re-registration, Moss is going to let me know if we may continue with a US registration.

The italics are mine: the crisis was Farrell's.

Betsy, as much as Farrell, Russell, Nasholds and Geddes Brown, was, in her inanimate way, an American citizen. But Hong Kong was most emphatically British, and this insistence on the plane's British registration by the British Civil Aviation Authority in British Hong Kong was a decisive element in the emergence of an independent Farrell–de Kantzow aviation venture in the Far East and, later, of the much bigger and wholly British version of it.

Both men saw quite plainly how desirable an operating base in Hong Kong rather than Shanghai would be. You had only to look at a map and it stood out a mile: Hong Kong was the region's very heart. It was a bit of a wreck, but it was also delightfully free of the political torment that so racked mainland China. And there was another pressing reason for giving up Shanghai as a principal base for air operations. The question of forming a Chinese airline was much in the minds of Chinese businessmen in Shanghai, and one in particular looked enviously at Roy Farrell's success: his name was T. C. Loong, a most powerful man in Chiang Kai-shek's China who was later to found another airline, Civil Air Transport (CAT), in Taipeh. Loong offered to buy Farrell's air operation and when Farrell demurred he turned nasty in retaliation. Farrell's planes faced arrest each time they landed in China. 'I realized then my hopes of an airline in China were non-existent,' Farrell told me. 'So that's why I decided to form a Hong Kong-registered airline instead.'

Thus Hong Kong entered the story as Cathay Pacific's permanent home.

CHAPTER 5

The territory of Hong Kong, which means 'Fragrant Harbour', looks unimpressive on a map, hanging like an insignificant pilot fish beneath the underbelly of the mainland Chinese province of Quangdong, formerly anglicized as Kwangtung. It comprises Hong Kong Island (32 square miles), the mainland peninsula of Kowloon (3.5 square miles), the mountainous New Territories and numerous islands that in 1946 amounted to 335 square miles: 370 square miles in all (later land reclamation has added quite a bit more). But this appendage to China is perfectly poised between South East Asia, the Far East and Australasia, with the Pacific on its doorstep and, beyond the Pacific – America.

What above all else gives Hong Kong the right to the title 'Gateway to South China' is the broad, natural harbour between the island and the peninsula. This expanse of water is protected to the west by a number of islands big and small, and approachable from the east through the quarter-mile-wide Lei Yue Mun Gap – a gap of great importance to aviators as well as ships' captains, as will be seen.

To the west, the largest island of all is Lantau, more than twice the size of Hong Kong Island itself and at its highest over 3,000 feet – a dragon-like shape pointing its straggly tail towards the broad western anchorage. And your aircraft, swooping in from Bangkok or Singapore over the grey mouth of the Pearl River, cuts first across Lantau to traverse the inevitable fleet of ocean-going ships at anchor, and then across pebble-sized Stonecutters Island before skimming the fluttering tenement washing on the threshold of Kai Tak's runway.

What of the Colony's air services between the wars?

Hong Kong's only airfield, Kai Tak was (and still is) situated in the northeast of Kowloon, its eastern edges skirting the waters of Kowloon Bay. Its name derived from the early part of the century when two prominent

Chinese businessmen, Sir Kai Ho-kai and Mr Au Tak, not remotely interested in flying, simply decided they liked the look of this remote piece of green, grassy land, bought it and enlarged it by reclaiming land from the Bay with the intention of making it into a 45-acre garden city development. Before that could come to anything, a group of British air enthusiasts spotted the land as ideal for the flying club the Colony lacked, and they talked the Governor, Sir Cecil Clementi, into agreeing to a compulsory purchase. Money was forthcoming to buy it and soon, in the early twenties, Sir Cecil drove out to declare the Flying Club open.

From that moment events moved rapidly. The interest of the Colony's ruler was now roused and thoughts of imperial defence came to mind. Sir Cecil agreed that yet more money should be put out to reclaim another 160 acres of Kowloon Bay and then, in partnership with the RAF, the government actually took charge of what was now the Colony's new and only official aerodrome. In next to no time a few Fairey Flycatcher aircraft of the Fleet Air Arm were based there under the eye of a Director of Air Services, who was also Harbour Master. Flight training in Avro Tudors began. The Portuguese Air Force wing in Macao was allowed to park a couple of its Fairey 1110 biplanes there. This was the beginning. It was the coming of the flying boats that proved the making of Kai Tak Airport.

Britain's Imperial Airways Empire Mail run from the United Kingdom to the East began the influx. Aviation enthusiasts, veterans of the First World War, had promised successive Hong Kong governors: 'We'll be flying out from London in seven days!' and eventually, with Imperial Airways' luxurious twenty-four-passenger, 164mph, Short S-23 flying boats, 'they' managed to do just that. Important developments across the Pacific, too, focused attention on Hong Kong. In 1937 Pan American Airways began a trans-Pacific 'China Clipper' service, with huge (for those days) four-engined Martin M-130 flying boats carrying forty-eight passengers at 163mph. They joined San Francisco to Hong Kong, touching down for fuel at Honolulu, Midway Island, Wake Island, Guam and Manila, connecting with Pan American's affiliate CNAC, the Chinese airline, on the Manila–Hong Kong sector. By 1938, as a result of this pioneering, 9,969 passengers a year were disembarking on the mud and grass airport where Sir Kai Ho-kai and Mr Au Tak's garden city might have been.

Then there was an interruption. On 8 December 1941, out of a clear sky, planes were seen approaching Kai Tak. The Second World War was well under way, of course, but people cheered and waved, thinking they were the long-awaited reinforcement of RAF planes coming to help defend the Colony against the Japanese. Help was certainly needed; the existing

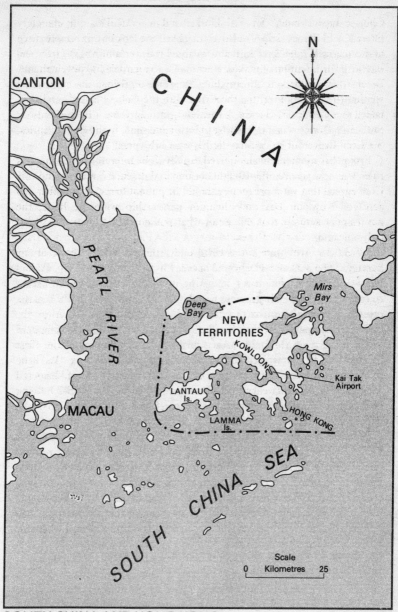

SOUTH CHINA AND HONG KONG

defence was laughable. Wing Commander 'Ginger' Sullivan, in charge of Hong Kong's RAF station, had at his disposal nothing more impressive than four Vickers Wildebeeste torpedo-bombers and a trio of ungainly Supermarine Walrus amphibians, which could just about make 100mph with luck and a strong tail wind. Unfortunately, the planes everyone was applauding were not RAF reinforcements but Japanese bombers. Their bombs soon began to fall on Kai Tak's single runway, and among the Wildebeestes that Sullivan had assembled near the seadrome so recently used by the Imperial Airways flying boats. For Hong Kong it was clearly all up. A few intrepid British pilots were skilful enough to land between the bomb craters at night to pick up a handful of British evacuees, but everyone else (and the Colony itself) went 'into the bag' on Christmas Day 1941. The Colony died, and nearly four years of Japanese occupation went by before anything in it came to life again. Roy and Syd arrived a year after the Japanese surrender. What did they find?

Needless to say, what they saw had very little in common with what one sees now. The bankers' playground of today, with its ultra-modern gold and ivory skyscrapers, its high-rise luxury housing, the urban sprawl that seeks to contain a relentlessly growing population that at present easily tops six million – everything that so impresses us today lay hidden in the unforeseeable future. At the time of the Japanese surrender in August 1945 Hong Kong was a disaster area. During their occupation the damage through looting and neglect – not to mention American bombing – had been immense. Roy Farrell took his first look at post-Japanese Hong Kong and saw a sad, end-of-the-road sort of place that seemed to have slipped halfway back to the nineteenth century. Its people had a depressing shabbiness about them. 'The Chinese looked like destitute coolies,' he wrote.

Furthermore, the Colony had been isolated from the world to a degree almost impossible to grasp in these days of jet travel. Shipping had been terribly disrupted, passenger and cargo ships scattered, wrecked or sunk. Hong Kong's harbour – formerly one of the busiest in the world – was still an abandoned and stagnating pool, its anchorage cluttered with the wrecks of eleven big ships and seventy-two smaller ones, some of them deliberately scuttled by the British as the Japanese came in, some victims of General Claire Chennault's China-based bombers, which the supplies flown over the Hump by the likes of Roy and Syd had kept flying. Kowloon's port facilities were in an atrocious state; shipping was at a standstill. Air services, of course, were virtually non-existent. There was no international telephone service. Public transport was so sketchy that it was a problem to get around the Colony at all – it was a bright thought of Farrell's to have imported two jeeps from Okinawa. On top of everything, the Japanese had made off with whatever they could lay hands on. Across the harbour in Kowloon the imposing and conveniently situated Peninsula Hotel (known to everyone as 'the Pen'), the centre of a slowly reviving social life, needed a lot of reviving itself. In spite of its busy lobby and rowdy bar furnished with heavy, hide-backed oriental chairs and huge blue Chinese jars, it was, Farrell thought, little more than an upholstered slum.

Little by little, a makeshift British military administration, overworked and desperately improvising, put together a few basic pieces of the Colony's disjointed life before the returning civilians took over once more in May 1946. Of course, Hong Kong's eventual rehabilitation was assured by the mere fact that it is uniquely situated at the centre of one of the world's most densely populated regions – something that is a good deal easier to see now than it was in 1946. Then, nothing was clear, nothing predictable. The entire Eastern world was a shambles: Imperial Japan a defeated cripple under American occupation; the spirit of China broken by war, its people and land fragmented between the Nationalists and Communists. In the colonial territories of South East Asia – Indochina, Malaya, the Dutch East Indies – the upheaval of war had exposed the essential weakness of the imperial powers, Britain, France and the Netherlands. The spirit of national independence was abroad, and nationalist leaders were planning violent confrontation with colonial governments from Burma to Vietnam, from Laos, Malaya and Singapore to the remotest islands of the Dutch East Indies. Only a born optimist like Roy Farrell could have been quite so confident in the future, quite so sure of making his fortune. 'Oh, things will pick up,' he told his associates. Of course things had to improve. But how long any serious improvement would be in coming no one could foretell.

Meanwhile, for expatriates at least, Hong Kong was an easy-going place and rather fun to be in. 'Syd and Angela were in a Peninsula Hotel suite for a while with her temple dog, Butch,' Roy remembers, 'and actually, we had the darnedest time. It was relaxed, you know. Syd and I used to roll in there from the Star ferry from Hong Kong Island late at night bawling out "San Antonio Rose". I guess you'd be thrown out for doing that today.'

The immediate postwar shortage of ships in the Far East greatly inspired and benefited the rebirth of civil aviation in Hong Kong. For one thing, the task of dragging China back onto its feet, of coping with its millions of ragged, barefoot and half-starved refugees, required every available form of transport and, given the distances involved in this huge country, aircraft played a most important role. Kai Tak soon became relatively busy again with civilian aircraft, most of them belonging to CNAC, flying to and from

China. At the same time British Overseas Airways (BOAC), the postwar successor to Imperial Airways, restored its flying boat service from Britain, once more delivering passengers, mostly senior government officials and businessmen, in just under a week.

A year later, British aircraft of companies to be nominated by His Majesty's Government were granted rights of setting down and taking up passengers at four Chinese airports, Kunming, Canton, Shanghai and Tientsin, and a BOAC subsidiary, Hong Kong Airways, began operating from the Colony under this Sino–British agreement. By 1948 aircraft from the United Kingdom, China, the Philippines, Siam (now Thailand), the USA and France were arriving at Kai Tak at a rate of about twenty-five a day, and in a twelve-month period the number of passengers amounted to nearly a quarter of a million, the majority still passing to and from China. The commonest civilian aircraft were recently demobilized DC-3 Dakotas and DC-4 Skymasters, but a new pride of the skies appeared, too – the 'Connies', the sleek, three-tailed Lockheed Constellations.

This was satisfactory for the time being, but Hong Kong's postwar bugbear was that by modern standards Kai Tak Airport left much to be desired. Aircraft had grown heavier. They needed more space in which to land and take off. Kai Tak itself huddled uneasily under an escarpment of forbidding rocks. The Japanese had increased the little airport's dimensions by ruthlessly demolishing acres of Chinese housing, and they had pulled down the ramparts surrounding Kowloon's ancient Walled City to use its massive stones in the construction of two longer runways. Even so, Chic Eather's first impression of Kai Tak in late 1946 was one of a muddy swamp. Duckboards led to immigration and customs 'offices' located in a cluster of old army tents near the seadrome, and Chic felt his spirits plummeting with every squelching step. Syd de Kantzow did little to raise them by walking him to the centre of the field and jabbing a finger at the enveloping escarpments to the east and north. 'Never,' he said, fixing young Eather with a hard eye, '*never* let yourself be a party to a take-off on Runway 31.' You only had to look at Runway 31 to see what he meant: it pointed straight as an arrow at Lion Rock, a 1,500-foot-high knuckle of vaguely leonine appearance into which a departing RAF DC-3 had ploughed not long before, with the loss of nineteen lives. Runway 31 was only to be used for landings, Syd commanded. A government report issued that year went so far as to state that 'Kai Tak, close under a range of steep hills of up to 1,800 feet, remains inadequate for heavy aircraft.' Furthermore, foreign airline operators were coming to the same conclusion, the report warned: 'There is a serious danger that international aircraft may start overflying the Colony.'

The thought of such a boycott struck panic into the minds of Hong Kong's officials and businessmen. In the event, Kai Tak was not boycotted, but the mere possibility of such a thing started agitated talk of building a new, better airport. Where? Anywhere ... somewhere in the New Territories. ... It was a debate begun in urgency that was to drag on for over a decade, find temporary solution in a compromise at Kai Tak – and then drag on again to this very day. Cathay's early inter-office letters and memos reverberate hopefully with excited chatter of the imminent construction of a big new airport fit for the twenty-first century. It would be, the memos promised each other, out at Deepwater Bay. But nothing happened. At last, in the early sixties, came compromise at the old Kai Tak site. Obstructive hills were levelled, their rubble dumped into Kowloon Bay, and where all had been water a new giant runway sprang out across the waves, aimed at the Lei Yue Mun Gap. The debris of those hills, suitably surfaced, is what you land on today.

CHAPTER 6

Quite soon Roy Farrell, as Texan as Texans come, found to his discomfiture that he was the wrong nationality for Hong Kong. At that meeting with Neil Buchanan, Mr A. J. R. Moss, the Colony's Director of Civil Aviation, let it be known that to qualify for registration there any aviation company was going to have to be two-thirds British-owned. Up to now, Farrell had shuttled nothing but freight between Australia, Manila, Hong Kong and Shanghai, but he and Syd – particularly Syd – now had regular passenger services much in mind, and Moss was saying that the predominantly American ownership of Farrell's company was a major – indeed an insuperable – stumbling block to any such thing.

Luckily, Mr Moss was a cheery sort of man, known affectionately as 'Uncle Moe'. In spite of his grand title of DCA he was, in fact, notably unpretentious, quite content to work out of an equally unpretentious Quonset hut in Statue Square. As it happened, Moss had very much taken to Syd de Kantzow and that was no end of a help. 'It is now definite,' de Kantzow exulted in a letter to Russell dated 30 August 1946. 'We have rights to carry passengers from here to anywhere in the British Empire, also being registered here the British Government will support our application to fly to China, the Philippines, and anywhere we desire in the world.' He reassured Russell, 'This is not baloney, but a damn good opportunity to get *a small profitable airline operating from Hong Kong*. The company is in the process of being registered now.' What about the American angle? Well, 'The local company laws require two-thirds British directors; so Roy, Neil and myself are the present directors.' The new aviation company – distancing itself from Farrell's indubitably all-American-directed freight trading company – was now British, above board and ready to operate.

Good old Uncle Moe, having given permission for both Betsy and Nikki to carry Hong Kong registration letters, directed them to be entered in the records of the Colony's Civil Aviation Department as VR-HDB and VR-HDA respectively. Overjoyed, Syd de Kantzow urged Russell, 'Please, have those letters painted on our two ships.' With this, Betsy suffered a strange injustice. Anyone can see that the pioneer from Bush Field, Georgia, should have become VR-HDA, but by a quirk of fate she was pipped at the post. For some obscure administrative reason Nikki got into the DCA's register first and Betsy, for better or worse, became VR-HDB. Nevertheless the glory was hers: because of her veteran's status, those five letters became – and remain – the most famous in the history of aviation in the Crown Colony of Hong Kong.

The articles of association of Cathay Pacific Airways, drawn up by Johnson, Stokes and Masters, Solicitors, of Hong Kong, were dated 24 September 1946, having been duly signed the day before by 'Roy Farrell, Peninsula Hotel, Kowloon, Hong Kong, Merchant' and 'S. H. de Kantzow, Merchant', of the same address.

Syd himself flew Betsy to Sydney to be repainted and then, on 25 September, the day after the official registration of the new company in Hong Kong, he flew her back on her maiden flight as VR-HDB. Another Australian pilot, Peter Hoskins, was with Syd on that historic flight and he remembers that they were carrying a cargo of 2,000 day-old chicks in cartons. It was terribly hot and steamy in Morotai, the stop before Manila, and some mechanical trouble kept them on the ground longer than expected; there was a danger that the chicks would stifle to death. 'We let them out of their boxes,' Hoskins says, 'and immediately the cabin was crawling with little birds. It took us ages to collect them after take-off.'

The partners' dreams, however, were not of chicks; they were of passengers . . . of more and frequent charter flights . . . of a scheduled airline. Syd had written to Russell of a need for 'a profitable airline . . . a company. . . .' That company was about to be created, and it was to be called Cathay Pacific Airways.

How did such a uniquely imaginative name for an airline come to be chosen – a name whispering of magical landscapes and mythical destinations, of Tartary, Xanadu and Shangri-La, a name to enchant the most jaded traveller with its promise of airborne romance. There are two slightly divergent accounts of how and where the choice was made. Chic Eather has it that Roy and his partners, racking their brains for a suitable name over drinks in the Cathay Hotel on the Shanghai Bund, decided at once to avoid any name with the word 'China' in it; nobody wanted to risk even an implied association with the land of Mao Tse-tung. This, it seems to me, smacks of hindsight. Though it would be perfectly plausible if the naming had come a

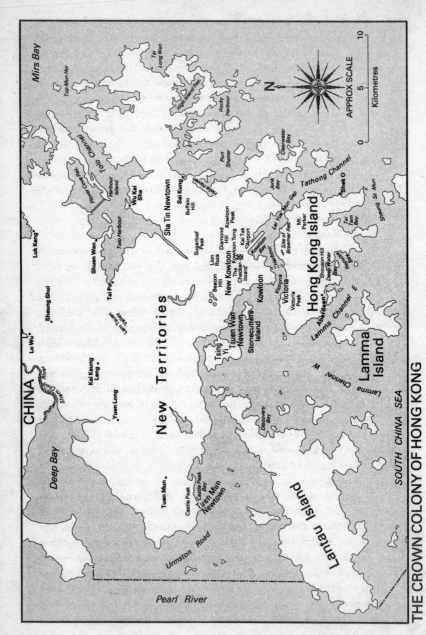

THE CROWN COLONY OF HONG KONG

few years later, few people in Shanghai in 1946 were aware that the Communists would soon be the new masters of all China.

In Roy Farrell's account, as relayed to me, the get-together was not in Shanghai but in Manila – to be precise, in the semicircular Tropicana Bar of the very grand Manila Hotel, formerly the harbourside headquarters of General Douglas MacArthur. Roy's story continues as follows:

'There were several foreign correspondents in Manila, and one afternoon I called three or four who were with *Time-Life* and *Newsweek*, and I told them to meet me in the bar. We got together and I said, "Look, boys, I want your help in picking a name for an airline I'm getting ready to incorporate in Hong Kong." There was only one prerequisite, I said. The name was to have "Cathay" in it. As we all know, Cathay has a kind of magic, doesn't it?'

'Marco Polo and all that.'

'Right.'

'The Silk Road, the Great Wall, Genghis Khan. . . .'

'Sure. All that. Well, after several drinks and much conversation we agreed on the name: Air Cathay. But, of course, that was not the end of it. The horseshoe-shaped Tropicana saw a good deal more of our hard-drinking little group before a *final* name was approved. You see, for me there was a fatal drawback to "Air Cathay". At that time, Milt Caniff was writing a strip cartoon series for several hundred papers in the United States. The strip was "Terry and the Pirates"; today it is called "Steve Canyon". Anyway, the setting of "Terry and the Pirates" was the Orient and Milt Caniff's drawings and his dialogue were exceptionally good and accurate. I kept up with the strip because my aunt back in the States would send me eight days' of "Terry and the Pirates" at a time. So I knew that Milt Caniff had just named Terry's airline "Air Cathay".'

A typical day's issue of the Terry and the Pirates strip of 1949 (drawn in this case not by Milt Caniff but by one George Wunder) shows in its first frame a DC-3 boldly labelled 'Air Cathay' ploughing through stormy skies somewhere in Asia.

'Good thing Terry kicked this kite upstairs just before the flood washed out the airstrip,' someone is saying in the passenger cabin, to which, 'Ah, phooey!' is another passenger's ungracious (and unexplained) reply. Up for'ard, Terry himself is granite-calm, unperturbed by floods or anything else. Blond, his fresh face as unmarked by fear or doubt as a nineteen-year-old's (he is already a veteran flier and the possessor of a peaked cap decorated with enough scrambled egg for an air marshal), he murmurs coolly to his co-pilot through tight lips, 'If our gas supply holds out, we'll make for Hong Kong.' But wait! –

'Sorry, chaps,' crackles the spoilsport voice of a pipe-smoking British air controller at Hong Kong [next frame]. 'Fog's just lifted here and we have traffic stacked up like the weekend's dishes. We won't be able to bring you in for some time.'

We see Terry struggling with the controls and his temper. His lips grow even tighter. His voice comes back, calm and firm: 'No dice. Fuel supply's running low. Air Cathay will take its business next door.'

A beautiful girl has been reading a newspaper at the Hong Kong controller's side. At the words 'Air Cathay' her head snaps up; she springs to her feet, flinging away her newspaper. 'Hey! That pilot mentioned Air Cathay!' she cries. 'That's the crowd Spray O'Hara disappeared with. Oh, lucky day!'

'Friends of yours, eh?' the pipe-smoker drawls, quick on the uptake, adding, with a smirk, 'Well, I gather they'll be landing across the bay in Macao.' He couldn't be more right, and the final frame is a happy one. It shows a Chinese rickshaw-driver in traditional wide straw hat and baggy pants cantering at breakneck speed across Macao's muddy airstrip [we know it's Macao because a sign says 'Adios'], urged on by the excited English beauty in the seat behind him. They make it on the dot – for at that moment, propellers whirling, the pride of Air Cathay taxies to a halt. . . .

'It was a good comic strip all right,' Roy said. 'More of a documentary really, but even so I didn't like the idea that my airline should have the same name as an airline in a comic strip. So that night we all stuck together drinking and discussing, and when the evening was over we had agreed on "Cathay Pacific Airways". You see, Pacific is another kind of romantic name, and anyway we thought we might be flying the ocean one day. That was it. We had a name. With that decided, Syd and I signed the corporate papers on 23 September 1946.'

In La Quinta Motor Inn with me all those years later, Roy summed it up. 'A new phase was beginning. We'd done extremely well. We had four planes flying and money in the bank. We hoped a new form of success lay ahead.' I could see him reliving that time as he thought about it, enjoying once more the memory of that early success. The glass of Coca-Cola raised to me now might have been one of those Cuba Libres at the bar of the Manila Hotel he had raised to Sydney de Kantzow, Bob Russell, Millard Nasholds and Bill Geddes Brown way back in 1946, toasting the future of a baby airline, newly baptized; toasting the unforeseeable empire of the air to which he and Syd were godparents: 'To Cathay Pacific Airways!'

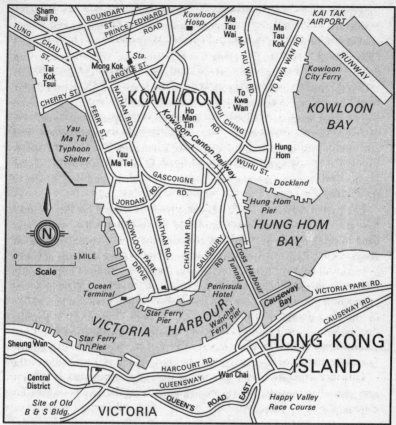

HONG KONG HARBOUR AND AIRPORT

Cathay Pacific was born – long live CPA! 'CPA. That's what it was then,' Farrell told me. 'In the beginning we always called it CPA.' In fact, CPA came to be regularly called by its full name only when those three initials ran the risk of confusion with the C, P and A of Canadian Pacific Airlines. These days, if someone refers to Cathay Pacific Airways as 'CPA' you can tell he is an old Hong Kong hand, betraying his generation as much as an Englishman does who refers to the radio as 'the wireless'.

Hong Kong, Australia and a good segment of the Orient were very soon hearing and reading about the new airline with the exciting name. 'Wing Your Way By CPA' said an early advertisement in the *China Mail*. 'Fly to

Singapore . . . Fare $880; Bangkok . . . Fare $528; Manila . . . Fare $600; Sydney . . . Fare $2,200. Baggage allowance 55lb. Freight and passenger bookings to be made at the office of CPA's new agent, P. J. Lobo & Co. at 4 Chater Road.' [In 1946 five Hong Kong dollars were worth one American dollar.] On 23 October Neville Hemsworth piloted VR-HDA (alias Nikki) with seventeen Chinese students aboard in the first of CPA's charter flights from Hong Kong to Gatwick Airport outside London: a thirty-day round trip on what was a pretty long haul for a twin 1200hp-engined 'crate'. He described the flight as 'very tough', but that charter was a milestone. And one month into the official life of Cathay Pacific the Roy Farrell Export-Import Co. (Hong Kong) Ltd. had chartered one of Cathay's two DC-3s for Hemsworth to inaugurate the first Roy Farrell 'airmerchandising' service to the United Kingdom.

The partial derivation of CPA's name from Terry and his Pirates must have struck a good many observers as apt, however much Roy would have liked to think otherwise. The new company *did* have a swashbuckling air about it. Chic Eather remembers hazardous flights along the coast of China to Lungwah field at Shanghai, relying on the eccentricities of unpleasantly low-powered radio beacons at Swatow, Amoy, Foochow, Wenchow and Ningpo – flights that on more than one occasion might have cost him his life in that storm-ridden region. Even so, Shanghai remained a popular destination with Syd's pilots – or Syd's 'pirates'. According to Chic, Lyell Louttit, the Radio Officer, found the Arcadia nightclub particularly bewitching when he was in the grip of the grape – and probably in the equally powerful grip of one or other of the club's blonde White Russian hostesses who, incidentally, very much fancied the skimpy Scamp swim-suits imported by Farrell.

Apart from Shanghai there were charters to Bangkok, Manila, Saigon and Singapore, and they were no less adventurous. On one occasion – it was certainly worthy of Terry and the Pirates – Eather's DC-3 from Bangkok was suddenly diverted, in full flight for Hong Kong, to Tourane in central Vietnam (later to be renamed Da Nang and become a major American base) by mysterious orders cryptically radioed to the aircraft's Captain, Dick Hunt, a former squadron leader in the Royal Australian Air Force. The war between the French and the Viet Minh nationalists was at its height, and it was a very bloody one in which anti-French guerrilla forces were becoming increasingly bold. Hunt and Eather spent a sleepless night in the villa the French Air Force general in Tourane had allotted them, listening to bursts of machine gun fire nearby; the shutters were tightly closed for fear of a Viet Minh grenade attack. At dawn next day they stumbled out to the airfield, hoping to discover why they were there. A few minutes later the Emperor Bao Dai of Annam and his entourage were driven up and escorted aboard their plane, and Hunt and Eather, stifling their yawns, flew the lot of them to Hong Kong and into exile. The French had decided that Indo-China was to have an independent, democratic government – though the exclusion from it of a certain Ho Chi Minh was to prove a costly omission.

Similar CPA escapades – one could say they were literally 'fly-by-night' – ensued during a three-week charter by Indonesian nationalists. The Dutch had thrown up an air blockade to isolate the forces of Dr Ahmad Sukarno's pro-independence government in central Java. Lyell Louttit, for one, was involved in surreptitious flights, often after dark, between Jogjakarta and Bukit Tinggi in western Sumatra before the whole devious adventure ended in the ignominious impounding of a CPA DC-3 in Singapore. Dutch officials there suspected the aircraft had been sold illegally by CPA to Sukarno, and it took Harry de Leuil, Syd's general manager, some time to convince the Directors of Civil Aviation in Singapore and Hong Kong of the company's innocence. It was a salutary experience, showing in those days of national independence movements how extremely unwise it was to mix commercial aviation with the violent imponderables of other people's politics. Far less risky were the chartered air shipments of refugees from Eastern Europe to Australia, and the series of two-month charters that Roy Farrell arranged to fly plane-loads of fresh fish from Kuantan in East Malaya to Singapore. True, the stink of fish permeated the aircraft from stem to stern and almost put the CPA crews off fish for the rest of their lives, but at least they weren't in danger of being shot down by British or Dutch fighters.

More charters were waiting to be picked up than Cathay could handle, and during these operations two aspects of the company became most obviously apparent. First, as I have already said, it was a distinctly shoestring operation. Second, its success was quite largely due to a very few people who were inspired to work – or rather, overwork – by an unusually high level of enthusiasm.

In next to no time Roy and Syd had to expand their staff. They had already added Harry de Leuil, a veteran Australian aviator, to run the CPA office in Sydney while Russell (and, later, Eric Kirkby) handled the Roy Farrell Export-Import Company's. In Hong Kong, Syd de Kantzow – by now, of course, specifically in charge of air operations – took on CPA's first local employee at Chater Road. This was Marie Bok, a strong-willed, intelligent, Hong Kong-born Chinese girl, who had previously worked with the Colony's Harbour Authority. They had met at the CPA ticket office in the Peninsula Hotel and Syd, wasting no time, had said, 'Come along and be my secretary.' Marie accepted the hard work and chaotic surroundings and stayed with the airline for thirty years.

Conditions were certainly spartan. 'We had one badly lit room,' she recalls, 'and our staff consisted of Syd (when he wasn't flying off somewhere), an accountant, and myself. That's all. We had to do everything – produce manifests, issue tickets, obtain clearances for this and that. Thank heavens the then DCA, Uncle Moe, was most helpful. He really adored Syd and wished him and CPA nothing but well.' She laughs at a sudden thought: 'You know, in those days payments were often made in cash and we carried these stacks of bank notes through rain and howling winds to the Chartered Bank wrapped in nothing more than a few sheets of the *China Mail*.' (Neville Hemsworth remembers Syd handing him wads of banknotes with no thought of accounting for them.) 'Shoestring? I'll say it was. Syd wouldn't spend what he thought of as unnecessary money, so we even had to borrow a cable code book and a long carriage typewriter from Roy Farrell's office.'

No one, least of all Syd de Kantzow, talked of office hours from nine to five; a twenty-four-hour day would have been insufficient to cope with the work, so Marie was relieved when two more stenographers were brought in, and overjoyed when – wonder of wonders – Syd agreed to pay for a couple of typewriters for them.

Today Marie Bok and her husband are the prosperous owners of a pearl emporium in Kowloon; she spends half the year there and the other half in Perth, Western Australia. A very handsome woman still, she remembers the 'happy old days' – Roy Farrell sauntering into the CPA office twice a week, so 'charming and outgoing', of Syd, sometimes a bit sulky or perhaps simply preoccupied. Roy's other partners, 'Nash' and Russell, she says, were 'more the cowboy type. High-spirited. Great blokes, but not great workers.' 'Nash', thickish-set and jowly, had poor health; he seemed to attract every passing local bug, and generally stuck close to home in Manila. Jolly Bob Russell, on the other hand, gravitated more and more to Hong Kong. He found it difficult to take things too seriously, and now and again Marie Bok had to file some unusual letters – like the one to Syd that began: 'To the Most Exalted Emperor and/or King of CPA. From: The After-hours House-boy.' Marie liked Russell's cheery grin and his unusually florid ties, one of which had jockeys' whips and horseshoes on it, a symbol of his frequent attendance at the Happy Valley racetrack where he gambled with mixed success but a passion matched only by his unrestrained enthusiasm for girls of all shapes and sizes.

Even so, Russell was not all frivolous. In fact, his 'Most Exalted Emperor' letter contained two perceptive remarks. 'At present,' he wrote, 'there are surprisingly few who know you can travel from Sydney to Hong Kong by air, but we can certainly change that when *permanent permissions* are granted.' And: 'After we advertise on a large scale we can obtain more passengers than we can handle.'

Passengers and advertising: Bob Russell had identified CPA's way to the future. It seems obvious now, but in the Far East of 1946 advertising was in its infancy and few people thought of flying; there were ships galore, after all, and surely ships were cheaper than planes. Roy Farrell had always been aware of the power of advertising. Very early on, for instance, his ads had plugged the unexpected availability in Hong Kong, thanks exclusively to CPA, of fresh Sydney Rock Oysters – a plug that sold CPA as much as the oysters. It was a modest beginning but in later years, of course, like everybody else, Cathay Pacific would spend millions of dollars on advertising. As for Bob Russell's mention of 'permanent permissions', it reflected a growing awareness among Roy's partners that CPA urgently needed regional landing and operating rights on a once-for-all basis.

The little fleet had grown to five by January 1947. Syd began to recruit more crews from Australia, sprucing them up by replacing the company's American-style uniform with shorts and summer jackets of white linen. Routes were consolidated and added to: the familiar ones to Sydney and Manila remained, but Cathay Pacific now flew to Singapore via Bangkok, a long haul which meant leaving Hong Kong at crack of dawn in order to get back next day. (There were no flights in or out of Kai Tak after dark.) 'A bloody awful time to get up,' the flight crews moaned, but no one challenged the necessity for Syd's gruelling work schedules if the line was to blossom for the benefit of all.

'Only one crew did the entire Hong Kong–Singapore–Bangkok flight,' wrote Chic Eather, a veteran of it. 'That meant a duty period of some thirty hours. One got a rest when one could – the aircraft being as good a place as any other until the close, humid atmosphere and the inevitable bugs and mosquitoes of Singapore's airfield drove the would-be sleeper out for a walk and some fresh air.'

Even in Hong Kong, their home base, the exhausted CPA crews had to doss down on camp beds in a couple of almost bare rooms in the Peninsula. Flight-time limits, palatial hotel accommodation and interesting stopovers lay in some distant and almost unimaginable future. The lordly aircrews of today wouldn't begin to tolerate the schedules which for Syd's fliers became routine. In any case, modern regulations quite rightly forbid them. Take

Eather's work period in the final two weeks of 1946, and imagine any pilot undertaking it today. One day he was in the air for eighteen hours and twenty-five minutes. He had two days off in the fortnight and muses wrily, 'I wonder how they managed to forget me for those two days. Perhaps they had no spare aircraft.'

Syd de Kantzow drove his pilots with an almost evangelical zeal, but pioneers *are* zealots and Chic's conclusion is fitting: 'Such a rat-race operation could hardly be justified, but the general dedication and willingness to do more than one's share must have contributed to the future fortunes of the company. It could be argued that if this attitude had been absent there would have been no Cathay Pacific and none of the comfortable flying jobs of today.'

Another de Kantzow-inspired step forward was the recruitment of CPA's first air stewardess. After all, any new air service in which passengers were more highly considered than woollen goods, Chinese silk hats and even oysters *must* have stewardesses. In Syd's opinion, stewardesses were a sure sign that an airline had 'arrived'.

One of Cathay's first and prettiest stewardesses lives now in happy retirement near Surfers' Paradise on the Queensland coast, having moved there after marrying Jack Williams, one of Cathay's Australian engineers. The smart little bungalow she shares now with her second husband sits back from the sea in a garden suburb that in its peacefulness is far from the roaring days of Syd's Dakotas. Though not really so far for Vera: ask her about that time and you realize you have started something; she laughs, runs to bring you a chair and a beer, dashes for her photograph album and in no time is acting out what they were like, the endless days and nights inside those rattling, bouncing, propeller-driven crates, as if she was playing a delightful game of charades. What *had* it been like to stagger about with trays and cups of tea on a heaving aisle hour after turbulent hour all the way from Hong Kong to Sydney – and then back again? Vera makes it sound as if those were the happiest days of her life – and perhaps they were.

Her album shows the young Vera, dark-haired with a big white smile, at the top of the steps at Betsy's open door. She is cool and petite in a dark blue double-breasted uniform, the long open collar of a white blouse flopping casually over its lapels, and a soft round hat gold-embroidered with the initials CPA enfolded in a pair of wings. Her high heels must have been the least ideal footwear for carrying babies' milk and airsick pills up and down the narrow aisle of a tossing aircraft, but she certainly added a welcome touch of beauty to the austerity of flying.

For there was no luxury in flying then. Consider that old warhorse, Betsy the DC-3. Unlike Vera, she was no oil painting. To be frank, she closely resembled a tubular sardine can with rivets. No upholstery brightened her dull interior. Her floor was a strip of metal; her seats were nothing but metal buckets, lightly cushioned, down each side of the fuselage. Structurally strong, Betsy was very thin-skinned. Her every riveted rib was starkly visible, and if you had happened to prod her metal skin too violently with the tip of an umbrella you might have found yourself prodding the air rushing by outside. A glance at her Meccano-like innards gave very little promise of an enjoyable two- or three-day flight to Darwin and Sydney, even without the virtually inevitable dust storms and thunder. Who could have wanted to fly? After all, you were not 'Vinegar Joe' Stilwell roaring over the Hump yelling 'Gung-ho!' to zap the Japs. . . . Yet Vera loved every flying minute.

The comradeship was a large part of it. When she pointed to a group photograph of smiling girls in CPA uniform, she glowed with happy recognition. 'That's Dolores Silva – she's in the States now, in Alabama. This is Margaret Wheeldon Pugh, she's in America, too. Who married first? Was it me? No, Terry Marquis, I think. Irene Machado, look, she's married to Ken Begg, an early CPA pilot. Oh, and that's Linda Fernandez. She was our air chief.' Her face temporarily lost its smile when she came to the next name: 'Delca da Costa. Oh, dear. She was killed in the Macao hijacking. . . .' And two minutes later the smile faded again: 'Olive Batley. She was on the one that flew into the Braemar Reservoir. She was a new girl, not long with the company.'

After a pause I said, 'Not just a line of pretty faces, were you, Vera. Brave as well.'

'Oh, I don't know. It was a job to do.'

Most of the first five or six CPA stewardesses were Portuguese girls born in Macao or Hong Kong. Chinese girls became the majority a little later, and oriental cabin crews were to become (and remain until now) a Cathay trademark.

Vera said, 'You only think of work in the plane. Think of the passengers. See they're well covered, that they have a pillow. Flying to Sydney tough?' She scoffed at the suggestion. 'We looked forward to the shopping, seeing the world.' She smiled. 'Even if we did have to wash all those dishes in Darwin on the way. A DC-3 carried only one stewardess, you know – there were only five or six of us in the company all told. But you could doze when the passengers had had their dinner.'

Dinner? In that tin tube of a plane?

'We served mostly sandwiches or salads. Nescafé in a thermos. Coca-Cola. But *proper* knives, forks and plates, please note – no plastic! Some passengers thought they were for them. We had to ask some from Saigon "Give us back our plates, please" as they left the plane.'

To complicate things, on the day-long Hong Kong–Singapore run there were often passengers from China who knew none of the three languages that CPA's first stewardesses usually spoke – Cantonese, English, Portuguese. And what about those famous storms over the South China Sea? 'Well, the planes *would* jump about, yes. Jo Cheng, our first Chinese girl, was carrying a tray of tea and the plane got into an air pocket. She went down and the tea all over her – oh, she was so funny about it!'

Hot tea all over? Funny?

'Dear Jo. So funny.'

In due course CPA bought four-engined DC-4 Skymasters with startling refinements – leatherette-covered chairs in rows, ceiling fans and cupboards. Luxury! At last it was just possible – just – when Vera and her friends served proper food – eggs and steaks – to shed the uneasy feeling of being trapped half-starved in a Tin Lizzie troop-transport. The steaks – and Vera serving them – would have made up for turbulence, fatigue, and even quite frequent mechanical shortcomings. She remembers how a CPA DC-4 lost an engine coming in on the approach to Bangkok. 'Don't worry,' Vera smiled to a trembling passenger. 'We've got three more.' Another engine went: 'Two to go,' she cried happily, adding for extra reassurance, 'The Captain says we'll soon be there.'

'Were you *never* worried, Vera?'

'I tell you, we were too *busy* to worry.'

Too busy to worry in the air, that is – but on the ground one thing made them worry a good deal: the constant possibility of offending Syd de Kantzow. Vera recalled, 'When I worked in our ticket office in the Pen, Syd and Roy Farrell used to come in. Roy, very tall, slim, polite, was always smiling. Syd was very strict. You sat up straighter. You always wanted to be neat and tidy with Syd.' And as she spoke, two visions came to my mind: the pukka wartime Syd in a well-pressed drill uniform; and the new Syd in his Hong Kong sales office, the respected martinet, master of himself and his own airline, controlling by example men, women and a fleet of expensive machines. 'He didn't talk to you much, you know – he would just look across at you from a table in the office and say quite quietly something like, "Get hold of Marie Bok, will you, please?" – by telephone to the Chater Road office, he meant.' Vera made a wry expression and laughed. 'Believe me, you didn't wait for him to say it twice.'

'An enigma,' that's what Chic Eather, who respected him, said of Sydney de Kantzow. And looking back at Syd's unusual story, not having known him, I am reminded of that literary classic of the 1930s, Antoine de Saint-Exupéry's *Night Flight*, and of its leading character, Rivière, the introspective, enigmatic director of a South American airmail network, a driven, solitary man who tolerated no flinching and could seem severe, even inhuman. Rivière in reality was anything but insensitive: launching his beloved planes 'like blind arrows at night's obstacles', he needed as much courage to issue orders as his pilots needed to carry them out. Yet whenever Rivière entered his office, in overcoat and hat 'like the eternal traveller he always seemed to be', a sudden zeal possessed the staff: the secretaries began bustling about, the typewriters began to click. I see Syd as Rivière – someone who constantly reminded himself, 'You must keep your place. Tomorrow you may have to order this pilot out on a dangerous flight. He will have to obey.' Behind the enigma Chic and others tried to fathom, behind the 'good fellow' and the moody, retiring disposition, the real Syd de Kantzow might easily have been silently agreeing with Rivière – 'Love the men you command – but without telling them.'

CHAPTER 7

CPA's 'Burma campaign' had a distinctly Errol Flynn atmosphere about it, even if the Company's fliers were not actually at war with anyone. It was certainly an adventure and there were plenty of flying bullets; too many for some. It began in early 1948 and was to continue until the announcement that enough was enough at the Company's Annual General Meeting in April 1950 – nearly two years after a new Cathay Pacific Airways had been born under the aegis of the great Hong Kong-based commercial house of Butterfield & Swire. So it covered a longish period of time.

'Swashbuckling' is a good description of the Burma story: it has a wonderful *Boys' Own Paper* air about it: you expect to find Biggles in it as well as Errol Flynn. More than any other part of the pre-Swire history of Cathay did it qualify de Kantzow's air crews for the nickname 'Syd's Pirates'. In November 1947, Millard Nasholds – a man so laid back (as they didn't say then) that Chic Eather believed 'he could sleep on a barbed wire fence in a typhoon' – arranged for a private Burmese company called Air Burma to charter CPA planes to help solve that newborn country's transport problems. And no one, certainly not he, could have foreseen that Syd's planes and crews would soon be caught in the crossfire of a lively civil war.

Burma had left the British Empire in June 1947 to become a republic, with a Prime Minister in Rangoon called Thakin Nu, and a Deputy Prime Minister and Commander-in-Chief called Ne Win, who would later rule the nation as President for many years. The new government had problems. At first the fledgling Burmese Army, largely composed of Christian Karens, a stocky warrior people who dwelt in the eastern uplands and despised the ruling Buddhist Burmans of the plain, found itself fighting a haphazard hit-and-run war with at least two indigenous Communist guerrilla organizations. Quite soon insurgency moved into a far more serious phase when the Karens themselves rebelled against Thakin Nu's central government. The

Communists alone, well equipped with a variety of discarded Second World War weapons, had created a major inland transport problem by blowing up railway tracks and bridges, mining roads and, equally important in a country that depends a great deal on water transport, by shooting up barges and sampans on the Irrawaddy and Chindwin Rivers. Now, with the Karens in revolt, the situation was critical. Would Cathay Pacific – for a very reasonable fee – provide the government with some air transport? Cathay Pacific would and did.

To start with, Roy and Syd bought two Avro Anson transports, relatively luxurious aircraft capable of operating into short up-country airstrips. The Burmese airstrips were not only short, they were often little more than muddy clearings left over from the recent war with the Japanese. Even so, there weren't enough of them and extra strips had to be created. This was done with eight-foot-long, eighteen-inch-wide perforated steel platforms known as PSP, an invaluable legacy of wartime invention. As Chic Eather says, PSP could transform a soggy paddy field into a usable runway in a matter of minutes.

Eather, as like Biggles as any of CPA's daredevils, loved Burma – but not everybody in Cathay fell in love with it. It is easy to see why. The two Ansons and their crews were based at Rangoon in barely tolerable conditions, and pilots' tours of duty were limited to three weeks. Those who stuck it out there boast about it over their beer to this day like proud men obsessed.

Take Bob Smith. He went to Burma as Station Engineer – indeed he says he was the only licensed engineer at Rangoon – and describes a startling situation there. There were no hangars for a start. 'A hangar? Never!' He throws up his hands in derision. 'Nothing but a small storeroom. We did all our work out in the open – and you know what the monsoons are like. We had to put up a sheet of green canvas and stick a light under it to see by. Talk about hot! A million insects got under there with you.'

Bob had been with Trans-Australia Airlines in Melbourne when a friend said, 'Why not join Cathay Pacific for £32 a week?' He was only earning £11 a week then, so he moved over to Cathay in Hong Kong and thence to his stint in Burma. Bob is a big, tough, no-nonsense old Aussie, with a collection of Cathay mementoes in his bungalow on Lake Macquarie outside Sydney that could fill a fair-sized museum, and a memory of Burma he will happily share with anyone prepared to drink beer and eat plum cake with him and his wife. One recollection has never faded – that of his living and eating quarters ('If you could call 'em that,' he said). The address came out pat, as if he was giving me his own. '102 University Avenue, Rangoon. That was the mess. And a den of iniquity, I can tell you.' Photographs of it showed a crumbling, colonial-style porticoed entrance, a high ceiling, and off-duty CPA pilots with bare, damp chests and long, old-style, wide-legged shorts, lolling in wicker chairs reading mail from home under inadequate fans. It was, Bob says, 'the only place anywhere you could catch amoebic and bacillary dysentery at one and the same meal. Although you could get equally exotic bugs at the real Palace of Germs, as we called it – the restaurant at the airport. As for our office – 4 Strand Road behind the Strand Hotel! Big rats. Big girls, too.'

But there were more serious hazards, potentially lethal ones, in the countryside – particularly with the Karens in rebellion. 'We were really joining in a civil war,' Bob Smith says. 'That was the British Embassy's view, anyway.' And the Embassy was right. Many of the air operations Cathay Pacific undertook were purely humanitarian – dropping salt, rice and flour to remote villages or army posts cut off by Karen or Communist guerrillas. But too often cargoes turned out to be soldiers, weapons and ammunition needed by the Burmese army for immediate military operations. On one terrifying occasion at least, a cargo of pre-war gelignite was wheeled up sweating with age and therefore so unstable that a goodish bump might easily have set it off. The pilot, Captain John Paish, promptly ordered it to be off-loaded despite hysterical threats by a Burmese officer to shoot the entire Cathay crew.

It was not long before the two Ansons proved too small and too underpowered to carry the large loads of military equipment that the Burmese government wanted transported round the country. In any case one of them was written off by the fleet captain, Morrie Lothian, when he undershot the runway at a small field on the coast of the Bay of Bengal. The second Anson was promptly withdrawn from use and left on a disused runway at Rangoon. Syd then sent three DC-3 Dakotas – the old dependables – into the firing line. One of them was Betsy.

That the war risks were no joke can be seen from the number of times Cathay's aircraft were hit by rebel bullets. Captain Jim Harper, Cathay's Operations Manager in Burma, got a bullet through the foot and another through his lower intestine while flying his Dakota at what he imagined was a safe height. How he managed to land it no one will ever quite understand. Sometimes Bob Smith worked on aircraft well into the night, with tracers and flares all over the place, and once a bullet ricocheted onto the steps where he was sitting. 'I kept it for some time,' he says, 'as a souvenir.' Bo Egan, another engineer, once drove a Dodge truck to the airport under heavy Karen fire, desperately waving an Australian flag as a sign of peace and neutrality. Naturally some Cathay crews balked at all this; it was not what they had signed on for. Others thrived on danger and look back on Burma with affection.

One pilot who joyfully joined Cathay at this point from Air Burma was Dave Smith, an ex-RAF man who had flown Mosquitoes and later DC-3s during the Berlin Airlift; he became Cathay's Operations Manager in Hong Kong and a director. Dave had piloted the Deputy Prime Minister, Ne Win, about the country and even survived a bad attack of amoebic dysentery. He remembers that when Cathay planes in Burma carried 'humane' cargoes – food for example – CPA stencils were used on the fuselages; when the same aircraft carried troops and ammunition, possibly the same afternoon, they were marked with Air Burma stencils, although, absurdly, the Hong Kong registration letters remained the same. In Hong Kong, Uncle Moe Moss worried that planes registered in the Colony were becoming part of the Burmese government's war effort, and that their crews would be taken for common-or-garden gunrunners.

One thing was obvious – before long the question of danger money would come up. Sure enough, a group letter was drafted in Bob Smith's sweaty little office and sent to Hong Kong.

'Danger money! What's all this about danger money?' Syd snapped – but he dispatched Captain Dick Hunt, his Operations Manager, to Burma to investigate this preposterous proposal. Chic Eather relates what happened.

On the morning of 5 March he arrived at Mingaladon [Rangoon] to fly out with Captain John Riordan and see conditions for himself. He unceremoniously told John to 'hop into the right-hand seat' and they took off for Meiktila in eastern Burma. All the way he lectured John on 'how bloody frightened you blokes have become, using every pretext to lever more money off a struggling impoverished company.' At Meiktila the airfield signals were correct, indicating the place was still under government control. As the engines stopped he said, 'Look, John. Must be a VIP coming back with us. We've got a guard of honour.'

John looked and said, 'Yes, we have. And they look like Karens.'

'Bloody rot!' replied Hunt.

Riordan went down to open the cargo door and as it swung back he received a precise salute from a diminutive officer whose serious expression was replaced by a grin as he said, 'I am a Karen.'

'I thought so,' Riordan said, returning the salute. He returned to the cockpit with the good news.

Hunt, in a subdued whisper, asked what they should do.

'Just what they tell us,' Riordan said.

The Karens locked the crew in a room. . . . At dawn the officer came and casually told them his assignment for the day was to capture Maymyo, about 65 miles north-north-east of Meiktila on the other side of Mandalay. Hunt and Riordan, he said, had been given the honour of assisting. They would fly troops to the airfield at Anisakan whence his men would proceed to Maymyo five miles on. They would go at once.

'What if we refuse?' Hunt snarled. The still-smiling officer unholstered his revolver, blew down the barrel and said quietly,

'Now, Captain, I hope you are not going to be difficult.'

The Karens captured Anisakan calmly and casually, according to Chic Eather's account, and then moved on to take the important hill town of Maymyo. Hunt and Riordan were not asked for any more help. They spent two further days as honoured guests of the Karens, and when they were released found their DC-3 had been spring-cleaned and shone like a new pin. Attaching Riordan's Cathay Pacific wing to his own breast, the smiling Karen officer said, 'When we capture Rangoon we'll make you the first Marshal of the Karen Air Force.' Chic Eather ends the story: 'Captain Hunt returned to Hong Kong and reported that the Burma operation did entail a certain amount of risk to the crews. They all got a 50 per cent pay rise and something like 30 rupees an hour danger money.'

The Cathay crews in Burma had to put up with all sorts of other hazards: atrocious weather, for instance, and, as Dave Smith recalls, the habit of certain 'little Burmese rascals who would wait till you were going through the engine checks in the cockpit, then slip a few friends on board, pocketing the money. Once, finding it difficult to lift off the aircraft, I stopped and found fifty on board. We were licensed to carry thirty-eight or so. There was probably a crate of arms, too.' Perhaps John Riordan was a victim of such sharp practice, or perhaps it was a drastic shift in wind direction that made him 'run out of airstrip' on take-off at Anisakan. At any rate, he wrote off a DC-3 and left Burma and Cathay at the same time.

Before me lies a photograph taken by Bob Smith many years ago. It was sent by a former Cathay radio operator called Peter Smith, and shows a typical Burmese airstrip at that time: an almost treeless plain, wiry grass, a group of Burmese admiring the streamlined nose and shiny engine cowlings of a parked Cathay Pacific DC-3, and, in the foreground, in the shadow of the port wing, two barrels of fuel and two fire extinguishers crammed into an ox-cart, the 'engines' of which – two yoked oxen – are sleepily ignoring the camera. 'Refuelling detail. Upcountry Burma' is written on it in pencil, and it reminds me of Betsy's narrow escape from fiery oblivion in 1949 near the Chinese border at Bhamo. Morrie Lothian was the pilot, and he was starting Betsy's engines with no co-pilot to help him. Betsy's starboard engine burst into flames during the starting procedure, but because he was alone and in the pilot's left-hand seat Lothian was unable to see this. Chic Eather says, 'Morrie then taxied the now merrily burning aircraft the full length of the runway, turned into the wind, and presumably made the mandatory magneto check. Just as he was about to commence the takeoff run, the starboard engine fell off . . .' In due course Betsy was fitted with a new engine and Bob Smith, with amazing ingenuity, attached a new starboard wing.

Of course, there were laughs in Burma, too. How could there not have been with such a Laurel and Hardy pair as the outsize Captain John Moxham ('Mox the Ox') and slim First Officer Mike Russell, who detested each other but time and again, by some quirk of destiny, found themselves flying side by side. When their mutual antipathy was really on the boil they would only communicate in the cockpit by scribbling notes to each other – even to such orders as 'Gear up' or 'Gear down'. On good days, according to Bob Smith who flew with them as Flight Engineer, they were able to channel their intense dislike into a dialogue of exquisite politeness – thus:

Mox to Mike (in an exaggerated whisper): 'Michael, don't you think the cylinder-head temperature on the port side is a little high?'

Mike: 'Yes, John old boy, I do believe you are right. What would you like it to read?'

Mox (after considering the matter): 'Well, Michael, the starboard engine is reading 190 degrees. What about making them even?'

Mike (having adjusted the output reading to the desired figure and beaming at his commander): 'I do hope that is satisfactory, John, old chap.'

Mox: 'Ah, thank you, Mike. That's much better. I feel happier now.'

And it was Bob Smith – although few had thought he had a syllable of poetry in him – who put Rudyard Kipling in his place on a world-famous point of literary geography. Chic Eather tells the story well.

Captain Johnnie Paish and Smith were flying home to Mingaladon at about 8,000 feet, when out of nowhere and without preamble, Smith declared, 'Rudyard Kipling is wrong.' Paish didn't know what he was talking about. Then he recited: 'By the old Moulmein pagoda, looking eastward to the sea.' He said that if the pagoda faced eastward it would face right into the middle of China. It couldn't possibly face the sea. He raised such an argument that Paish got fed up, and said they would go across and see. He landed at Moulmein on the other side of the Gulf of Martaban and proved Smithy right and Kipling wrong. Smithy was so pleased he bought them a curry lunch at a little native eatery just below the Pagoda. The meal was first class. When they went to re-start, they couldn't get a peep out of the starboard engine, and found that a Karen bullet had sheared the connecting drive of the starter. A replacement starter had to be flown over next morning.

Some time later Syd de Kantzow said, 'Do you mean to tell me you would ground one of my aeroplanes for 24 hours and use hundreds of gallons of fuel just to prove Kipling right or wrong! I know who started that argument – it was Smithy, wasn't it?'

Bob Smith has told me: 'I don't wish to seem too harsh about this, but the flight to Moulmein story is a complete fable.' He adds: 'There is in Kipling's poem "Mandalay" a line, "An' the dawn comes up like thunder outer China 'crost the Bay". During a rather "liquid" discussion at the CPA mess one evening I remember arguing that this could not be so. East from Moulmein lies Thailand (Siam).'

By 14 April 1950, by which time Roy and Syd's CPA had come under the management of Butterfield & Swire, the government of Burma looked set to nationalize all domestic air travel. Accordingly Mr Charles Collingwood Roberts, Swires' Chairman, told a meeting of his directors in Hong Kong that Cathay's Burmese days were at an end.

CHAPTER 8

On 16 July 1948 the violence that underlies the pleasant face of the Orient had come to pay Farrell and de Kantzow a visit much nearer home. At six o'clock that evening, high above the water ten miles from Macao, a Chinese criminal called Chio Tok fired a .38 bullet into the base of Captain Dale Cramer's skull, and the CPA Catalina flying boat he was piloting with twenty-six passengers and crew nose-dived to the bottom of the Pearl River estuary. The Catalina's name was 'Miss Macao'.

Miss Macao was one of two Catalina amphibians recently bought in Manila by CPA and chartered to the Macao Air Transport Company (MATCO), a subsidiary company that Roy and Syd had set up in conjunction with P. J. Lobo, the successful Macao-born trader who owned Cathay's Chater Road office. 'See the beauty of Hong Kong from the air,' the new MATCO advertisements urged readers of the *South China Morning Post*. 'Fly to Macao next weekend. You will see so much in twenty minutes.'

MATCO had been started up for a specific purpose. When Hong Kong Airways ploughed a plane into the Peak – the highest point of Hong Kong island – scattering gold bars far and wide with much publicity, the shouts of 'Gold!' had struck a resounding chord in Farrell's always active imagination. Roy, Syd and Millard Nasholds were soon rapping excitedly on the door of P. J. Lobo's son Roger (now Sir Roger).

'I told Roger,' Roy explains, 'that the importation of gold into Hong Kong would be stopped as Britain was a signatory of the Bretton Woods Agreement which forbade its signatories from trading in free gold. I also pointed out that Portugal – which owned Macao, of course – was not a signatory and therefore not bound by the restrictions. I asked Roger to go to Macao, see his father and start the paperwork for our joint importation of gold into Macao.' Syd was enthusiastic, too: 'The shortest hauls pay best,' he assured Roger Lobo. The Lobos, father and son, soon agreed and the four of them shook hands on the new deal.

There was a small problem. Where were Cathay's DC-3s to land in Macao? The Portuguese colony – a mole on China's cheek so tiny as to make Hong Kong look like a great wen – had no airstrip. But, as Roger Lobo remembers, Roy and Syd had an interesting idea: why land at all, they asked. Why not simply pack the gold into barrels covered with gunny bags and kick them out of the doors of the DC-3s over the Macao racecourse – a method they had used most effectively in wartime Burma when delivering rice supplies to Chiang's beleaguered troops? Unfortunately gold weighs more than rice – the heavy barrels of gold disappeared into several feet of Macao mud. Next idea?

'We decided to pay for the racetrack to be cleared for landings. This was done in a day, and our glorious inaugural flight was to be received by the Governor of Macao and every notable in the place. Really posh. The red carpet was out. Speeches were to be made. Very grand.' Hong Kong's civil aviation authorities and the press came aboard at Kai Tak, and peering down as the DC-3 (in fact, VR-HDA alias Nikki) approached Macao, they could see not one but *two* bands playing on the racetrack. Roy and Roger Lobo and his wife were also on board, Syd was co-pilot, 'Pinky' Wawn was at the controls – and they zoomed in with all the slapstick dignity and meticulous execution of the Marx Brothers in *Animal Crackers*.

'Trouble was,' says Roy, 'the sea wall had not been knocked out and as we neared it I felt sure were were too low. Darned right, we were. As we passed over it two struts stuck noses up through the right and left wings. Wawn made a good job of a belly landing with no landing gear left, and we made a skidding halt directly in front of the reviewing stand. . . . The crowd was stunned by the brilliance of it all and the bands stopped in the middle of a bar. We didn't have to climb down from the plane, we simply stepped out.'

Groucho could not have timed it better. Some onlookers even clapped. Few realized what had happened, Mrs Lobo merely remarking in sweet ignorance to her husband, 'I say, that was a short landing.' But Syd looked at Roy in a meaningful sort of way and murmured 'Sea planes' – and next day Roy flew to Manila. He knew where to find sea planes, having already started a local air service there, Amphibian Airways, which used Catalinas to bring fresh fish to Manila from the provinces, and now he bought two of them.

From that day those graceful, snub-nosed amphibians with the two large overhead engines carried passengers and gold from Hong Kong to Macao – gold that had been shipped from South Africa, the United States, Great Britain, France and elsewhere to Hong Kong by the giants Pan American World Airways, BOAC, Air France and KLM, who were all prevented from flying to Macao by the lack of airfields. A lot of that gold went strange ways, though most of it was, no doubt, pocketed by Chiang Kai-shek in China. But many ordinary Chinese had a hankering for gold, too: mistrusting postwar paper currency, they stored it like squirrels preparing for a harsh winter – underground, under their beds or even in their teeth. Among those who ached to get their hands on some of the golden loot were four Chinese from the island village of Nam Mun, south-west of Macao – and they made a plan.

On 16 July Miss Macao's outward evening flight from Hong Kong to Macao was uneventful. So was her stopover and take-off from Macao for the return to Hong Kong. Then something went terribly wrong.

It was some time, however, before the authorities in Macao or Hong Kong became aware that anything was amiss, for those were days when communications between even such short distances were primitive. There was no means, for example, by which Cathay's representative in Macao could have been in radio or any other touch that night with Cathay Pacific in Hong Kong or with marine police patrols. All the same, the Catalina's failure to arrive at Kai Tak was noted by Roy Downing, air traffic control officer there, and at 7 p.m. he alerted Hong Kong's Water Police that the plane was overdue with twenty-three passengers aboard. Vera Rosario, in the CPA sales office at the Pen, remembers that she said uneasily to Bob Frost's deputy, Tommy Bax, 'Odd, Miss Macao's not back yet.' And they telephoned Syd de Kantzow. However, with night coming on nothing very constructive could be done. Next day at dawn, instructed by Syd de Kantzow, Captain Dick Hunt flew the other Catalina to Macao to assist if necessary in a search. There he learned the worst.

The first sign of disaster had been the appearance in Macao harbour at 9.15 p.m. the previous night of two fishermen in a motorized junk with the waterlogged body of a half-drowned Chinese, still breathing but incapable of speech. Police swiftly identified him in hospital as one Wong Yu, a twenty-four-year-old rice farmer from Nam Mun. For the moment he could tell them nothing, but one of his rescuers related that shortly after 6 p.m. he had seen an aircraft passing over his boat towards Hong Kong, that it had made a sharp turn to the left followed by a turn to the right and had then dived directly into the sea. The aircraft, he said, had hit the sea with a great splash and exploded. The second fisherman described an exactly similar phenomenon, though without the explosion. According to him the erratically turning aircraft had been making a strange 'popping noise' in the air. Then he had seen a man – Wong Yu – in the water, supported by a seat cushion. Neither fisherman was able to pinpoint exactly where the plane had hit the water. 'No accurate picture can be gained of what happened,' Syd told the Hong Kong press in an early statement, for Wong Yu, recovering in hospital, remained silent and bad weather delayed a serious search operation.

The first body was sighted near the breakwater at Macao two days later; it was of a passenger, an oil company executive called Stewart. But this time search equipment had been brought up and sweeping operations had begun over a wide area between Macao and Lantau Island. Dick Hunt flew a second CPA Catalina to Macao, this time bringing Syd de Kantzow, Uncle Moe Moss, Roy Farrell (who had flown in from Manila) and Roger Lobo.

Roger Lobo recalls: 'We had a floating crane, a fleet of barges and a couple of motor launches out there trying to locate the wreckage. A typhoon held us up at one point. Always full of ideas, Roy had us all spread out over the area with pieces of cord with weights on the ends of them methodically probing down trying to make contact with metal. Well, we found the wreck in the end.' The Catalina was lying in four fathoms of muddy water not far from an outcrop of rocks called the Nine Islands, west of Lantau Island. The divers were hampered at first by fast-running tides and silt, but at high tide the clear ocean water flowed into the Pearl River's mouth and they were able to recover some bodies and debris.

Moss's initial report began with a series of bare melancholy facts: 'Aircraft: PBY 5a "Catalina" VR-HDT. Engines: Two Pratt and Whitney R-1830/43. Owners: Cathay Pacific Airways Ltd. Pilot: Capt. Dale Cramer – missing presumed killed. First Officer: K. S. McDuff – killed. Flight Hostess: D. da Costa – missing presumed killed. Passengers: 23 – 10 killed, 12 missing, 1 survivor.'

First Officer McDuff was stated positively to have been killed, since he was the only one of the crew whose body was recovered. (He lies today in the cemetery in Hong Kong's Happy Valley.) The fact that he was comparatively unmarked meant, said Moss, that he could not have been in the pilot's compartment at the time of the crash, for the compartment was completely wrecked. But that did nothing to explain why Miss Macao had dropped out of the sky. There was no sign of fire or explosion. Everything looked as if the plane had been flying normally. What on earth had happened?

The beginning of an answer came while the main portion of the aircraft was being examined in Macao Naval Yard: a discharged .38 calibre shell was discovered. Then, in the mud and silt inside the aircraft, three more exploded shell cases were turned up and two other shells that had misfired. That was enough for the Hong Kong press: 'Fantastic Air Piracy Attempt,' announced the *China Mail* after a few guarded remarks from Mr Paletti, the

Macao Police Commissioner, and that was what it turned out to have been. To be precise, Miss Macao was the victim of the first act of piracy for gain in the history of aviation.

The key to the unravelling of the complete story was the confession of Wong Yu, the survivor, and the Macao detective force went to imaginative lengths to get it. At first he was incoherent, so a recording device was concealed near his hospital bed. In addition police officers disguised as patients were placed in neighbouring beds, and from time to time elderly 'relatives' came to sit by them and hold their hands. In time Wong told all he knew, and from his confession and from papers taken from the Al Capone-style clothing of his three confederates, whose bodies were also recovered, Captain Paletti and his men were able to round up six or seven other Macao Chinese for questioning. Between them, the Chinese told a remarkable story.

There were four chief conspirators in the plot, which had been some time in the making. The leader of the four, Chio Tok, for example, had taken the trouble to learn to fly Catalinas in Manila, and together with the others had studied the flight paths of the Cathay amphibians as they flew regularly back and forth between Hong Kong and Macao. Of course, like everybody else they had heard the mouth-watering reports of cargoes of gold bullion – and Tok had had a thought. Why not hold up a Catalina crew at pistol point, take over the controls in mid-flight, and divert the aircraft to some obscure place – a hidden bay near Nam Mun perhaps – where it could be looted at leisure? The Nam Mun villagers were relatives or friends of the plotters; the Catalina's passengers and crew could be held on some neighbouring island and with any luck ransomed for an additional chunk of coin. It must have sounded a pretty good idea. On the appointed day the conspirators bought three handguns and boarded the flight at Macao, fortified with a last-minute cup of coffee at a restaurant near the harbour. All four were neatly dressed in new, if cheap, wide-lapelled suits and broad-brimmed hats of the kind familiar to fans of Edward G. Robinson in *Little Caesar* or James Cagney in *White Heat*, and thus attired they scattered themselves strategically about the interior of the aircraft. Chio and a companion, Cheong, were careful to sit just behind the pilot, Captain Dale Cramer, and Keith McDuff, his First Officer. McDuff's fiancée, the Flight Hostess, Delca da Costa – Vera Rosario's friend – took her usual place on a hinged seat near the boarding door. The only other Cathay employee aboard was Robert Frost, the Company's Sales and Traffic Manager from Hong Kong, who at the last moment had asked if he might come along for the ride – to kill time, actually, while his wife was having her hair done.

77

Soon after take-off, with Miss Macao soaring smoothly into her heading to Hong Kong, the gangsters drew their guns. While two of them shouted at the astounded passengers to move to the starboard side, and with Cheong covering McDuff, Chio Tok pointed his gun at Cramer's head and told him to get up and hand over the controls. Dale Cramer was a war veteran, a former US Navy pilot, who had been with Cathay nearly a year. He had taken the place of the original pilot, Dick Hunt, who had bad earache. A couple of Chic Eather's photographs show him to have been a friendly-looking, blond man, smiling on the wharf of Macao 'after another successful gold delivery' and drinking with friends on the penthouse roof of the Banque de l'Indochine, the Cathay pilots' home-from-home in Saigon. Obviously a good-natured man, and one with a strong jaw signifying resolution – enough resolution, at any rate, to destroy all Tok's careful plans. For Cramer looked down the barrel of Tok's .38, heard Chio's command 'Get up!' – and refused to budge. At the same time, McDuff swiftly stooped for the Catalina's iron mooring-pole near the co-pilot's seat and cracked Cheong over the head with it.

At that point all hell broke loose and bullets flew. In the whirl of astonishment, panic and confusion, it seems probable that one of the passengers, a Chinese millionaire who had started life as a gangster in Macao and was well known for his short temper, tried to grab the pirate nearest to him; at least his body was found with a bullet through it. Those who knew them thought that both Bob Frost and another passenger, Major Hodgman, a noted Hong Kong amateur jockey, would certainly have intervened. At any rate it is not difficult to imagine the pandemonium in that confined space: the cries of anger and the screams, the shots, the smell of cordite, the struggling bodies in the aisle. The essential thing about the desperate mêlée inside Miss Macao that evening was that during it, Tok, appalled that Cramer had not instantly handed over the controls according to plan, panicked and put a bullet into the back of the captain's head and several into his body too. Cramer's dead weight slumped across the yoke of the control column, pushing it forward, and Miss Macao put her nose straight down and dived into the sea.

The legal aftermath was something of a farce. The self-confessed pirate Wong Yu was never tried for murder or piracy, since the British considered his evidence inadmissible in a Hong Kong court and the Portuguese authorities took the position that they had no jurisdiction over piratical acts on a British plane. According to some, Wong Yu slipped across the Chinese border a free man and disappeared. But when Roy Farrell, visiting Hong Kong many years later, asked an old friend – a well-informed Chinese businessman – what finally became of Wong Yu, he was told that the pirate had been released from the prison where he had been detained during the investigation at about nine o'clock on the night of a particularly bad typhoon. Flying debris struck and killed him only a block or two from the prison gate.

Of course, there have been numerous airborne hijackings of various kinds since the Miss Macao disaster, but at that early time Sydney de Kantzow believed the only solution to this new hazard was to run metal detectors over passengers and baggage at every departure point. He did not consider practical the suggestion that the door to the flight deck should be locked, and Chic Eather, a very experienced pilot, agrees with him.

'The flight deck is connected by interphone with the several cabin attendants' points and I do not think as pilot I could place myself above the welfare of a hostess or passenger threatened with summary slaughter if I refused a hijacker's instructions to open the crew door. I could see a situation where every passenger could be executed while I, with grim determination, held on to the flight deck. This is not the action of a commander; his main duty is to protect each and every life placed in his care.'

Poor Dale Cramer had no opportunity to make any decision at all.

Late in 1947, after only a few months in existence, fate knocked for Roy Farrell's CPA. As Roy tells it, 'A. J. R. Moss, the Director of Civil Aviation in Hong Kong, cabled me in Manila saying he needed to see me, so I checked in with him the following day. He told me that the Governor had been advised by Whitehall that every government considered communications and transportation vital to national security, and they couldn't see an American owning a British-registered airline. I had to reduce my interest from a third, not to exceed 10 per cent. I asked what would happen if I failed to comply, and I was advised my landing rights would be cancelled. Still, Moss did tell 'em I could have adequate time to find a legitimate purchaser.'

'Adequate time'. . . . Roy and Syd and their partners were not to know just what that meant, so Moss had given them food for urgent thought. But he had not panicked them. They knew they were sitting on a good thing. They had a profitable operating fleet of aircraft; they had experienced and devoted personnel; they had an air maintenance setup at Kai Tak. They might be obliged to sell – but at least they had something worth selling. And at that juncture, like one of those blimpish figures in knockabout farce, along came Brigadier General Critchley of Skyways, London.

Skyways was a British air transport company newly formed in the aftermath of the war by a trio of accomplished aviators. Brigadier General A. C. Critchley, its chairman, had been the wartime Director General of BOAC (the new name for Imperial Airways); Captain R. J. Ashley, the Managing Director, had been his personal pilot; and Sir Alan Cobham was a famous aviation pioneer. Skyways owned Avro Yorks and Lancastrians, and had a lucrative contract with the giant Anglo–Iranian Oil Company to fly their employees and freight between the United Kingdom and the Persian Gulf. It also flew charters to Europe, Palestine and Africa, and operated an embryo Hong Kong–Singapore service.

Critchley disliked Roy and Syd almost on sight; and decidedly the antipathy was mutual. The Brigadier was less than diplomatic. He and Skyways seemed to think they were God's gift to Far Eastern aviation, coming to save a tinpot organization from instant dissolution and penury, but they were alone in this belief – certainly as far as Roy and Syd were concerned. No doubt serious discussions of a purely technical nature relating to a possible Skyways takeover of CPA did take place between the two parties, but what emerges from the Skyways episode as a whole, before the inevitable collapse of serious negotiations, was pure slapstick.

'After our first meeting,' Roy says flatly, 'I realized Critchley was trying to steal our airline.' Syd concurred, and in next to no time Critchley found himself in a kind of hellzapoppin' scenario for which nothing in his past experience had prepared him.

For a start, Syd turned up at their first meeting smoking a monstrous cigar which filled the room with dense clouds of smoke and considerably upset the Brigadier – he had come to deal with a cringing suppliant, not Ronald Colman playing the part of Lord Beaverbrook, blowing arrogant smoke rings at him with a Corona-Corona. At that first meeting Roy and Syd learned that Critchley hated to be kept waiting, so for the second meeting they contrived to turn up twenty minutes late.

'This meeting accomplished nothing,' Roy told me, 'but we agreed to a third.' For Critchley this was a mistake. They all met, Roy recollects, in a suite of rooms at the old Hong Kong Hotel. This time Roy and Syd were thirty minutes late.

Roy says: 'When the General's blood pressure got back to acceptable limits, I told him I had three propositions for him.

'The first proposition was that he should pay our price. This he violently refused.

'My second proposal was to let me keep the airline for eighteen months with all landing rights and at the end of the eighteen months I would give him the airline. His reply was "Don't be a bloody fool."

'My third offer was that I would play him eighteen holes of golf to see if he would double my price or nothing. The General was an excellent golfer and he immediately shouted that I was a bloody fool and that he would beat me, to which I replied that I knew his handicap and I knew mine and he wouldn't have a chance – after all, I'd played barefoot with the caddies in Calcutta. With this he exploded and said he would have me run out of Hong Kong.' The meeting, not surprisingly, was at an end.

Roy and Syd consulted Uncle Moe Moss at Civil Aviation, anxious about Critchley's threat to have them run out of the Colony. Uncle Moe had a word with the Governor, and no more was heard of that.

'And so,' Roy says, 'some months later we started negotiations with Jock Swire, and about eighteen months after Critchley we sold 80 per cent to Swires and their associates.'

That was in June 1948. How this momentous change of life came about for Roy, Syd and everyone else connected with CPA I shall try to explain a little later. But meanwhile I must introduce the great and noble Hong Kong house that John Swire built.

PART TWO

'JOCK'

CHAPTER 9

The Times of London of 25 February 1983 carried the following obituary notice.

Mr J. K. Swire

Mr John Kidston Swire, head of the £1000m Swire Group in Hong Kong from 1946 to 1966, died on February 22 at the age of 90.

It was Swire who, with typical courage and resolution, led the old-established family shipping and trading business after the war into large-scale air transport and property activities, so that its Cathay Pacific subsidiary is now the largest regional air carrier in that part of the world. Son of John Swire of Hubbard's Hall, Harlow, Essex, he was educated at Eton and University College, Oxford, and served with the Essex Yeomanry in the 1914–1918 war. He became a director of John Swire and Sons in 1920 and chairman in 1946.

A handsome man of strong character and great integrity, he played a leading part in building up what is now one of the leading British companies operating in the Far East.

He married in 1923 Juliet Richenda, daughter of Theodore Barclay of Fanshaws, Hertford, by whom he had two sons – John, now chairman of the Swire Group, and Sir Adrian, deputy chairman – and two daughters.

How far is it from the house where postmaster Clint Farrell's son was born in Vernon, Texas, to John Kidston Swire's home at Hubbard's Hall, Harlow, Essex? Cathay Pacific, the regional airline that grew up to span continents, links both men and both places. Yet to J. K. Swire – universally known as 'Jock' – parts of the Far East had become as familiar as his own backyard long before Roy Farrell flew Betsy into Shanghai. How did he come to be there?

We need to go back two generations to find out. His grandfather, John Samuel Swire, born in 1825, was the initiator, later to be known to all who worked for him as 'The Senior'. In 1847 he had inherited *his* father's

Liverpool business, John Swire & Sons, which imported cotton from America until the Civil War disrupted that trade. Thereafter he turned instead to China and Japan, taking on a Bradford wool mill owner named Richard Butterfield as partner. The partnership was short-lived for Butterfield resigned after only a few years, yet the company remained Butterfield & Swire for nearly a century, a much respected trading name in the East. When word came that Fletcher & Co., the partner's Shanghai agents, had gone broke, Swire sailed out East to see things for himself. The oriental die was cast.

Swire was not a man to waste time. He stepped ashore in Shanghai on 28 November 1866; he rented an office in Fletcher's Building on the Bund; he staffed it with five Europeans; and on 4 December he announced in the *North China Daily News* that Butterfield & Swire would open for business on 1 January 1867. The announcement read:

NOTICE

We have established ourselves as Merchants under the Firm of Butterfield & Swire.

Richard Shackleton Butterfield
John Samuel Swire
William Hudson Swire

Corner of Foochow & Szechuen Roads
formerly occupied by Messrs. Fletcher & Co.

Next, according to local custom, he needed a House (or 'Hong') name for the new company, and with the help of a sinologist of repute and imagination chose the ambitious name 'Taikoo', a combination of two Chinese words meaning 'Great' and 'Ancient'. He himself, also in keeping with local practice, would, as head of the new Hong, be referred to as its Taipan ('the main plank in its roof'). The Taipan of Taikoo. . . . In next to no time, John Samuel Swire had become a leading performer in the Far Eastern commercial arena. It was a turbulent region.

In the quarter-century since Shanghai had been opened up to Western trade there had been frequent rebellions and wars on a large scale, even for China. The Chinese City of Shanghai had been attacked and captured, and on one occasion occupied by rebels for as much as eighteen months. Luckily for him, John Samuel Swire happened to arrive there in a period of lull and had time to look around in peace. The three-quarters of a mile stretch along the curve of the Whangpoo River now known as the Bund was, he saw, already occupied by a number of fine two-storeyed European buildings belonging to the Hongs, the big commercial houses; there were churches, a Customs House, a club and a racecourse, and broad streets running inland beyond the four-mile-long walls of the Chinese City. Gracious living was possible – among hazards: disease, for example. One of his staff, invalided home in the spring, died halfway there at Aden; his replacement died the same autumn. A newly admitted partner survived only eighteen months. There were other deaths, but no time to waste in mourning if you were, like Swire, struggling for a foothold on the China coast. He began trading at once in tea, silk, cotton and sugar. He opened a Yokohama branch and three years later an office in Hong Kong, too. At this point William Hudson Swire retired and John Samuel took in a partner, J. H. Scott; Swires and Scotts have been closely associated in the direction of the firm ever since.

In 1872 – a major milestone – Swire established a shipping outfit, the China Navigation Company, known as CNCo; its purpose was to run steamers up the Yangtze River. At first two vessels, the *Tunsin* and a paddle steamer, the *Glengyle*, plied twice weekly the 600 miles between Shanghai and Hankow, and later vessels reached Ichang in Hupeh Province near the Yangtze Gorges. 'We are going to run the River,' John Swire declared, and the hitherto dominant American company, Russell & Co., sold out quite soon, leaving B&S by far the biggest foreign operator on the Yangtze. Presently Butterfield & Swire expanded CNCo's operations to the coastal trade, running profitable north–south grain charters carrying soya beancake from Newchwang and Dairen in Manchuria to Swatow, Hong Kong and Formosa, where farmers used it as fertilizer. By 1883 CNCo operated fifteen coasters for the beancake trade, reinforcing this success by building the Taikoo Sugar Refinery in Hong Kong and later the Taikoo Dockyard there. By 1905 the Taikoo fleet had expanded to no fewer than fifty-four vessels, some of which carried passengers from Shanghai to Tientsin, and from Amoy to Hong Kong and Manila.

If you examine The Senior's portrait, the hard jaw and the confident eyes, it is difficult to imagine John Samuel Swire reduced to a 'state of fear and trembling', but that is the state he liked to claim he was in when he took the plunge into passenger transport. In 1886 he had ordered four large passenger ships to provide a regular liner service between Foochow, Hong Kong and Australia – and the immediate result was the magical appearance in the South China Sea of the *Changsha*, a beautiful yacht-like steamer with two tall masts and one tall slim funnel: a ship to dream of; a ship almost worth building even if she lost money from the moment of launching, which was not the case. There were to be three more *Changsha*s in the years to come, but none more beautiful than the first.

The steamers all made money, though it was not an era when circumstances conspired to make every shipowner rich. A Sino–French war in the south of China, a Sino–Japanese war in the north and the alarums and disruptions of the Boxer Rebellion at the turn of the century – despite these horrendous events Swire's activities prospered in a number of directions, particularly after The Senior, with extreme patience and diplomatic skill, had evolved a *modus vivendi* with an imperial Chinese government notoriously given to periodic bouts of xenophobia. 'In future, we must share the same bed, celestials and terrestrials,' John Swire murmured soothingly. And he insisted that terrestrials, too, had to bunk down together from time to time. A live-and-let-live agreement to keep competition more or less within gentlemanly bounds was arrived at with Swire's rival Hong, the oldest and most powerful commercial house, Jardine Matheson, supreme in the region since the Emperor of China had been obliged at the end of the First Opium War to cede Hong Kong to Great Britain by the terms of the Treaty of Nanking of 1842.

Daily sailings by Swire vessels became the rule on the Lower Yangtze and on the Middle River from Hankow to Ichang, while on the Upper River Swire ran a passenger and freight service up to Chungking, 1,310 miles from the sea. Yet another service opened from Hankow to the lake port of Changsha and Siangtan, and small motor vessels even penetrated up to Kiating, little more than two hundred miles from Burma. Thus the Taikoo flag reached far into the heart of China.

After 1918 there were important changes in favour of passengers. CNCo sold the beancake fleet and moved over completely to scheduled berth services up and down the coast, and to Hong Kong and Manila as well. The move coincided with a major development that would greatly influence decisions when B&S came to give serious thought to aviation as a complement to their shipping. This was the sharp growth in importance of the southern sea routes from Swatow and Amoy to the Straits Settlements (Singapore, Malacca and Penang), and from Swatow to Bangkok because of a dramatic escalation in the number of emigrants from China. To sustain these new and immensely profitable routes between the two world wars, Swires commissioned from Scott & Co. of Greenock, or built in their own Taikoo Dockyard, at least a dozen good-sized passenger ships. And so, despite the Depression, strikes, earth-shaking political developments and the appalling disruptions of modern warfare, Taikoo and CNCo prospered.

By the time John Samuel Swire, The Senior, died in 1898, aged seventy-three, Butterfield & Swire Ltd was solidly set. With its offices up and down

China, its ships, its sugar refinery and its Hong Kong dockyard, it could now stand beside the older Hong, Jardine Matheson Ltd, as one of the two great commercial houses of the Far East. John Samuel was succeeded by his two sons, John and Warren, and it was Warren, something of a martinet, who introduced his nephew Jock to the Swire organization in the Far East with a personal letter to their No. 2 man in Hong Kong:

Dear Edkins

I hope you will make that young nephew of mine work, as he has had a very good time for the last three years and hasn't done a stroke of work. He may therefore be tempted to think that there is no need to work. I don't think for a moment he will, when he is given a definite job which he has to carry out or else add to another man's work, as he is a *very* good fellow and has an uncommonly square head; but any way he is *not* in China for his own amusement, but to learn as much as he can of the China end of the business as soon as he can. We have lots of work for him here as soon as he has enough experience to do it, which I hope he will acquire in the course of the next five years. . . .

As it happened, the First World War broke out five months later and immediately most of young Jock's energies were devoted to getting into it. In a sense Jock Swire was as much made for the army as for a life in high commerce; at any rate he seems to have been a born cavalry officer. After Eton he had gone to University College, Oxford, to read Law, and there attracted his contemporaries' attention both as a horseman and as a star of the University's Officer Training Corps. In the University magazine he was singled out as *Isis* Idol number CCCCLXXXVI, and the profile's undergraduate author refers to Jock's great height ('growing like a tree'), to his horsemanship ('learning to stick like a limpet to the saddle'), and to his 'immense enthusiasm for life'. His football and his cricket 'are marvels of gymnastic skill. Did he not once trundle out the City Police?' As for his performance in the OTC: 'As a trooper he was adequate, as a lance corporal he competed favourably, but when he came to adorn the dizzy rank of a subaltern his true *métier* was found. He set a fitting seal on his military and equestrian career', the profile added, 'by captaining the winning Oxford team in the inter-Varsity jumping competitions at Olympia'. *Isis*'s last words were: 'We hear that he is bound for the Far East. . . .' Bound for it – and to be bound most intimately to it for the rest of his life – that is, for the next seventy years.

Jock joined the family firm in the autumn of 1913, aged twenty, and next year sailed for Hong Kong on a ship of the Blue Funnel Line, a Swire associate. War broke out on 4 August 1914 and he had to wait until Christmas to rejoin his regiment, the Essex Yeomanry. He filled in the time in fine military manner attached to the Duke of Cornwall's Light Infantry, patrolling from Deepwater Bay to the fishing village of Aberdeen, mostly at night, on his pony Shanghai, and so earning the affectionate description 'Deepwater Bay Hussar' among his friends. (He was, he said, on the lookout for the German sea raider *Emden*, then at large in Far Eastern and Pacific waters.) Circumstances took a grim turn. Almost as soon as Jock returned to Europe, his brother Glen was killed in action at Ypres. His Oxford contemporaries died in droves. Jock himself was wounded twice in France, the second time at the battle of Loos where a close call from a mortar bomb resulted in permanent partial deafness. His directness of character made him popular with his men; they seem to have taken to his sense of humour, too. After the war he liked to tell of the occasion when, on leave from the trenches, he called at a London chemist and ordered a thousand condoms for his battalion – he was worried about the ill-effect that fraternization with the French *filles de joie* was having on his men's health. 'A thousand? Certainly, sir,' said the chemist, handing them over. Then, as Jock made for the door with the package under his arm, he called after him, 'Enjoy your weekend, sir.'

Jock returned to Hong Kong at the end of 1919, and this time he arrived as a director of the firm with 'special responsibilities for Overseas Staff'. It was a job perfectly designed to bring out the extraordinary warmth, straighforwardness and simple humanity behind the tall, moustached, unmistakably military appearance he presented to the world. By now he had strong ideas on man management. 'Money is not everything by a long chalk,' he noted in his diary shortly after arrival. Improved terms of service were long overdue for employees below management level – home leave on full pay with a free passage for man and wife, a wage of £400 to £1,800, and a profit-sharing scheme based on salary and service. He went on:

> The reason why B&S lack *esprit de corps* is because (a) London are not sufficiently human or sufficiently acquainted with local colour. (b) Too many deadheads at the top out East. (c) Heads of Departments' posts should be made real plums, and no one kept after fifty. (d) No Taipan should be kept after fifty. (e) London and Eastern Taipans must say 'Thank you' more often. (f) The staff don't know their Directors personally.

We recognize the tone of voice of a recently 'demobbed' officer accustomed to looking after his men. It is a tone, robust, sensible and kind, that sounds again and again.

Any requests must always be acted on at once. It is not only what you give, but the way that you give it. . . . Men should always be told to look for another job the very instant it appears certain that they cannot get to the top. Don't breed deadheads deliberately.

B&S's female employees to a large extent owed their 'liberation' to Jock. He inspired a new company rule, giving managers

discretion to appoint any of the outstanding women clerks, who are qualified, to desks for which regular staff members only have been considered; that is to put them on the footing of permanent members of the staff and to pay them accordingly. . . .

The idea of promoting women was a revolutionary one in the buttoned-up, commercial world of colonial Hong Kong, and Taikoo boxwallahs might have been a little startled by a communication from London: 'A shorthand-typist *ought* to be attached to each of the big departments.' The Senior himself had once ruled against the use of female clerical staff and his words on the subject (as on many others) had achieved the status of holy writ. At the turn of the century a Hong Kong Taipan had had the temerity to urge London headquarters to allow him to employ a stenographer, preferably a woman. He received a rap on the knuckles. 'Remember how our late Senior discouraged the immoderate use of pens, ink and paper. Business is not built up that way.' Such a sententious retort has a Dickensian ring; it might have come from the mouth of some pompous character in *Dombey and Son*. Certainly Jock Swire, the Deepwater Bay Hussar, would never have offered it. Twenty-seven years old and back from the first modern war with his already experienced wits about him, Jock was going to make some changes.

In his capacity as director in charge of Overseas Staff, Jock probably had the best opportunity of any man in John Swire & Sons to explore the remotest nooks and crannies of the company's Far Eastern ramifications. Luckily he was intensely inquisitive by nature and an obsessive recorder of events and impressions. Throughout his adult life he not only dictated countless letters and memoranda in the normal course of business, but he also kept a diary. The earlier entries give a fair idea not only of Jock Swire's mentality but also of how things were Out East in those remote pre-Second World War days: what it was like to travel in China and Hong Kong through foreign eyes; his private view of people working there and how things should be done. Entries are frequently pepped up with Jock's 'Thoughts Along the Way'. As a former cavalry officer and army riding instructor, he was given to the odd equestrian phrase: he would say of some bombastic bore 'Terrible old blow-hard', and throughout his long life he earnestly advised younger members of John Swire & Sons 'Never, never buck.' A favourite word was 'flat catcher', meaning an undesirable, part-bounder, part-conman. His bitterest commercial rival couldn't accuse Jock Swire, sometimes acerbic but never devious, of being a flat catcher.

Jock made private notes of a six-month working journey to and from the Far East in 1930. The result is a ragbag of observations, snatches from which – endearing, dated, even trivial – I hope will do something to recapture a distant era and the character of Jock who lived it.

Friday January 10 Left Victoria 11.20 by Blue Train to Marseilles.

Saturday January 11 Embarked at 8.30 on SS *Aeneas* at Marseilles and sailed at noon. At table with Mr and Mrs Holt, Miss Severs, Mr Dudley Ward and Mrs Leonard. Capt. Wallace in command.

Monday January 13 Really quite cold & I have a nasty little chill on my tummy. Wearing summer suit and thick underclothes. Passed through Straits of Messina in the morning.

Thursday January 16 Arrived Port Said 10 a.m. Cold and showery. Miss Severs left and going to Cairo . . . . Still wearing thick underclothes. Fur coat at night. . . .

In the Arabian Sea, Jock sized up his fellow travellers like Hercule Poirot musing over a group of suspects in an Agatha Christie mystery.

Thursday January 23 Great humidity and very hot in the cabins. The nice people on the ship are Lt Comm. Havers, Davidson, Mrs Leonard; Moss, quite a nice Tientsin padre called Scott, and Dudley Ward is passable. A Mrs Strong seems all right but her husband is awful. A boy called Chaplin going out to Borneo seems a good lad. . . .

Thursday January 30 Fancy dress dinner and dance. Everyone played up & it was the greatest fun. I went in a Dutchman's costume that I had bought at Simon Artz, Port Said. Mrs Leonard, Havers, Davidson and Chaplin dined with me & we all thoroughly enjoyed ourselves.

Penang was a disappointment: 'A very poor imitation of Hong Kong . . . I was very much impressed by the way the Chinese have completely swallowed up the place. It is purely and simply a Chinese colony.' The call at Singapore brought a request from the manager of the Singapore Cold Storage for an exciting commodity called 'dry ice', and with the British commanding general Jock discussed the question – a serious one, then as now – of piracy. Mr Jenkins, in charge of CNCo in Singapore, supported Jock in pressing for British soldiers to be posted on ships at anchor in the Roads. The general was cool to the idea and poor Jenkins proved, in this instance, a broken reed. He collapsed, Jock noted, 'with a bad go of Denpers [diarrhoea]'. On Sunday, 9 February, Jock arrived in Hong Kong to find the B&S Taipan half crippled by lumbago but still able to discuss piracy. To Jock's way of thinking the whole problem was due to the fact that 'the Army, Navy and Government are shirking their responsibility entirely'. The sympathetic British admiral on the China Station agreed. 'The piracy menace is as bad today as ever,' he said and told Jock he had so informed the Admiralty, though without much luck. But for Jock and other shipowners, the worry over piracy was obsessive.

The diaries, again at random, give a good idea of his attitudes to employees, the recruitment of Far Eastern staff, and more.

To Canton: Met by Webb and went back to the Hong for breakfast and then motored straight to call on the Governor of Canton, General Chan Ming Shu. Had $\frac{1}{2}$ hour talk with him through his secretary Leung. Getting him down to launch *Tsinan* [a Swire ship] was a stroke of genius & I am sure it has done inestimable good. . . . Went over *Newchwang* [another CNCo vessel]. Capt. Green, a sour rather bolshie young fellow. . . . On *Szechuen* [yet another ship]: Atkins C/O; Appleton 2/Engineer, a ginger fellow with a chief's ticket who is desperately keen to get married . . . a nice fellow but rather unbalanced. Pollard the 3rd Engineer struck me as touched but is said to be quite a good engineer. . . . Shaw suggests Knight should go to Hankow and Fisher, who is better with men, to Shanghai. . . .

Shaw does not think *anyone* should retire on less than £300 after 20 years & thinks £500 more like it. I like C. C. Roberts [later to become Cathay Pacific's first chairman] more than ever; he has a grand jaw on him. . . .

Went all over *Antung* [a CNCo ship] with a view to deciding how we can protect against pirates. A very difficult job. Expanded metal all round the officers' deck and turn the music room into a guardroom with the NCO in a first class cabin seems the cheapest and best way. . . .

I believe we ought to get six university candidates every year, send them all for three months to the School of Oriental Languages in London and those that are passed as likely to do well in China should be sent to Nanking four at a time to learn Chinese and study China until they are wanted on the staff. I believe under modern conditions that this would produce the sort of fellow we want for the future far better than the London probationary staff does.

This last entry pointed the way to one of Jock's most enduring staff innovations – the hand-picking of undergraduate recruits from the universities, specifically for service in the Far East. He expanded the idea on board the SS *President Madison* en route to Shanghai:

[In the past] foreigners made no effort to understand the Chinese, their language, or their customs. No foreigner can continue to trade in China for the future without doing so. . . . Our foreign staff must be good linguists & thoroughly understand the Chinese. We must therefore change our method of recruiting and training and adapt for the future. We must err if anything on the side of being in advance of the times & not be afraid of taking risks. . . . Only the very best will be recruited & a good man should never be missed, vacancy or no vacancy. While at Nanking they would study the Chinese language at the College & absorb Chinese manners and atmosphere. They would work part-time in the office & come into B&S after not less than 6 months or more than 18 months. The London probationary staff should be cut down to 3 or 4 who should be public school men recruited from Glasgow shipping offices etc. . . .

This idea – which underlies Swires' recruiting practice even today – carried over into its logical corollary: that hand-picked Chinese, too, should be taken into top jobs at high salaries.

In Shanghai, Jock acted on his new idea at once.

Proceeded straight to Hazelwood [the Taikoo mansion] where I found Brown, Lamb, Yu Ya Ching, & Wang [all Swire employees] just sitting down to dinner. Our relations with China, the Nanking Government, & important individuals is quite excellent. Yu says there will be no war, Nanking is stronger than ever. . . . While we were talking yesterday, the most attractive young Chinese I have ever met called Chow came to ask Brown for a job. He is a BA Cantab & has been practising at the English Bar. He speaks and writes perfect English. Brown and I enormously impressed but in view of his age 36, his education and experience he could want a bigger job than we had to offer, Brown turned him down. I am convinced there is a place in our organisation somewhere for this man & when discussing the Wuhu agency this morning, I said to Brown, 'Let's send Chow.' He has not stopped bubbling with enthusiasm since!! . . .

Later, there was politics:

Dined at the Cathay – the Keswicks [owners of Jardine Matheson], Porter, Kent, Brown [B&S executives], Shun, Hu Hsueh, one of China's greatest intellectuals, and George Sokolsky. The latter is a pure-bred Polish Jew educated in America aged 55 with a Chinese wife. Was with Borodin in Canton & now lives in TV Soong's pocket [Soong was Chiang's powerful Minister of Finance] & writes amazingly good articles for the press. . . . I should not be at all surprised if he is not Russia's chief spy in China. He was a communist but claims to have changed his outlook. I listened to him for two hours & very interesting it was. He considers that the real Chinese revolution is still to come & will come soon. . . . The heads of Government are governing the country by cash, murder, prison & repression & the young men must sooner or later push through the crust & push them out. There will be a very ugly stage before a proper modern government is set up. As regards the armies [of the warlords] they are all hard at work making gas & mechanising themselves . . . but it is all on the surface & will have no bearing on fundamentals. The Germans surrounding Chiang are the worst he has ever met & are forever preaching the domination of the country by force. . . . There was an interesting discussion on the Russian Revolution, on Lenin, on Gandhi. On the complete impossibility of any but a penniless man leading the masses. . . . In fact a throughly high-brow evening.

Jock's six months' safari round the Swire offices and ships on station reveals a resilient mind and a constitution rather prone to chills and colds. Despite them, the tour took him hither and yon and high and low, frequently snuffling or sprinting for the nearest lavatory. It included Ningpo and Shanghai, many isolated riverine ports dotted along the length of the Yangtze – Lower, Middle and Upper – among them Nanking, Wuhu, Kiukiang, Hankow, Changsha and Siangtan, Chengling, Ichang, Chungking. In unreliable trains or on the quivering decks of overcrowded steamers and long-funnelled river boats he crisscrossed southern China (Swatow and Amoy), northern China and Manchuria (Tsingtao, Tientsin, Peking, Newchwang, Dairen, Fusan, Antung), and Japan (Kobe, Yokohama), dossing down on the tumbledown verandahs or – less often – luxuriating in the comfortable living rooms of the company's staff houses.

Thoughts and impressions went down in note form. On future promotions, for example: 'The order for the Management is Mitchell, Masson, Lock, C. C. Roberts. T. is departmental-minded and not a leader. We *must* have leaders in future. . . .' Notes on staff housing: 'The Taikoo house, Hankow, is in an awful state, the carpets are worn out, the curtains the most ghastly Victorian things . . . just like a dentist's waiting room. Impossible for a woman. The kitchen range doesn't work. The coolie carries all the bath water through the dining room.' In the far-flung outposts of B&S problems of temperament abounded. At Nanking X's sarcasm and Y's inhuman execution of London's policy were having a disastrous effect on the morale of the Chinese staff. The manager at Wuhu was 'completely insensitive and devoid of imagination', and had been the cause of a spate of resignations. Genially breezing and sneezing in and out of offices up and down the coast, Jock brought comfort and reassurance.

Much time was given to the question of how best to use the Taikoo fleet on the Yangtze – a wonderful collection of craft with stovepipe funnels, bulldog noses and tight canvas sun-awnings, but also with serious shortcomings. Take, for instance, the *Shengking*: 'Engines broke down at midnight between Nanking and Wuhu, 4 a.m. and 7 a.m. This ship is a public disgrace. There is only one bathroom & wc for all the men on the ship. As we now have so many saloon Chinese, the wc's should be labelled in Chinese so as to keep them out of the ladies. The galley is like a furnace and the unfortunate cook is almost melted. . . .' As for the officers: 'Mr McArthur [Chief Engineer] is quite charming; Johnston, the 2nd Officer, a good lad. Captain E. is the nastiest man I ever met & a menace on the river. T. is mad. . . .'

The river could be a dangerous place; the civil war between the Nationalists and the Communists raged up and down its banks. 'The *Peterel* [a British gunboat] was at Shasi, as there are a lot of communists in the neighbourhood. We saw nationalist troops rounding up a village. Three steamer loads of troops left Shasi with us. . . . Saw Admiral McLean who has the wind up about the Upper and Middle River' – and the lawlessness could get on people's nerves. 'Shasi is a dreadful place for a young fellow to live entirely alone for eight months. Tippin was very shaken there and should leave the river.'

Fortunately with Jock, humour was never far away – even in one blackly comic incident almost too terrifying to be funny. In later years Jock must have smiled over it more than once from a First Class seat in one of his own Boeing 747 jumbo jets, but at the time. . . .

On 15 March 1930, Jock Swire and John Scott caught an aeroplane from Shanghai to Nanking. Jock's notes on what happened are brief and decorous:

John & I left the Bund at 7 a.m. & caught the 8 o/c aeroplane from Lungwha aerodrome. It was very foggy & rough & after a very eventful voyage landed at Nanking 10.30. It was our first flight for both of us. We had two American pilots, one of whom had his wife (?) on board who sat on his knee & drove the machine a great part of the way. Very terrifying. The car was full to overflowing with six passengers; the president of the company's wife, Mrs Price, was very sick into a newspaper & in trying to throw it out of the window, the wind caught it & blew it over John & me; very unpleasant!! I think it will be some time before J.S. flies again!!

Luckily, there are more explicit accounts. Arriving in Hankow a few days later, Jock was shown the following extract from the *Chung Shan Daily News*:

When aeroplane 'Wuchang' started its return trip from Shanghai to Hankow (via Nanking) on the 15th instant, there were three foreign lady passengers. Among them was one American who was an acquaintance of the American pilot. While the plane was flying up in the air, the couple began flirting with each other, then sitting together and embracing each other and then, while piloting the 'plane, they practically carried out their love affair. Consequently, the machine became very unsteady and was much shaken and the passengers felt vomiting and dizzy. This aroused the wrath of the China Aviation Co. to report the matter to the authorities, asking that such obscene conduct of the pilot be stopped and the safety of the passengers carefully looked after. But the staff said that they did not dare interfere with the pilot. After much consultation, it was permitted to have the assistant pilot changed and the No. 1 pilot was thus allowed to fly on to Hankow with his lady friend. When the plane was coming down at Hankow, the pilot still held her close, kissing her all the time and the spectators in the Airdrome were amazed to see them doing so.

Jock revelled in recounting the incident. In 1979 he told an interviewer:

I do not think John Scott had ever flown in his life before and I do not think I had. But we got on board an amphibian aircraft to Lung Wa Lake with a very drunk American pilot and his girlfriend on board and there was thick fog. It was an awful old ramshackle aircraft. We did not begin to know what we were doing. And we took off into the fog. Then to our horror, the pilot had his girlfriend through in the cockpit on his knee. And John Scott, I remember, leapt to his feet – he was about six-foot-eight – and shouted, 'Fetch that woman in.' And he cracked his head on the top of the thing and went down with a wallop to the bottom. . . . There was a wonderful report of the thing in the papers. No one dared report the pilot.

An experience like that might have put a lesser man off flying for life. Jock gulped, laughed and not only went on flying but created an airline of his own as well.

The last entry in a diary of an exhausting and exhaustive four-month Far Eastern tour is typically spry:

July 2 1930. Arrived Liverpool Street Station 8.38 after a perfectly delightful journey.

Considering the illness, the human problems and the mental and physical fatigue that such a long working journey entailed, there is a good deal of the indomitable Jock Swire even in that.

CHAPTER 10

An interest in aviation – or in 'going into Air' as the phrase was – crops up in Swire company correspondence at least as early as 1933 ('Air' in office letters was usually spelled with a capital A). A letter from John Swire & Sons' London office to B&S in Hong Kong and Shanghai at the end of that year reported with some excitement: 'We have had a talk with the General Manager of Imperial Airways . . . and eventual extension to China clearly forms part of their plans.'

Imperial Airways were the forerunners of BOAC; their passenger–cargo services even then ran to Singapore via Bangkok, and Butterfield & Swire already had an eagle eye open for any chance to become the IA agents in Hong Kong if it expanded in that direction. The Imperial Airways regional representative in Singapore, Captain Barnard, was already pointing out to residents of Hong Kong and China how useful the weekly IA services operating from Singapore to England would be, 'particularly as the Siberian Railway route is liable to interruption' – i.e. the Japanese occupation of Manchuria. Moreover, newspaper reports from Nanking predicted a link-up of CNAC's China air network with the Imperial Airways service connecting Britain, India, British Malaya and Hong Kong.

In due course, B&S formally applied for the direct agency for Imperial Airways in Hong Kong, China and Japan, 'confident that our experience as shipping agents and the widespread nature of our organisation will enable us to give Imperial Airways Ltd. satisfactory service'. B&S suggested that the Taikoo Dockyard, an extensive repair and engineering facility, might be put to use as an aircraft maintenance unit too. 'A major factor, that,' Captain Barnard agreed.

But was IA's hoped-for extension to the Colony and beyond feasible? China in the midst of war was volatile and violent. Aviation of any kind was bound to be subject to a tangle of military controls and political priorities as long as the hostilities with Japan continued, and hostilities showed no sign of ending – on the contrary. Good policy, B&S thought, to use this uncertain period to make friends with Imperial Airways, to demonstrate Swires' unique fitness to act as their active advisers when the time came. Unfortunately that time never came. Soon all local Chinese air services were out of commission and most aerodromes in military hands because of the danger of Japanese aerial bombardment. It would be madness, B&S's Shanghai office reported, to risk any neutral planes in the region until further notice.

What of Hong Kong? Swires' Taipan there tried to look ahead. 'We consider [he wrote to London in September 1937] that, as air-travel between the Far East and Europe is only in its infancy and is capable of tremendous expansion, there may be possible developments in the future which may make a close B&S/Imperial Airways connection a valuable one for us.' Hong Kong, he added, despite a somewhat inadequate airfield, was certain to be a nexus for commercial aviation. But he was not dreaming of a Swire air fleet. His thinking was based on the still prevailing idea of Swires as nothing more than agents for somebody with planes of his own.

The Second World War stopped most speculation dead. Who could tell what would happen after the war? When would 'after the war' turn out to be? Hitler had overrun Europe. The Japanese army was approaching Hong Kong; some Europeans of the Colony were being evacuated and others called up. Yet at that distracting time, Walter Lock, a director of Butterfield & Swire, wrote his London directors a letter of startling foresight, based on a conversation he had just had with a Commander Murray of Imperial Airways who was busy closing down his company's Hong Kong office in anticipation of Japanese occupation. Part of it read:

> In discussing the future Commander Murray tells us that it is practically certain that they [Imperial Airways] will wish to re-open their own office when their machines come here again, and he also tells us that as a matter of policy after the war they will be operating main lines only. . . .
>
> Intended main lines for the Far East are the present from London to Sydney, which will probably omit Bangkok, and a second line from London to Vancouver, via Calcutta, Rangoon, Hong Kong, Shanghai and Japan. This means that there should be a real opening for private British aviation, both between British possessions in the Far East and from British to other territories, and there is at present a possibility of opening a line from Hong Kong to Singapore via the Philippines and Borneo, which was until recently a project of Imperial Airways. . . .

It seemed to Walter Lock that a Swire air service from Hong Kong to

Manila, Sarawak and Singapore should be a wonderful idea. With it B&S would acquire two priceless benefits: a start in the air and a working knowledge of the air business. Lock's train of thought went further. It would be advisable, he wrote, to start with three machines – not flying boats, but DC-2s which he understood to be entirely suitable and cheaper to run. He had heard that the American airlines were switching over to DC-3s and selling off their DC-2s; one might be picked up for about £15,000. Perhaps three machines and 'a good lot' of spare parts might be bought for £50,000, although American pilots would probably be needed and they might be expensive. As for maintenance, CNAC had an engineer in Hong Kong who might help out; otherwise, of course, there was the Taikoo Dockyard and B&S might have to get their own man. . . . 'You may think this rather a wildcat suggestion,' Lock ended, a touch defensively.

It was certainly a bold one for 1941. Pearl Harbor was attacked in early December that year, Hong Kong fell to the Japanese on Christmas Day, Singapore surrendered the following 15 February and Burma was overrun (Roy Farrell and Syd de Kantzow would soon be in India running the gauntlet of Japanese Zeros over the Hump). It must have seemed like the end of everything. And Walter Lock, at his desk as the shutters went up around him, was calmly proposing a Swire-owned airline from Hong Kong to Manila, Borneo and Singapore. He had sown the seed. A few years later Swires would have such a thing, and much more, but Walter Lock would not see it. He died with the Polish leader, General Sikorski, in the Gibraltar air crash of 1943.

With the war and the nightmare of Japanese occupation over at last in 1946, it was time to pick up the pieces – if the pieces were to be found.

Jock Swire had spent the war in London, not only as a director of Swires but also as Chairman of the London Port Employers and as the representative of the Minister of Shipping at the Ministry of Economic Warfare. He survived the Blitz and watched with a kind of miserable fascination as disaster after disaster overtook British military and naval forces in the East, disasters that meant the destruction of the commercial and shipping empire built by The Senior and his successors, and the internment of many Swire staff in the soul-destroying rigours of Japanese prisoner-of-war camps. On the night of 10 May 1941 John Swire & Sons' offices at 8 Billiter Square in the City of London had been totally destroyed. Jock and the staff were at first offered temporary refuge in the offices of their Hong Kong rivals Jardine Matheson, but before the move was made accommodation was found at Cornhill, in the 'palatial' offices of the Scottish Widows Fund, whose staff had been evacuated to Scotland. The firm remained at Cornhill for twelve months before taking up residence on the first floor of 22 Billiter Street until the end of the war.

The morning after the bombing Jock wrote to his mother:

> . . . The office was completely gutted by fire on Saturday night, which is rather a bore, as all our records have gone. So now we have nothing and must start from scratch.
>
> I've been walking the City all day looking for accommodation, but all our friends are burnt out too. I never saw such a shambles in my life. A large part of the City is just in ruins and that's all about it. However, we will get in somewhere. At present Jardine Matheson have taken us in.

And on 13 May 1941—

> . . . We got into Billiter Square today and found most of the things that really matter still intact – if only we could get at them. The whole area (a good 400 yards square) has been roped off as dangerous, as some of the buildings are falling down as they cool and no-one is allowed in. Also we could not open the safes for a week or two until they cool off and there may be another blitz by then. I have never seen such ruins outside Ypres.
>
> We got a lovely new temporary office today, at 28 Cornhill, and moved in this afternoon. I am now hard at work collecting such things as typewriters, which are unobtainable, I got 4 from Windolite this evening.

When the German bombing of London reached its full height, Jock, with typical generosity, moved his entire staff into his mother's house at Harlow in Essex, and he and they commuted to the City together. When Jock referred to his employees as 'his family' it was no empty phrase.

By the time the war ended, Swires' Hong Kong industries, like the Billiter Square offices, were little more than rubble, most of CNCo's ships had disappeared and the very future of the Colony as a viable port was in considerable doubt, threatened as it was by turmoil in China. The embryo British administration that had moved in after the Japanese faced monstrous problems, including among much else a breakdown of law and order and a lack of public services, of food and of hospitals. It was going to cost a very large fortune indeed to put commercial Hong Kong together again. Would the Hongs, Swires and Jardines be able to raise the money? Yes – thanks largely to the unstinted support of the Hongkong and Shanghai Bank, whose directors came across with loans on almost imaginatively generous terms. But even so, it is fortunate that Jock Swire had a talisman to hand for use when things looked bleak. Kipling's poem 'If' had been dinned into all

British public school boys of his generation to stiffen their upper lips in times of trouble, and an uplifting line or two from it seemed very appropriate for Jock's situation at the war's end:

> [If you can] watch the things you gave your life to broken
> And stoop and build 'em up with worn out tools. . . .

In January Jock Swire was out East again to face the worst, a familiar soldier-like figure in a crumpled trilby stepping from a BOAC Sunderland flying boat at the Kai Tak seadrome. One thing he was prepared for – the Taikoo Dockyard at Quarry Bay had been smashed to bits by American bombing raids towards the end of the war. To this day in John Swire & Sons' office in London there is an excellent US Air Force photograph of the bombs actually exploding; the reconstruction of the dockyard was able to go ahead at once, thanks to such photographs and the foresight of Warren Swire, who studied them in London and assessed the damage. Two hangars from Dorman Long and one each of the essential machines were rushed out to Hong Kong, and a new *caisson* for the dry dock had already reached Colombo by the time peace was declared. Quick thinking. By the time Jock arrived the yard was in operation again.

Inspecting Butterfield & Swire's property, Jock discovered an unexpected problem. 'Peak House [a Swire house] has now been practically stripped of everything as also Mt Kellett [another Swire house]. They are now taking away the bricks from Mt Kellett servants' quarters. It really is the limit in a British Colony.' Overworked British officials were unhelpful. 'Called on MacDougall [Colonial Secretary] and complained about looting. . . . His only answer was that it is up to us to install watchmen. I think the only thing to do is to find out what it would cost to loot the houses ourselves and, if not too dear, do it and wait. . . .'

Personnel and ships were other problems. Some members of the prewar staff could be brought back at once, but those who had been prisoners of the Japanese needed long rehabilitation leave. Jock met them: 'Saw T. S. Marshall, looking bad. John's bursting with health. Cheverst aged and tired. Trueman O.K. Lindsay aged but tough. Tippin O.K. physically, tired mentally' – and so on. Eric Price and C. C. Roberts, both prewar China hands, were invaluable in pulling things together. As for CNCo, its ships had been dispersed, requisitioned by the Japanese or sunk. On his way to Hong Kong, Jock had found two CNCo vessels stuck in Calcutta, their officers impatient to get back to sea, and he was comforted to learn that British Naval Intelligence knew where all CNCo's Japanese-captured ships had gone to, their Japanese names and where they were now.

Roy Farrell waves from his US Army C-47, alias Betsy.

Sydney de Kantzow in 1946.

Betsy's first flight from Shanghai to Hong Kong and Sydney, 1946. Roy Farrell (left) with Bob Russell.

Kai Tak Airport, 1947.

Vera Rosario became Cathay
Pacific's first air hostess in
1948.

John Kidston Swire
(1893–1983).

Swires' Hong Kong headquarters from about 1897 until 1960. Butterfield was dropped from the title in 1974, although Butterfield ceased to be connected with the company in the 1870s. An example of the Swires' innate conservatism!

Jock Swire as Deep Water Bay Hussar. Hong Kong, 1914.

All that was left after the Braemer Reservoir crash in 1949.

A Cathay Pacific DC-4. Range: 2,100 miles. Cruising speed: 200 mph.

Jock Swire with his daughter Gillian and John Browne (above) and with members of a Cathay Pacific crew.

Left: Adrian Swire with Michael Miles. *Right:* Lord Maclehose of Beoch, Sir John Bremridge and Mr Duncan Bluck at a reception held at HAECO Hangar No. 2 to commemorate the arrival of the first Cathay Pacific B747-200 on 31 July 1979.

Patrick Tsai and Chester Yen, two of Cathay's Chinese senior executives.

A Cathay Pacific Lockheed Electra, one of two in the fleet from 1959 to 1967. Range: 2,700 miles. Cruising speed: 400 mph. Seventy-five passengers. In the foreground, the southernmost tip of Kowloon, the Star Ferry Terminal. Top left: Kai Tak Airport in the haze and hills of the New Territories.

Above: A Cathay Convair jet. Range: 2,800 miles. Cruising speed: 590 mph.

Left: John Nott, British Minister of Trade (standing), at the Dorchester Hotel in London, announcing his dramatic decision to allow Cathay Pacific to fly the Hong Kong to London route and giving John Swire (left) a night to remember.

Below: At Sydney Airport little Betsy, newly repainted in the Cathay uniform, gets ready to 'race' one of the company's giant 747s home to Hong Kong – and retirement.

Jock's diary provides useful vignettes of the postwar scene at about the time that Roy Farrell and Betsy were flying into Shanghai.

Dined with Price. Most depressing account of Shanghai where lawlessness appears to be unbelievable. . . . John Keswick [of Jardine Matheson] thinks Chiang Kai-shek will be out by the end of March. . . . Very gloomy about Russia in Manchuria. . . .

Japan: Lot depends on what MacArthur has in mind for Japan and it may well be five years before Japan has any trade with the outside world except what may be necessary to pay her debt. Japan is a mess. Yokohama completely flat and full to the brim with American shipping. Tokyo and Kobe also flat. . . .

Revisiting China with John Scott, Jock found one or two CNCo ships to take them to Canton, Amoy, Shanghai and Tientsin. Both well over six foot, the two middle-aged Englishmen must have seemed to the Chinese an imposing couple of 'red barbarians' as they moved around that battered coast. Sailing up to Tientsin in Swires' old *Shantung*, they somehow managed to tuck themselves into the wireless operator's cabin, and the old tub rather bore out Scott's opinion that Swires' existing ships should be replaced; she was thirty-one years old and pretty far gone, leaking everywhere. 'Cost someone a packet to put straight,' Jock sighed to his diary. And the *Shantung* was not the only thing out of date. Both men were soon obliged to agree that the former glorious days of CNCo's Yangtze River fleet and China coasters were past reviving.

Wednesday, 10 April. There is no hope of our getting back onto the river under the British flag. . . . Went to Tsu Yee Pei, the Governor of the Central Bank, and had my hat stolen. He thinks labour troubles have reached their worst. . . . Lunched with Cheng of Nat. Egg Products at Sun Ya Restaurant. Poisoned at lunch and on the run all night. Feeling frightful. Dr. Burton gave me sulfaquanadine. . . .

Shanghai: Very depressing talk on CNCo's future. John would sell such ships as we have; I am not so sure. The industrialisation of Hong Kong may well make HK a base port not dependent for cargoes from China.

A fair prediction. And Jock added an important suggestion:

We are proposing Shanghai/Amoy/HK/S'pore/Batavia [Jakarta]. . . . Our new ships should be 4,500 tons dead weight, 16 knots. They should carry 40 cabin passengers and a quantity of refrigerated space.

A concentration by CNCo on the China–Hong Kong–Straits passenger and cargo trade – that was to be the big idea now. As if nothing much had happened in the last five years, Chinese were once more shuttling busily between South East Asia and the Fukien coast of China. Family links, holiday visits and trade had revived immediately after the Japanese collapse. And this had a great significance for the future of Swires in the East, for it made them think seriously again of 'going into Air'.

'We must protect the Air over our ships' – whoever first uttered it, that phrase began to sound round Swire boardroom meetings and in memoranda like a bugle-call to rally jaded soldiers to fresh glory and adventure. Perhaps someone had thought it up during a long night's German Blitz during the war, and it sounded like Jock. At any rate it concentrated the Swire mind on the wonderful idea of *themselves* 'going into Air' at last, of carrying on from the day when the shutters came down on the Imperial Airways office as the Japanese approached, and Walter Lock's thoughts turned to a B&S air service from Hong Kong to Singapore via Manila and Borneo.

Jock returned to Hong Kong from China and on 11 May made a most significant, if laconic, entry in his diary: 'Morton gives a very good account of Holyman of A.N.A.'

R. W. Morton, from CNCo's agent Colyer Watson Pty Ltd of Australia, was visiting Hong Kong, and Holyman was Captain Ivan Holyman, Managing Director of Australian National Airways, a great man of Australian flying and an outstanding personality among airline pioneers. It was to be with Holyman's expert advice and cooperation that Swires would be able to get off to a good start in Air, a new area of activity of which – canny traders and veteran shippers though they were – they knew nothing.

In June Jock and John Scott were in Melbourne dining with Ivan Holyman and discussing with rising excitement the ANA air service to Hong Kong on which Holyman had set his heart, despite strong opposition from the leader of the ruling Labour Party, Mr Ben Chifley, to the very existence of privately owned and independent airlines like ANA. Jock enthusiastically supported Holyman: 'Agreed [he wrote] we must get HK Government to ask for Air Service at once as ANA are at present the only people who can put on a service. Holyman is obviously a fighter,' he added approvingly. The very next day things went a stage further: 'Spent the afternoon with Ivan Holyman fixing up [for B&S to have] the ANA agency for HK, China and Japan.' Jock's liking for Holyman knew no bounds, and that evening he noted, 'This is quite the most outstanding man we have yet met.'

Ivan Holyman and ANA had been brought to Jock Swire's attention by R. A. Colyer, who in a letter to Warren Swire the previous year had urged a getting together of B&S and ANA – 'a dovetailing' was the way he had put it. Colyer pointed out that Holyman not only had experience in air transportation stretching back to the early 1930s, but he 'was also unflinchingly straight'. ANA had initially been keen to operate a service to China on their own, but Colyer had assured Holyman that Swires' experience of the region would serve a very useful purpose. To this Warren Swire replied that 'we are seriously interested in these kind of projects in your direction'. He went on to visualize a possible ANA air service: 'I should think Australia/Java/Indo-China/New Guinea/Borneo/Hong Kong.' Furthermore, B&S had the engineering background of the Taikoo Dockyard, which should be available to ANA. And he echoed Walter Lock: 'Another possibility is *a Hong Kong company in which we might take an interest.*' (My italics.)

When C. C. Roberts, Swires' Taipan in Hong Kong, approached him, Uncle Moe Moss, the friendly Director of Air Services, was encouraging. He knew and approved of Holyman and ANA, and appreciated the desirability of setting up a cheap and unsubsidized British line between Hong Kong and Australia before any Chinese or Americans could push their way in. Aware that Holyman wanted to use Skymaster DC-4s on the proposed route, Uncle Moe confirmed that DC-4s could land at Kai Tak, although they were the largest aircraft able to do so. (Incidentally, Moss also disclosed government plans for an entirely new airport with minimum runways of 3,000 yards 'capable of accommodating any plane at present in existence or likely to be for some years to come'. The image of this 'entirely new airport' will come and go like a mirage as this history progresses. It is an exciting idea and remains one to this day. In 1988, it is still the merest gleam in many an ambitious Hong Kong developer's eye.)

Jock Swire and John Scott left Sydney for London in a euphoric state of mind that was undiminished by a breakdown in Darwin of the Qantas flying boat, necessitating a twenty-four-hour wait on board in acute discomfort; by a dust storm that forced them to overfly Basra; and by a starboard engine struck by lightning that forced their plane back to Marseilles and delayed their arrival at Poole seadrome by three hours. 'Rather frightening,' Jock admitted – but it wasn't going to put him off Air.

Nevertheless, government obstruction defeated private enthusiasm. Despite all Holyman's fighting qualities and Jock Swire's support, an independent ANA Australia–Hong Kong link was not to be, thanks to the Australian Government's opposition and the contention of the British Ministry of Civil Aviation and the government-subsidized airline BOAC that this route should be reserved for the Australian Government-owned Qantas, with which BOAC was affiliated. Nor were the efforts of Holyman's colleague, Ian Grabowsky, to engage CNAC in a China–Australia service any more successful. Thus it was that the aviation ball bounced back, so to speak, to the original exciting idea – that of a Hong Kong-based air company in which B&S might take a leading interest. Was there such a company in existence already, they wondered? Or would it be necessary to create one from scratch?

The following note dictated by Jock Swire in early 1947 gives the first reference to the Roy–Syd combination:

> Roy Farrell Export-Import, Hong Kong Ltd. is a serious concern, an American–Australian company with largely American capital, frowned upon by the Ministry of Civil Aviation in view of the American holding. At present they are only tramp owners and therefore able to fly where they like. . . . Skyways Ltd., a Critchley concern, have sent a Mr Curtis to Hong Kong to investigate the possibilites. . . .

Those possibilities were considerable. Roy, Syd and CPA had come to a crossroads – perhaps the end of a line. Despite the unquestionable success of their operations, the times were changing and with them international attitudes to commercial aviation. Tramps were on the way out; the age of hotly competitive *scheduled* airline operations had begun. It would be an age, as we all now know, of regulation, of rigid controls, so to launch a scheduled airline meant obtaining franchises – or licences – to use certain routes on a regular basis. The power to bestow the necessary franchise to operate a Hong Kong-based air company lay exclusively in the hands of the Colony's Government as represented by the DCA – a unique franchise for a single company. As it happened, the Colony's officials were strongly sympathetic to CPA, yet the fact that it was partly owned by Americans told fatally against it. Furthermore, CPA (and potentially Swires) had a rival: Hong Kong Airways. HKA had been formed just after the war by Swires' competitor, Jardine Matheson, but still lacked a single aircraft to start operations.

Hankering for its own company in Hong Kong, BOAC, backed by the Ministry of Civil Aviation in London, strongly opposed the enfranchisement of CPA, and now persuaded Jardines to sell them HKA with which to lay claim to the coveted franchise. The Hong Kong Government, however, refused to grant any franchise until CPA had been given a chance to dispose of its American holding. Just then Skyways arrived on the Hong Kong scene. At this dramatic juncture, that company might have seized for itself a great Far Eastern future by buying CPA from Roy and Syd for a reasonable price, making of it a brand new British-owned company (newly christened Cathay Pacific Skyways, or what you will) and thus run away with the Hong Kong franchise. But it didn't. For Mr Curtis's 'investigation' led to Brigadier General Critchley's botched bid for Roy and Syd's pet company – a bid they both had considered outrageously stingy and which Roy had repulsed with his offer to take on the Brigadier at golf, barefoot if necessary. The way was open for Swires to move in, and the lines of destiny guiding John Swire & Sons and CPA finally came together.

CHAPTER 11

Letter from B&S to John Swire & Sons Ltd, London:

Hong Kong, 12th December 1947.

Dear Sirs,

Air

Cathay Pacific Airways. Ian Grabowsky [of ANA] has had conversations with these people. As you know, they were early in the field here following the [Japanese] surrender and Roy Farrell was looked on as the leading spirit. His interest, however, had been withdrawn and the Manager is an Australian – de Kantzow. Grabowsky knew him in Australia and New Guinea and we know something about him also. He appears to have packed a good deal of adventure into his young life but was at one time one of CNAC's ace pilots. He has, however, married and appears to have settled down here. We had a talk with him and Grabowsky, and de Kantzow struck us as a keen, quiet spoken young Australian of not more than 35.

He expressed himself most interested in coming in to any side ANA and ourselves would lead. There is still American money in the Company but he has been having conversations with the [Hong Kong] Government [which] wants the company to reduce the American holding to 10% so that they can continue to have any privileges as a British Company. Government appear to be keen to give them a helping hand. . . .

Grabowsky is obviously fond of de Kantzow and would welcome him into the fold. Incidentally, de Kantzow made it clear that he wants to retain his holding in the Company. . . .

It might be useful to build a Company to embrace all the various operating interests and co-ordinate policy etc. . . .

To this last sentence, someone at Swires in London (possibly Jock) has added a pencilled note: 'Let's form a new company. ANA, Cathay Pacific, Far East Aviation and as far as necessary or advisable, B&S. Skyways?' (Far East Aviation Co. Ltd owned the Hong Kong Flying Training School, a trio of diminutive and out-of-date aircraft and very little cash, but it was a Hong Kong company.)

'Let's form a new company' – at last it was in writing!

Syd de Kantzow was all for a new company. He wrote to his friend Ivan Holyman that CPA was quite prepared to discuss how ANA, B&S and CPA might merge to 'undertake and operate an airline service and maintenance overhaul factory in the Far East initially and possibly later elsewhere'. CPA, he added proudly, had by far the largest airline maintenance and overhaul organization, had its own Board of Directors and was subject to direction by its parent organizations on broad policy only. For himself, he wanted membership of that Board and a senior executive or managerial position. And to retain his financial holding in the new company. Jock read his copy of Syd's letter and scribbled on it, 'So far so good.'

Indeed, CPA represented Swires' only immediate hope of getting into the air: it already had the right to operate a Hong Kong–Singapore service, and its airline maintenance station at Kai Tak could become the new Air Repair Depot B&S envisaged. FEA's main appeal as a partner was that it would bring a little extra local standing in the eyes of the Hong Kong Government; as for ANA, it was Swires' 'first love'. Holyman as a character had really bowled Jock over, and more practically speaking could provide all the flying and technical experience that Swires lacked. Apart from that, Holyman thought the world of Syd and could handle him – a most important point, for handling Syd, Jock thought, might well be a knotty problem. Syd was proud; Syd was touchy. B&S must show him no condescension – indeed should *feel* none. True, a potential part of that problem was soon resolved. Syd and Roy and everybody else had agreed to accept Ian Grabowsky's expert evaluation of CPA. There was no ill-natured haggling as with Critchley, so that was one major hurdle virtually overcome.

Yet there was an obvious problem to be faced: just how independent was the new CPA flying or operating company to be from the parent companies Taikoo and ANA? Holyman and Grabowsky seemed to think that the new flying company should maintain a wholly separate identity: an independent organization, they argued, has more drive and energy than one that is 'lost' in a large concern. Swires for their part fought shy of giving unfettered control of 'their' CPA to de Kantzow. They were an old, successful and experienced firm, extremely cautious and generally conservative, and with

Air they felt they were moving into a strange and possibly treacherous world. They did not want to have to rely on de Kantzow's judgement on all matters of policy that might arise. They wanted a hand on the brake. Furthermore, Taikoo's object in 'going into Air' was to complement its shipping activities, and from this didn't it follow that both Shipping and Air should both be under Taikoo management? Of course, on the other hand Swires recognized that without CPA they would have no airline to operate and no prospect of getting one; they would have no ground at Kai Tak except the Flying School's patch, and they would have no equipment. Worse still: if Swires declined to play, CPA could perfectly well turn round and sell out the whole caboodle to the opposition, Jardines, who would no doubt snap it up greedily.

The truth was that the B&S people could not suppress a lurking unease for what one might call 'the Syd's Pirates factor'. For instance, it had been alleged (particularly by Skyways) that Syd had allowed CPA to operate without much regard for Certificates of Airworthiness, loadsheets, and such like. Was this true? According to Chic Eather: 'It was a justifiable criticism. Don't forget the CPA lot had come up in a hard school. They'd been fighting a war. We were all a bit too young and foolish.' One can see that, and yet still agree with Swires that any future accident which inquiry showed to be the result of slackness of any kind would have a disastrous effect on the good name of the new operators, with repercussions for Swires. One couldn't ignore that. Hence the insistence at Taikoo on keeping an eye, though a comradely one, on all flying operations managed by de Kantzow.

At this point Skyways reappeared. Since Skyways had recently abandoned their agents, Jardine Matheson, and moved to B&S, Jock urged Critchley to forget their falling out with Syd and Roy and join the new CPA: perhaps Roy had 'opened his mouth too wide' with him. This was not (nor is it now) Farrell's view. He considered he had opened his mouth just wide enough, considering he 'hadn't cared a rat's ass' [one of his favourite expressions] whether the Skyways–CPA deal fell through or not. It was no doubt easy for people from London to underestimate the immense pride he and Syd took in the airline they had built up from nothing, and to fail to appreciate how little these tough-minded war veterans were prepared to put up with patronizing attitudes from anyone, particularly 'Pommie bastards'. It was as simple as that.

Nevertheless the fact was that those talks with Critchley had inflamed Skyways against the character of our heroes. Neither Maurice Curtis nor Captain Ashley, Critchley's Managing Director, made any bones about their belief that the Cathay Pacific people were a bunch of adventurers living to a large extent on what they earned from carrying gold to Macao, an operation they had started up some time previously. Ashley said quite bluntly that he had no opinion at all of de Kantzow, whose sole value, as he saw it, lay in his influence with Moss, the DCA. Ashley evidently was also deeply jealous of ANA, claiming to believe that the Australian Government would soon 'see them off'.

How could Skyways possibly become a partner in the merger if that was their attitude? Ashley indeed sounds like a very embittered man, and he cut no ice with Jock Swire, who shrewdly regarded his attempts to belittle de Kantzow as a deliberate effort to wreck the whole merger. For this part, in continuing dealings with Syd, Jock found him quite prepared to cooperate. 'De K.,' he wrote, 'is very amenable to advice from ANA and ourselves and regards us as his friends. He cannot see why Skyways should be in the thing at all and is still very sore at the way Critchley treated him last year.' And to his directors in London Jock repeated a final warning: 'De Kantzow is no rabbit. He has other buyers waiting at the door and will not hesitate for one moment to tell us to go to hell if he thinks we are treating him unfairly. He has implicit faith in ANA, and the freemasonry of these Australians is extraordinary. David and Jonathan are as nothing compared to Grabowsky and de K.' Of course, Jock admitted, Syd was such an individualist that he *might* suddenly tire of working in a team and go off on some adventure in some other part of the world. He would be less likely to do so if Swires gave him his head to a reasonable extent on the operating side and made a success of Cathay. Of course, only time would tell: 'Personally, I'm hopeful.'

Jock found two other sources of hope. The first was a visit to Kai Tak, where CPA had just bought five huts in the centre of the airfield to serve as a repair depot and where he talked with Bill 'Hokum' Harris, the No. 1 there, whom he liked enormously. And second, Swires' people at CNCo were delighted to take Air under their wing, and everyone agreed that Swires' shipping staff, with their commercial experience and local knowledge, could take care of CPA's business management side.

The negotiations that led to the new ownership of Cathay Pacific took a long time; letters, cables and memoranda flew back and forth between the interested parties in London, Hong Kong and Melbourne through the early months of 1948, filling a number of fat files. Bridget Swire, Jock's daughter, was acting as his travelling secretary at this point and still remembers the drama of it all. 'I remember Grab arriving in Hong Kong with a few dozen Australian oysters for my father. We all had them for lunch out at Shek'O [the Swire Taipan's house near the south-eastern point of the island]. The long talks afterwards were clearly a success and I was told that the matter was very hush-hush. The whole atmosphere at the time was one of secrecy and suppressed excitement that B&S were "going into Air".' There was even a proposal (from someone in London) that the airline should change the wonderful name Roy and his partner had chosen for it:

> We ourselves [said a letter with an unreadable signature] should prefer to see a new name as indicative of a newer and bigger venture than Cathay, as to the goodwill value of which there is at least some doubt, although admittedly cast by antipathetic Skyways. We rather like 'Far East Airways', though you may be able to improve.

Luckily B&S in Hong Kong spiked this uninspired idea.

From time to time Jock escaped from this flurry of paper and resumed his travels. His genial, bear-like figure, greying moustache and soft hat were to be seen moving indefatigably about the East – taking ship (and his delicate stomach) once more up to the China coast and to Japan, flying back to Hong Kong, down to Sydney and Melbourne, back again to Hong Kong. Dutifully he filled his diary with the multitudinous problems that he, as Chairman of John Swire & Sons, was required to handle with the aplomb of an expert juggler.

Shipping:

> Madness to hang on to the *Shasi*. She could never be used anywhere but Hankow/Changsha now and who would invest £60,000 in that trade today? . . . *Chunshan* very decrepit . . . *Chuchow* should definitely be scrapped.

> *Shanghai*: Went on board *Hanyang* to look at passenger accommodation and found Capt. W. R. blind. However he does not sail until tomorrow noon.

Politics:

> *Peking*: Called on General Li Tseng Ren . . . now C-in-C of Chiang Kai-shek's armies. Also General Fu Tso Yi, G.O.C. North China. . . . Sung the same song that China is fighting Russia not only Communists; that if they lose Manchuria, they lose China and if they do that the world is doomed to Communism. . . . Edmund Clubb, the American Consul-General, a really good man . . . says chances of them holding Manchuria are pretty slim. They should pull out of Manchuria and concentrate on the Yangtze Valley. . . . If they lose 250,000 men in Manchuria they haven't a hope.

His own health:

> *Shanghai*: Oxford and Cambridge dinner at the Sino–British Club. Cambridge won the Boat Race. . . . Got badly poisoned somehow and feel like hell. . . . No lunch tomorrow. . . .

Another aspect of Air:

> BOAC have bought 5 Constellations, making 9 with Qantas. Goodbye to the
> Flying Boats.

Air again:

> *Hong Kong*: Long talk Grabowsky [ANA] and wired London and John [his
> eldest son]. . . . Grab values CPA assets at about £170,000 and de K at
> £180,000 and neither will budge. The answer looks like £175,000 and not a
> bad bargain at the price. . . . I like de K quite a lot. An Aussie of Aussies but I
> think straight but very ambitious and a go-getter. CPA made over £200,000
> sterling last year.

At one point Jock sighed to himself, 'This air business is certainly terrifying
and they talk the most fantastic figures.' But after another visit to
Melbourne he was more satisfied than ever that 'ANA are really good
people' – it was a point he had to hammer home again and again to his ultra-
cautious colleagues in London.

At last a Basis of Agreement was arrived at, and initialled on 5 May 1948
by John Swire & Sons, ANA, CPA, Skyways and Far Eastern Aviation
Company, for the formation of a new company to be called Cathay Pacific
Airways (1948) Ltd. By the terms of this draft Agreement, Syd de Kantzow
got what he wanted: the management of the flying company, a seat on the
Board and a 10 per cent holding. Roy and his partners, too, retained a joint
10 per cent holding. B&S were to hold the booking agency and John Swire &
Sons and CNCo were to have the right to appoint the Chairman and
Managing Director.

Before this Agreement was finally ratified, to nobody's surprise or great
regret Skyways and FEAC dropped out. Jock's diary at this point reads:
'Heard from London that Skyways are going to double-cross us and go in
with Jardines and H.K. Airways. . . . I think the immediate step is to get our
own show set up under our management.' Wasting no more time, the new
partners ratified the Agreement on 1 June, and the new company began
operations in July. It was registered on 16 October with a nominal capital of
HK$10 million: CNCo and ANA both held 35 per cent of the shares, John
Swire & Sons 10 per cent, Syd de Kantzow 10 per cent, and Cathay
Holdings Ltd (representing Roy Farrell and his American friends) 10 per
cent. Its Chairman was C. C. Roberts and its Managing Director M. S.
'Steve' Cumming, while the other directors were Jock Swire, Ivan
Holyman, Ian Grabowsky and Sydney de Kantzow. (Skyways, after a series
of ups and downs, ceased to exist in 1962.)

By now, the Cathay fleet consisted of six DC-3s (including Betsy) and one Catalina that Syd wanted to keep 'for general purposes'.

As for CPA's Macao gold runs, a decision was urgently needed: whether to take them over or drop them. Ashley had been slighting, but the fact was that certain of the consignees in Macao, China and elsewhere had dubious reputations. 'The profits,' C. C. Roberts of B&S admitted to Jock, 'are enough to make anybody's mouth water but we ourselves would not feel disposed to have our name associated with that trade.' MacDougall, Hong Kong's Colonial Secretary, privately encouraged Roberts in this view: 'The trade has a pretty nasty reputation even in smuggling hardened Hong Kong. We would not like any such smell to attach to us.'

So the Macao option was not taken up while, in another parting of the ways, Syd dropped his connection with the Roy Farrell Export-Import enterprise.

Everybody in the Swire empire, in London as much as in Hong Kong, was now keenly aware of the importance of good relations with Syd. As Jock had patiently pointed out to one and all, this did *not* mean giving him a free hand to run wild. What it did mean was that Syd must be allowed first word in all technical matters, on questions of air politics or on air operations, while B&S looked after commercial matters, matters of common sense, China politics, finance etc.

'Start by wholehearted faith in de K backed by ANA,' was Jock's instruction to C. C. Roberts, the first Chairman. 'Do everything you can to increase his sense of responsibility. If you are not satisfied, appeal to Melbourne [i.e. Holyman].' To make him feel 'one of the team' Syd was encouraged to move his office from P. J. Lobo's at Chater Road to one in the imposing B&S office on Connaught Road between the cricket ground and the harbour; while, as a physical symbol of ANA's participation, Grabowsky was to remain in Hong Kong for a few months to see things on their feet. Jock Swire, back in London, winged a cheering cable to C. C. Roberts: 'Good luck to new Cathay welcome Kantzow and old Cathay staff.' Swires were in Air at last.

And what of Roy? In his room at La Quinta Motor Inn on the Dallas-Fort Worth highway, where he had told me the early part – how he'd slipped the case of Black Label to the friendly sergeant at Bush Field and how he'd flown Betsy all the way to Shanghai across a world strewn with the wreckage of war – he said, 'Syd did all the negotiating with Jock. I had no say in it, but I had great faith in Jock, having seen him. Syd bargained in good faith, I've no quarrel with that. And Grab did a good job too, and got a fair market price for our equipment and spare parts. Only thing, I think we should have gotten something for goodwill.'

An interesting observation. Later I read part of one of Jock's letters of those days that said, 'Syd might well have asked to be given a 20 per cent holding free in return for goodwill, but he has accepted our somewhat doubtful contention that he has in fact no goodwill to sell. . . .' I hadn't read that when I talked to Roy. But evidently goodwill or its absence wasn't something the old adventurer had lain awake grinding his teeth about in 1948. The fact was that his first wife had developed health problems so serious that he was obliged to wind up his affairs in the Far East quite soon after the Swire takeover of CPA. Roy sold the American 10 per cent in Cathay Pacific Airways and headed back to Texas, where he has been in successful business of one sort or another ever since. He is very much a family man; his two sons are successful and he has several grandchildren. As for his former partners, Bob Russell and Geddes Brown followed him home and so, later, did Millard Nasholds, after a spot of trouble (a smuggling charge) with the Taiwanese authorities. Roy had fired Neil Buchanan some time earlier.

About Roy himself, Ross Tattam summed up for me what most people thought. An Australian who was with him in his export-import company and who, with Eric Kirkby, took over the Sydney office when Roy returned to the United States, he talked to me not in the States, not in Farrell's home-from-home Hong Kong or in Manila, but in the aggressively ultra-Australian atmosphere of the Randwick Rugby Football Club near Sydney, where Poms are not automatically very highly considered and Yanks run them a close second. There in a bar hung with historic rugby sweaters, among large men gripping cans of Foster's lager, Tattam told me: 'He was the best boss I ever had. A great guy to work with. A big bloke. Thought big. One of his secrets – he was courteous; he'd listen.' A pause for a swig, and he added, 'Look, I'll tell you one thing – those Hump pilots who came to Burma and Hong Kong never had a bad word for him.'

Roy himself seems to have no regrets. 'I wanted an empire out East – oooh, yes. Perhaps I could have done things differently. I could have changed my nationality, I suppose. And if it hadn't been for my first wife's illness. . . .' He shrugged, and I thought he was going to brush that bit of the past impatiently away. But he went on, 'You know, I didn't want to sell Cathay Pacific. I actually cried when my last plane – not Betsy, but a DC-3 – took off from Manila at three in the morning. Well, there are ups and downs in life.' He flashed me his big, warm, cowboy smile. 'And, oh, the ups are wa-a-a-a-y ahead.'

CHAPTER 12

The fact that Cathay Pacific was now a 90 per cent British company in strong local hands certainly did not mean that Jock's, Syd's and Ivan Holyman's troubles were at an end. On the contrary. The next few years were a period of extreme difficulty, reflected in a multitude of anxious letters and memoranda. In some ways 'getting into Air' turned out to be more of a problem than the London-based directors of John Swire had bargained for – something like graduating in one bound from a provincial tennis club to Wimbledon. 'We here,' Jock in London admitted to Eric Price in Hong Kong, 'readily appreciate how very much quicker the ball goes backwards and forwards over the net in this air business than it does in anything else to which we have been accustomed.'

There were some oddly bouncing balls to cope with. Hong Kong Airways, for example. Although wholly owned by BOAC, HKA was still pressing its claim to be given the Hong Kong franchise – for BOAC continued to dicker with the idea of being a regional and an international long-haul carrier at the same time. Over many months, the parties concerned dragged out their claims like doubles partners engaged in a protracted contest on a waterlogged Centre Court.

Holyman had early on stated his view that Hong Kong could not support two air companies: he was attracted by the idea of a CPA amalgamated with HKA into a single Hong Kong line, especially when it appeared that BOAC was moving away from regional ambitions and intended to sell the local company back to Jardine Matheson. Jock, however, was not so sure. He argued, from Swires' experience of the region as shipowners, that Cathay had the advantage of catering (in the main) for a different kind of passenger from BOAC and HKA.

The secret of Cathay's success, he maintained, lay with the small Chinese trader who had previously used Swires' ships and who, now that they flew,

116

did not call for all the 'expensive paraphernalia' either in the air or on the ground that BOAC was (and HKA would be) obliged to provide for European travellers with greater expectations of comfort. These people knew Cathay already, trusted it and would use it. There were a great many Chinese, after all: 'China being one of the most thickly populated countries in the world and having adjacent territories at handy air operating distances which are much less thickly populated, there is a constant coming and going. Take, for instance, movement between Amoy, Swatow, Hong Kong and the Straits Settlements. . . .' This, of course, would soon prove quite unrealistic; very shortly the Communists would take over in China and there would be no such traffic for about a quarter of a century.

Yet Jock's basic conviction that Cathay was – and should remain – a regional airline was sound. 'I know little of the intricacies of international politics,' he said, 'but I cannot help feeling that the trunk routes of the world, with all their political implications, will always be covered by nationalised airlines, but that governments will be compelled before so very long to live and let live, and leave what corresponds to the local coasting and short-sea trades to private enterprise.' Concentrate, he urged, on the region. 'It will be time enough, when that has been done, to consider spreading our wings further afield.' This was to be his belief for years to come.

In the event, the Government of Hong Kong in the person of the Governor, Sir Alexander Grantham (egged on by Uncle Moe Moss), proposed that all regional routes should be divided between the two companies in a way that appeared to give HKA by far the worst of the bargain – they were allotted the region north of Hong Kong, and Cathay Pacific the routes south of it. The proposal meant that HKA would be handed the doubtful gift of permission to fly to and from a Japan still in the straitjacket of American military occupation and a China about to go communist. Naturally, Holyman, quick on the uptake, dashed off a letter to Jock saying in effect, 'For God's sake, we must accept.' Dreaming perhaps of all those potential passengers in and out of China, Jock at first marked the margin of the letter with a large question mark; but on second thoughts he agreed with Holyman. The question now was: would HKA accept Grantham's lopsided proposal? Would any airline with its head screwed on voluntarily confine itself to those northern routes of such doubtful immediate benefit? Yes: HKA would.

On 13 May 1949 an agreement was signed by Cathay Pacific (Jock's hand holding the pen) and BOAC (on behalf of Hong Kong Airways) along Grantham's lines of allocation. Cathay secured the valuable routes to and from Bangkok, Singapore, Manila, Haiphong, Saigon, Sandakan, Jesselton (now Kota Kinabalu) and Labuan, and Rangoon (with an extension possible later to Calcutta). That left HKA with Canton, Macao, Shanghai and Tientsin, not, after all, Japan.

The 'Battle of Hong Kong Airways', as Jock called it, did not end here. It dragged on for another ten years. In November 1949 BOAC sold HKA back to Jardines, but it soon ran for cover to another 'big brother', in a charter association with the American company Northwest Airlines on the Taipei and Tokyo services. Absurdly, HKA was still an airline without planes of its own. Then, in 1953, the British Government attempted to bring about a merger between Cathay, BOAC and HKA to form a single regional airline. This came to nothing for two reasons: first, disaster hit BOAC in the quick succession of two Comet jets and a Constellation, and, secondly, HKA was doomed to be a dead loss in anyone's hands. Later still, BOAC came back having decided to try once more to bring HKA to profitable life. Two new short-range Viscounts arrived in Hong Kong in an attempt to make something of the Tokyo route. But there was still no profit in that, and finally Lord Rennell of BOAC meekly approached Jock Swire to ask if he would be willing to swap HKA for a parcel of Cathay shares. Jock said he considered HKA worthless and a liability, but nevertheless, as of 1 July 1959, Cathay took over HKA – though spurning the two Viscounts – and BOAC got 15 per cent of Cathay's shares and a seat on the Board.

Bill Knowles, Cathay's Chairman at the time, told his directors that he hoped this absorption of HKA as a wholly owned subsidiary 'would enable us to inaugurate a properly rational service with the arrival of the Electras' (the Lockheed turbo-prop aircraft the company had just decided to buy). Cathay now absorbed HKA's northern routes, which later were to become immensely profitable; and indeed went on to make an international airport of Osaka after Japan's miraculous revival. At long last the battle was won, but, as we shall see, there had been important casualties.

Syd's operations continued throughout this period. Burma showed a good profit; of other routes, the Hong Kong–Manila service did best, with 95 per cent of all the Company's passengers, the majority of them Chinese going to or coming from Amoy.

Now that the CPA office had moved to the impressive Butterfield & Swire building overlooking the harbour behind the Hong Kong Club (where the Furama Hotel is now), Syd, with Marie Bok, set up a grander sort of shop on the first floor there, only separated from the Private Office (the Swire Taipan's sanctum) by what Marie describes as 'a little balustrade thing'.

The CPA ticket office remained in the lobby of the Pen (located left of the front door, where today you find Van Cleef & Arpels). There Cathay's Sales Manager, Tommy Bax, the convivial Australian successor to Bob Frost (lost in Miss Macao), held bibulous and occasionally uproarious court – a popular man who by repute seems to have become a legend in his lunchtime and possibly a legend at breakfast, mid-morning, mid-afternoon and much of the night as well.

Syd's habit of command at once seemed reinforced by the new ambience. He was moved to issue a stern decree: 'As the Company has now entered the stage where it has to a large extent left pioneering behind, stricter discipline and a greater respect for recognized systems and procedures are necessary. For some time past, it has been constantly apparent to me that definite action has to be taken.'

Ian Grabowsky agreed with him, announcing his own unhappiness with CPA's cavalier approach to accounting up to now – it was so hit-or-miss, he said, that it was sometimes impossible to tell profit from loss. Even more radical, he began agitating for a change in the pay and flying hours of Cathay's pilots. It had been the habit to pay captains a basic salary plus so much per flying hour. Consequently pilots had been flying up to 170 hours a month (over 2,000 hours a year) to earn big money. 'This is a bad principle,' Grabowsky said, 'as pilots fly to the point where fatigue is not recognized or given way to.' To the Cathay Board he proposed a fixed limit of 100 flying hours per month. Since, according to Ivan Holyman, the secret of ANA's success was a very high utilization of aircraft – up to 4,000 hours a year each – an increase in the number of Cathay pilots seemed called for, and perhaps more aircraft too.

The era of 'Syd's Pirates' was approaching its end. It was tragically ironic, therefore, that, only eleven months after the Miss Macao piracy, disaster struck Cathay for the second time. In the left-hand seat this time was Captain Johnnie Paish, the man who had flown Bob Smith down to Moulmein to confirm Smith's contention that Kipling had turned the old pagoda there to face in the wrong direction. The front page headline in the *China Mail* of 25 February 1949 said:

AIR MISHAP KILLS 23

CPA Dakota Crashes in Fog in City Outskirts
Flight from Manila

Below were photographs of the plane burning on the edge of the Braemar (Taikoo) Reservoir, five miles from the centre of Hong Kong. The paper listed the crew – Captain J. C. Paish; First Officer A. Campbell; Radio Officer N. W. F. Moore; and Flight Hostess O. Batley. Olive Batley, aged twenty-four, was Vera Rosario's friend, educated partly in Shanghai, partly at the Italian convent in Hong Kong. She had been a dance band singer and, as Vera told me many years later, she was a new girl, only six months with Cathay. The nineteen passengers were Chinese, all of them on their way to Swatow. There were no survivors.

Eric Price in Hong Kong flashed a telegram to Jock as soon as he heard the terrible news: 'Aircraft from Manila crashed here foggy hillside above harbour circling after sighting airfield subject enquiry apparently human error details later.' Next day, after consultation with Mr Moss, he made a fuller report:

> The aircraft was on her way back from Manila with a quite unusually large complement of passengers. The weather was brilliant to within the outskirts of the Colony but on and within the circle of hills there was heavy but patchy cloud and mist. The pilot, who was one of the soundest and most experienced of our men, asked for permission to come in after a long wait. This was granted by the Kai Tak Control on condition that visibility was 3 miles. The aircraft came in safely, saw Stonecutters Island from near Lantao, and when approaching Stonecutters reported to Air Control that he was able to see the airfield and asked for permission to land on a certain runway. Immediately after this was granted he corrected his request and obtained permission to land on another runway. To do this involved circling; in the course of this he ran into heavy cloud which covered all the hills behind Causeway Bay and Lei Yue Mun, and the next news was of an aircraft at low altitude heard to crash in the neighbourhood of the main Taikoo reservoir. The aircraft is a burnt out wreck and all the occupants must have been killed instantly. From all the facts we have, it is a case of human error. . . .

Having read this preliminary report (many years later of course) I decided to visit the site of the tragedy, and on a foggy February day very like that of the accident I drove there with Captain Martin Willing, a Cathay-747 pilot and amateur aviation historian. We both wanted to try to understand how an experienced flying man like Johnnie Paish, an ex-RAF pilot with 2,500 hours on DC-3 types of aircraft and a CPA Burma veteran, could have made such a mistake. We took with us a copy of the official report of the disaster.

Fog had closed Kai Tak earlier in the morning and it was now 10 a.m. Even down at sea level on the harbour front, under the flyover to Causeway Bay and Chai Wan, there were dense swirls of mist, and foghorns sounded balefully across the water. I could make out a green and white trans-harbour ferry cautiously feeling its way, some sort of freighter at anchor 200 yards away was a dark grey blob, and the high-rise buildings of Kowloon on the other side of the bay were a mere smudge.

Pointing at the smudge, Martin Willing said, 'That's where the Hung Hom beacon was. See how close – how quickly a plane would reach here.' Descending to land over Stonecutters Island, Johnnie Paish had been cautioned by the Kai Tak Air Controller, Roy Downing, that the moment he could not see at least three miles in front of him he was to turn to the right, swing over to Hung Hom beacon and climb away to a safe height in order to try again. This instruction Paish acknowledged. And then, as Eric Price had reported, he suddenly asked for (and received) permission to divert from his present approach, to circle and try another runway – a manoeuvre that would bring him over the Hung Hom beacon on the Kowloon side of the harbour: evidently he had lost the three-mile forward visibility. From the Hung Hom beacon to where we stood on Hong Kong Island was close, as Martin Willing had just pointed out. 'You see, over the beacon he should have turned east-south-east and headed for the Lei Yue Mun Gap, then turned left again for the other runway. But he crossed the beacon – and turned south. Into the hill behind us.'

We drove up a twisting but well tarmaced road to the site of the former reservoir. It is under development now, like almost everywhere else in the Territory of Hong Kong, but beside a narrow ravine full of rubble you can still see part of the reservoir's walls. Behind and to the left is a brand-new supermarket and beside that white high-rise apartments. The hillside lifts sharply here, a grim rock-face of granite slabs and yellowish sandstone, scrub-covered. It was towards this rising hillside that an eyewitness had seen the DC-3 VR-HDG heading, dangerously low, bursting out of one cloud bank over Kowloon and roaring into another, the one which masked the all too solid hills of the island.

We stood there, 'seeing' the plane coming. Martin Willing said, 'Paish has got the wheels down; a little flap, too. Now, instead of the Lei Yue Mun Gap he sees this bloody great fog patch and he's heading at 90mph straight into the reservoir – "Oh shit! Gear up!" he yells and eases sharply back. Maybe banks a bit. But he's already at 300 feet over the coast. Too late.' The plane clipped the leading edge of the reservoir wall at 452 feet with a terrible metallic bang – screamed upside down over the water – and disintegrated against the granite hill-face. As it would be today, by the car park of the new supermarket.

The official report, signed 'A. J. R. Moss, Inspector of Accidents', attributed the disaster to 'an error of judgment by the pilot in that he flew into conditions of poor visibility and low cloud when requested specifically on several occasions not to proceed unless three miles visibility could be maintained'. Second, he should not have kept going over Hung Hom beacon but swung left, as was the normal practice. Of course, there remained that unanswered question. Why did such an experienced pilot – one who knew Kai Tak so well in all its moods – make such a mistake?

Many people have puzzled over that. One of them was Chic Eather, who knew Johnnie Paish well. He is inclined to think that Paish was misled, or at least confused, by the fact that a Hong Kong Airways aircraft had landed just in front of him without apparent difficulty. Admittedly the HKA crew might have made use of their unorthodox but frequent method of approach, which relied on *downward* rather than *forward* visibility. Even so, according to Eather, Paish erred in direction: 'As he crossed the coast near the Ritz nightclub the ground was rising faster than his labouring aircraft could climb. For many seconds the crew on that flight deck must have known that they were about to be dashed to pieces.'

I felt a tremendous unease as I stood on the broken lip of that crumbling reservoir. It was easy to imagine the scene, nearly forty years before, of an inferno of burning fuel and torn metal, of police cordons, of frantic groups of firemen, investigators and doctors, reporters and press photographers; details of the disaster had filled the front page of every newspaper in the Colony. Now where we wandered gloomily about there was nothing to show that such a thing had ever happened. A few workmen were busy on the edge of the ravine at the site of what a hoarding promised would eventually become the St Joan of Arc School for Girls. A stiffish breeze was whipping the slope where we stood, 400 feet up. The hillside was impassive; too impassive. With the visions we carried in our heads suddenly both of us wanted to leave it. As we walked to the car I glanced towards the bay. Below, the evil grey mist still crept low across the water hiding the runway at Kai Tak.

Ten years long, the 'Battle of Hong Kong Airways' left different casualties. Indeed it almost did for Cathay Pacific itself. It certainly led to Sydney de Kantzow's early retirement from the company. Despite Jock Swire and Ivan Holyman's best efforts to make him feel at home under the management of Butterfield & Swire, de Kantzow, the free flier, found it impossible to adapt to the Hong style of operation. Big companies, like large animals, move slowly and cautiously. Men like Roy and Syd live on calculated risks, on decisions taken in a single telephone call – snap! like that. It's what keeps their adrenalin flowing.

Syd was impatient – in his view the company should get on and spend money on expansion, or pack up. Even in 1948 the DC-3s were no longer enough, and with Swires' approval he had flown to Europe and bought a four-engined DC-4 Skymaster which entered service in September 1949 – but only after arguing in vain that Cathay needed not one, but three. His widow Angela remembers Syd groaning to her, 'How do they expect to keep the show going with one four-engined plane that keeps breaking down?' And he let all within earshot know his view that too much money was going in management costs, and that his was too small a holding for all the work he had to do as Flight Operations Manager. He and Angela lived well – at first in a suite in the Peninsula, then in a two-storeyed house over Deepwater Bay with an impressive garden and a fine view over the South China Sea. But it wasn't comfort he was after – he was after a stiff challenge and the independence to lick it in his own way. Syd was an original, an explorer. With B&S in overall charge, he felt dominated, sidetracked, frustrated. He wasn't used to that. His impatience wasn't anyone's fault. But there it was.

Inevitably the split came. In the letter he wrote to Jock announcing his retirement from the company he had helped to create, Syd spoke of 'our very pleasant association during the past three pioneering years in CPA'. He felt sure, he added, of an extremely brilliant future for the company. But to a friend in another trading firm, the Borneo Company, he still complained of how much B&S's management and maintenance were costing 'above any sum one would normally expect an airline to spend on such services. I myself am suffering financially, so rather than continue with an arrangement which ultimately will leave me with nothing I am taking the preferable alternative of disposing of my stock while I may. . . .'

It was agreed that Syd would retire from the Board and managership of CPA on 30 April 1951; the company would pay him three months' salary, and ANA and John Swire & Sons would buy his 1,500 CPA shares. There was no public falling out; everybody behaved in the most gentlemanly manner. The local press, reporting his departure from Hong Kong, quoted Syd: 'Now that Cathay Pacific is fully established on its routes in the Orient, there appears to be little likelihood of it being able to develop further in the predictable future, owing to the political situation. China is the logical sphere of expansion for operations in the Far East, but we know that is not possible. As a pioneer I now find there is little scope for me in the Far East.' The handsome Ronald Colman face in the accompanying photographs wore a cheerless expression.

Before returning to Australia, Syd and Angela leased a villa in Cap Ferrat on the south coast of France for six months. After that Syd went on to investigate a new flying career in East Africa (where he found his newly arrived friend Dick Hunt), but it was the beginning of the bloody Mau Mau uprising and there was no future to be found in East Africa. Soon he was back in Australia again. He put money into a wholly admirable building scheme for ex-servicemen in Sydney; and next he talked of opening a ski lodge. Then, when he was still only forty-three, on 16 November 1957, a car in which he was a passenger left the road in the Snowy Mountains near Cooma, outside Canberra. Two friends were with him, one of them Pinky Wawn, his old flying mate, when the car somersaulted through a fence at 60mph. A surgeon told Angela there was a chance that an operation might save Syd, so somehow she found an old Avro Anson and flew with him to St Vincent's Hospital in Sydney. But Pinky Wawn was the only survivor.

When we talked about it in her flat outside Sydney, under an old wall map of the Indian state of Cooch Behar where she'd first met Syd, Angela told me, 'You see, I flew over the Hump, too. I flew CNAC with Syd from Calcutta to Shanghai. We lost an engine taking off from Kunming on the Shanghai leg. Great fun. Did you know we were married in the Anglican Cathedral in Shanghai? Honeymooned there for ten days in the Grand Hotel.' She considered a short while. 'I'll tell you something. Syd always said he'd been born a hundred years too late, there were too many restrictions now. He'd have been an empire-builder. So much energy. So much "go".'

Later, Syd's sister Eve said, 'Of course, he should have stayed with Cathay. Of course.'

I don't know. I don't think they could have held him. I see Sydney de Kantzow as Saint-Exupéry's Rivière, but I see him too as F. Scott Fitzgerald saw Munroe Stahr in *The Last Tycoon*: 'He had flown up very high to see, on strong wings, when he was young. And while he was up there he had looked on all the kingdoms, with the kind of eyes that can stare straight into the sun. Beating his wings tenaciously . . . he had stayed up there longer than most of us, and then, remembering all he had seen from his great height of how things were, he had settled gradually to earth again.'

Syd was not a tycoon like Stahr. He was an expert flier and a pretty good organizer. He was liked and respected by most people who knew him well, disliked for a certain aloofness by others. Above all, he was an adventurer who, like the fictional Stahr, had the courage and vision to breathe life into a great enterprise. He lost that vision when others took on, with the best will in the world, the job of guiding it – it was not something a man like him could share. Perhaps in time those eyes that could stare straight into the Himalayan sun would have found a new path to follow, preferably in the air.

But there was nothing for him in Africa, a housing project in Sydney, and then everything ended on that misjudged curve on the way to a ski lodge in the Snowy Mountains.

CHAPTER 13

In time Jock came to agree with Syd that to survive Cathay needed three DC-4s, not one. Later still he preferred the larger DC-6: 'We really ought to have an aircraft that can do HK–Bangkok–Singapore–HK in twenty-two hours.' The trouble was there was not enough money: all through the early and mid-fifties, a shortage of capital tormented him and threatened the existence of the airline. A diary entry for January 1951 said, 'I am terribly worried and depressed about Air but cannot see daylight.'

Despite the gloom, Cathay's air operations, now depending on two DC-3s and the DC-4 (VR-HEU), continued apace. The single DC-4 Skymaster could take forty-three passengers and seemed to be everywhere at once, never out of the air. Her arrival had aroused considerable interest. When Captains John Presgrave and Dick Hunt inaugurated the Singapore flight, a reporter from the *South China Morning Post* who was aboard could barely contain himself: 'The blue of the Gulf of Tonkin appeared to outshine the Mediterranean when I passed over it at 8,000 feet in the new Cathay Pacific Airways Skymaster. . . .' And in a gooey advertisement for the Saigon service, an unctuously smiling salesman announced, 'That's right, Sir – You get SKYMASTER COMFORT'. Vera Rosario hadn't recalled much Skymaster comfort, but it turned out to be a popular plane with Chinese passengers: they felt safer with four engines than they had with two. H. H. Lee, Cathay's (ex-CNAC) man in Singapore, a most important destination for Chinese businessmen, recalls: 'The DC-4 called three times a week. HEU – How Easy Uncle. Everyone knew her – she was the only one we'd got! She'd leave Hong Kong in the early morning, touch down at Bangkok, and reach Singapore in the evening. Kai Tak had no night landing lights then, so the plane would take off from Singapore at 8 p.m., reach Bangkok at midnight, then leave at dawn for Hong Kong. We had a DC-3 from Rangoon and Calcutta, too. Our allies in ANA were running a scheduled service from

Sydney to Singapore and Colombo, so Cathay from Hong Kong and ANA from Colombo met in Singapore and complemented each other.'

That the use to which the Skymaster was put was extremely high no one knew better than the Cathay representative in the midway stopover, Bangkok. He was an unusual man with an unusual name, Duncan Bluck, and had come across to Air from Swires' shipping offices in Tokyo, Kobe and Yokohama. He was to be decisively involved with Cathay for more than thirty years and end up as its Chairman.

From an office in the Trocadero Hotel Bluck went out to meet VR-HEU, often in the middle of the night, marvelling that Cathay's only Skymaster was in such hectic use. In such use, indeed, that a puzzled Chinese businessman who flew in her regularly once asked Duncan quite innocently how it was that Cathay Pacific seemed to be the only airline to give *all* their DC-4s the same registration letters. He would have asked the same question had he visited Borneo and seen VR-HEU on the strip at Jesselton, surrounded by Dusun chiefs in loincloths and hornbill feather headdresses. The *China Mail* described her as 'overflying the world's most exotic orchids, the home of the tapir, rhinos, the orang-utan. Such delicacies as birds' nests can now be flown to Hong Kong in forty-eight hours.' She certainly got about.

Captain Laurie King saw a less romantic side of VR-HEU: 'On the Singapore–Hong Kong run, the refuelling was done at Bangkok by the co-pilots themselves and usually at 2 a.m. and in pouring rain. Filling eight tanks in pouring rain was a feat requiring effort. You had to strain the fuel through a funnel with a chamois leather filter to keep the water out. It would take at least an hour in the rain. I had joined Cathay from BOAC where you always had ground staff to do such things. I was quite indignant!' (At Saigon coolies would take the passengers' dirty plates and wash them under the aircraft in an old tin bath. The toilets were emptied, too – on the grass.)

The worry to Management in all this, of course, was pilot and metal fatigue – the wear and tear on men and machines all involved in trying to get the last ounce of employment out of a very modest fleet of aircraft. Some of it was self-induced. Granted that the first of the two days' flying time on the Labuan run took nine hours fifty-three minutes, there was, according to Chic Eather, a purely frivolous reason for crew-fatigue after the overnight stop at the Shellbourne Hotel in Manila. This drab building was reputedly haunted by the ghosts of victims of the Kempeitai, the Japanese Gestapo. Any new and impressionable hostess would be fed this story 'with the well-based expectation that she, after checking into her room, would soon appear at the door of the bravest member of the flight deck to be protected and comforted through the long dark night'.

Captain Dave Smith, who would follow Laurie King as Operations Manager, recalls a 'bad story' – the case of Cathay's Chief Pilot, Pat Moore, an old wartime flier, 'having an engine fail during take-off from Singapore, another failure as he turned back, and on the final approach a third engine coughing and spluttering. . . . This was an overhaul problem.' There were a good many examples of engine trouble in those days. Too many. . . .

In 1952 Dave Smith's work hours read as follows:

February	119 hours
March	111 hours
April	118 hours
May	127 hours

and so on until

November	143 hours
December	149 hours

Sixty to seventy hours might be the average today.

'I was single at the time,' Dave says, 'and we didn't think of exhaustion. We had to have a medical, of course, after every hundred hours, so we'd call the doctor up:

' "I've done over my time, doc."

' "Well, do you feel all right?"

' "Oh, yes, doctor."

' "Very well, then." '

Jock's diary at this period sounds a note of despair:

HEU's engines are worn out and we can never hope to make CPA pay without another Skymaster. . . . Discussed CPA with Bill Knowles. The pilots are being grossly overdriven. . . . The engine trouble losses last month were staggering and a few more like it will bust us. . . . Very unsatisfactory telephone talk to Walsh [Holyman's No. 2] in Melbourne. He clearly wants to pack up and won't hire us engines to go on with. If we pack up we lose all. . . .

Oh, the headaches, the imponderables, the expense of Air! A man might lose his shirt.

Cathay Pacific's losses for 1951 were HK$1,492,381; three years later they added up to well over HK$2 million. 'If this is not as good as we hoped for,' B&S's then-Chairman J. A. Blackwood blandly told his Annual General Meeting, with commendable restraint, 'blame the severe restrictions which all countries in SE Asia place on the movement of

Chinese.' (The communist takeover in China was indeed a major reason for a drastic fall in passengers.) Jock could find comfort in a single positive factor: Cathay's aircraft had acquired – and retained – an excellent reputation for punctuality.

What was to be done? The future offered two options. Either Swires could wash their hands of Cathay Pacific entirely and shrink back with relief from the hurly-burly of Air to the calm, familiar world of shipping. Or they could continue in Air – acknowledging that to be able to do so depended on finding new capital, on improving flying conditions, on improving the company's engineering and maintenance facilities at Kai Tak, and on buying bigger and better aircraft. It was all put succinctly by John Scott, Jock's old friend and travelling companion: 'We have now reached the point at which we must decide whether we are going to raise a pretty large sum of fresh capital for CPA or pack it in and get out while we still can get our money back.' Scott admitted he was torn in two on this question, but thought that the purchase of a DC-6, larger than the DC-4 and pressurized, would give Cathay a lot of face in the whole Far Eastern world. And above all, he hated the idea of dropping the enterprise to which they had put their hands. To start something and then run away from it had not been The Senior's way. Nor was it Jock's.

With considerable help from providence, Cathay quickly recovered from this desperate situation. Jock now set his sights on a DC-6. If Walsh thought Holyman 'wanted out' – too bad. 'A DC-6 is in fact the only answer today. We'll get nowhere unless and until JS&S Ltd and CNCo take their courage in both hands and buy a DC-6, alone if necessary.' Indefatigably, he took to the air with his old soft hat and his old suitcase tied with rope in an urgent search for new capital that led him once more to Australia, Hong Kong (where for a heady moment he thought the Governor might come across with a subsidy) and America. Luckily, he also stopped off in Canada. There, in Vancouver, he met Grant McConachie, the President of Canadian Pacific Airlines, and after a long talk noted joyfully: 'This is a second Holyman and I like him a lot.' Another diary entry gave a clue to his own character: 'Grant, Ivan Holyman, Syd de K. are all in the same mould and definitely "adventurers". I can't think why, but we all fell for each other at first sight.'

He poured out his problems and McConachie, like Scott, said he was sure Jock would be wise to acquire a DC-6. 'I think I have made a friend,' Jock confided to Scott, and it was true. The 'second Holyman' was going to prove a godsend sooner than anyone could imagine.

Despite their warm relations McConachie declined Jock's invitation to put capital into Cathay, but soon that problem was resolved anyway, for back in London P&O, the shipping giant which had turned down an approach from Jock Swire the previous week, changed its mind and decided to step into the breach. It paid HK$2.5 million for a 31.2% shareholding in the Company, and, coming in the nick of time, this decisive development acted like an explosive charge, ensuring Cathay an immediately viable future.

At this juncture two outstanding personalities in the development of the airline reported to the Cathay office in Hong Kong: Captain Kenneth Steele and a senior engineer called Jack Gething.

Steele had been seconded in 1953 from ANA to check and train crews and to draw up new flight manuals. Having reported the general standard of flying to be satisfactory, he had stayed to become a permanent fixture with the title of Flight Superintendent, remaining with the company until 1963.

Jack Gething was an outstanding engineer with considerable experience of flying in Australia and New Guinea. He now set about creating for Cathay a superb air maintenance service. Up to the fifties, two aircraft engineering companies had existed at Kai Tak: the Jardine Aircraft Maintenance Company (JAMCO), originally a BOAC associate to service their flying boats, and the Pacific Air Maintenance and Supply Company (PAMAS), associated with CPA. In 1950 the two amalgamated into one company called the Hong Kong Aircraft Engineering Company (HAECO). It was a very different set-up from Roy and Syd's small aircraft maintenance store, kept running by 'Hokum' Harris, Neil Norquay and Jack Williams. These men were fine engineers operating on not much more than a shoestring – 'a tin shed operation,' Dave Smith called it – and coping with far too many engine failures.

Now things began to improve out at Kai Tak. Not that they became what you might call de luxe overnight. Everything was crammed into an office under the control tower, near the terminal shack. Steele's office was there, and the teleprinter office, and a corner canteen consisting of a long cane table and a few chairs, and everything was periodically pungent with cooking smells from the flight kitchen. 'Ma' Sanders ran that. She was a formidable English character, now laughing, now scolding, telling Ken Steele and Captain Pat Moore, the Flight Operations Manager, to buzz off home to their wives while she lined up the Chinese 'boys' and gave them their worm pills or whatever she felt they needed. Cathay already had a lot of Chinese mechanics, and by then most of the air hostesses were orientals too. 'Ma' was a mother-figure to them – indeed to everybody. Her flight kitchen took over the whole office space in the end, and everybody else moved to a Nissen hut. Jack Gething's Engineering Department was simply a lean-to against a hangar. But the important, unforgettable thing, Dave Smith thought, was a oneness; a family feeling. When Jock came out from London he'd know every expatriate by name and quite a few of the Chinese too.

Angus Macdonald had recently joined HAECO from the Royal Navy: 'Work? The engineers would be up to their elbows in oil, and the Chief was really on their backs all the time, really riding them. You couldn't have it now; you'd have all hell. But then we never had a walkout. A go-slow now and again, perhaps, but no strikes.'

At first HAECO's staff included a number of Americans and Australians from JAMCO, but the Americans soon moved out. 'The top engineers' – Angus Macdonald again – 'were two-thirds what Chinese call *gweilos* [white ghosts] and one-third Hong Kong Chinese, while the ordinary mechanics were Chinese.' Nowadays most of HAECO's qualified engineers are Hong Kong Chinese. Cathay's apprenticeship schemes turned out Chinese engineers second to none – certainly the best in Asia, Macdonald thought. And Bob Smith thought they were the best sheet metal workers he'd ever seen.

'Most impressive,' Jock said when he saw how HAECO was getting on. In fact, Gething was in at the birth of a miracle child. By 1957 HAECO was providing engineering services to thirty-three aircraft operators of twenty-four nationalities; by 1959 to over seventy operators of thirty nationalities. Chic Eather, looking at HAECO from the viewpoint of today, calls it one of the great success stories of the aircraft engineering industry. The tin shed operation at old Kai Tak had grown into one of the largest organizations of its kind, not only in the Far East but in the world, thanks to the high technical standards achieved there by 'Hokum' Harris, Spencer Cooper and Tony Wakeford (both of whom came across from JAMCO when that folded), Jack Gething, Don Delaney and the rest of Cathay's engineers down the years.

To return to 1954: Cathay's skies were brightening after the infusion of P&O capital. The DC-4 (VR-HEU) was flying seventy-one hours a week, close as usual to her limits. There were two DC-3s in reserve – although Betsy, Roy Farrell's 'baby', had been sold to Mandated Airlines at Lae in New Guinea in 1955. But the airline's history was not, the reader may by now have realized, a smooth, unimpeded, upward-soaring flight to success.

That year VR-HEU was shot down, Captain Phil Blown achieved world-wide fame – and Cathay faced extinction once again.

CHAPTER 14

There was no radioed challenge; no warning shots. The Chinese fighters moved in on the Cathay Pacific Skymaster at 9,000 feet and opened up from both sides with cannon and machine-guns at about 150 yards range. They were cream-coloured, propeller-driven planes, each with a full red star on the side of the fuselage and a red nose. The Cathay co-pilot, Cedric Carlton, was the first to see the one on the starboard side. Captain Philip Blown glimpsed the second fighter immediately afterwards, just before the DC-4's No. 1 engine burst into flames. After that the aircraft was full of flying 50-calibre bullets, and the Radio Officer, Stephen Wong, began to yell out an emergency signal – 'Mayday! Mayday! Losing altitude, engine on fire!' Then the No. 4 engine and the No. 4 main fuel tank were ablaze, the radio aerial was shot away too and no one could hear Wong any more, though he continued to clutch his mike and shout his message to the world until the plane hit the water.

VR-HEU was carrying six crew and twelve passengers from Singapore and Bangkok to Hong Kong, passing as usual eighty to ninety miles south of Hainan Island in the international air corridor regularly used by all civilian aircraft on that route. There was never any doubt that the Chinese fighters came from the military airfield on Hainan. Nor that they intended to destroy the aircraft and everybody in her. Phil Blown's immediate concern was how to ditch a DC-4 from 9,000 feet with two engines and a wing in flames while all around him, as he told me many years later, the explosive heads of 50-calibre shells blew holes a foot and a half wide the length and breadth of the aircraft, with a deafening noise. Survivors said they had had no doubt that this was it. Mr Peter Thatcher, a Connecticut American, told reporters at Kai Tak how Leonard Parrish, of Iowa Park, Texas, travelling from Singapore with his wife and three children, was sitting with him at the rear of the plane, and the first he knew was when he saw fire on one of the engines. Mr Parrish got up and went over to take a better look. 'When he returned,' said Thatcher, 'I asked him what had happened and he replied: "We have had it. There is nothing to be done." I got up from my seat and was immediately hit by something on the inside of my left thigh.' The last he saw of Mr Parrish was him crouching over his son to protect the boy from the bullets that were streaming into the plane, cracking and roaring.

Phil Blown's cool thinking in that mad outbreak of explosion, flame and disintegrating DC-4 strikes one as something miraculous. He began to take evasive action, swinging the plane from side to side. Each time he did so the fighter on the side opposite to the way he was heading fired bursts of heavy machine-gun bullets into the plane, which was going down at about 350mph. At 5,000 feet the aircraft's rudder control was shot off; at 2,000 feet the right aileron went and Blown checked the plane's automatic right turn by shutting off Nos 1 and 2 engines and fully opening No. 3. He yelled to Cedric Carlton, to his Engineer, George Cattanach, and to Stephen Wong to brace themselves ready to ditch.

Looking at it calmly all these years later, I could see that Phil Blown is the sort who would deal with what followed as well as, if not better than, the next man. That is, when I could find him; it was not easy. I had to drive out of Sydney to the fringes of what seemed like the outback. A sign on a tree actually said 'Road Ends' by a red mailbox, and it did end, running off to expire in a gully full of trees.

Phil Blown is still a stocky, square-shouldered man of medium height, neat and soft-spoken, not unlike James Cagney with glasses. 'There are only two Blowns in the phone book here,' he said, 'myself and my son. I think the name must be German by origin, or Dutch.' His father had been a Yangtze river pilot for Swires and Phil was born in Tientsin, so he grew up among the China Hands. He and his wife Bunty, like Sydney and Angela de Kantzow, married in the cathedral in Shanghai. Since he retired as Cathay's Chief Pilot, Phil and Bunty have lived in the bungalow in which I found them on the edge of a far-flung township with a close-cut lawn and a dark red prunus tree and a small forest of blue gums that rise like a barrier between them and the open spaces of New South Wales. Phil had started flying with the RAAF, and after the Second World War got a job in the Deccan with a fleet of DC-3s belonging to the Nizam of Hyderabad. Then he answered a Cathay ad. With CPA he piloted the first DC-3 flight to Kuching in Sarawak where Syd (who was on board) 'had fixed up this publicity thing with a bunch of Dayaks. They wore feathers and had plugged padlocks through their earlobes. Beautiful.' A few years later VR-HEU was corkscrewing down the sky off Hainan, barely under control, and later still, here was Phil opposite me in an armchair holding a beer and chatting about it.

'The angle was pretty steep. The quicker I could get her down onto something solid or semi-solid the better. I saw Stephen Wong lying on the floor braced against the bulkhead talking into the mike. Luckily I was able to level her out. But still we came to the water at about 260 knots and it was hard to wash out [reduce] that speed. We had no flaps, you see. We just had to wait patiently, bouncing on the rough water like ducks and drakes. Then the starboard wing hit. It clipped a wave and sheared off and we waited – the seconds seemed like hours – for the real impact. And that was a hell of an impact at 160 knots as our nose ploughed into a huge roller somewhere near the top of it. The port storm window was shattered and the starboard window by the second and final impact. Ced and I were thrown forward very hard against the rubber crash guards above the instrument panel, the safety harness snapped, a lot of green water poured in, and I scrambled out of the front window with Ced after me.' Phil smiled. 'I think a little angel was sitting on my shoulder. And Cedric's.'

That corkscrew from 9,000 feet to sea level had taken about two minutes, and the Chinese only stopped shooting at 1,000 feet. One of the two Flight Hostesses, Rose Chen, was killed in the stream of fire on the way down; so was a Mrs Finlay; and Leonard Parrish, the son he had tried to protect, and one of his two little daughters. It was a stroke of luck, Phil Blown says, that only five months before he'd seen the Mae Wests all lying about on the luggage racks, looking pretty frayed. He'd suggested to Dick Hunt they should be put into a canister, and Hunt had agreed. 'And when we hit the water and the tail broke off, the Mae Wests floated clear. And a life raft, a yellow thing, bobbed out too, near the wreckage, and Ced Carlton grabbed it.'

VR-HEU started to sink almost at once. Nose-down, she was soon gone.

'I saw Mrs Parrish clinging to some wreckage with her daughter, and then Mr Thatcher in a Mae West swimming around about thirty yards away, supporting a woman with a deep gash in her throat. She was grey. Beyond I saw Ced Carlton and Mrs Thorburn [a Singapore passenger] clinging to something. Ced called to me that the Mae Wests were over where he was. I was hanging onto a mailbag and I swam over in his direction. I noticed the bodies of three more people and one was Mrs Finlay, another Rose Chen and the third was one of the Parrish children. I felt all three and found no sign of life. By this time the rubber dinghy was inflating and Ced was helping Mrs Thorburn and Esther Law [a Flight Hostess] into it, and I climbed in myself and dragged other survivors to safety.'

Ced Carlton had noticed, just before the ditching, Stephen Wong and George Cattanach lying side by side on the floor at the rear of the step leading into the cockpit, braced for the terrible shock to come. Neither of them was seen again. Carlton, too, was almost trapped in the cockpit, finding himself under water 'like a goldfish in a bowl'. He spotted a vague glimmer of light in the nick of time and made for it. Surfacing, he grabbed a Mae West, found the life raft and inflated it. Then he and Blown began searching for the others. As the last survivor scrambled on board the raft, he happened to glance at his watch. It showed 9 a.m., which meant that thirteen minutes had elapsed from the time of ditching to the time the last of the living was hauled safely into the life raft.

It was lucky that the Chinese fighters left the scene once they had seen VR-HEU disappear under the water. It was also lucky that Stephen Wong's prompt call on the high-frequency radio telephone – 'Losing altitude engine on fire' – was heard at Kai Tak. The position was calculated from the last report and a Search and Rescue operation got under way at once – an international effort of considerable scope. The first plane on the scene was an RAF Valetta, diverted from her Saigon–Hong Kong route, and her signals drew back two RAF Hornets which had previously missed the tiny life raft. They, in their turn, sent urgent signals. An hour later a British Sunderland flying boat arrived and was ordered to keep the raft in sight whatever happened. Wanting to do more, the Sunderland pilot looked around for a possible place to land, but seeing eight- to ten-foot waves below him decided not to risk his giant aircraft. Shortly after this, two amphibious Grumman Albatrosses of the US Navy from Clarke Air Base, north of Manila, reached the scene and were guided to the life raft by the ebullient captain of yet another aircraft, a French privateer from Tourane (later Da Nang), who clearly wanted to go after the Chinese but who restrained himself long enough to drop a marker flare with great accuracy near the raft.

What happened next is best told in the deadpan words of the American pilot of Grumman Albatross AF 1009, Captain Jack Woodyard, who now displayed a degree of airmanship that filled all who saw or heard of it with admiration and wonder.

The sea appeared fairly rough, being complicated by a ground swell system running 60 to 70 degrees to the main flow as we approached Hainan. I estimated eight to ten foot seas were running and the wind was southerly at twelve to fifteen knots. I prepared to land three miles north of the raft off the south-east coast at Tai Chou Island just off the Hainan coast, where the ground swell was dampened. A normal rough water landing was made without difficulty – the ground swells were barely touched before stalling on the swell crest. This eliminated any trouble from the ground swell. The sea conditions were approximately as evaluated, and after clearing the protection of the island taxi-ing was slowed considerably and on occasions the wing floats and pedestals were completely submerged. During periods of extreme roll when the props hit the water it was necessary to use idle reserve position to avoid straining or killing the engines.

The French privateer guided me to the raft, and on approaching it the engineer was posted in the bow with a throw-line and the radio operator and medic were stationed at the rear hatch with a throw-line and boathook. The raft was circled to check the condition of the survivors and to see whether they were able to assist during the pick-up. The first approach was successful, a single-engine approach, cutting the port engine before reaching the raft so the prop would stop and be properly positioned. Nine survivors were taken aboard.

The Captain of the downed Skymaster was among them and immediately came forward to the flight deck where he stated: 'We were shot down. Watch out for yourself. There may be other fighters in the area.' I immediately called Captain Baker in '2 Dumbo 46', told him of the number of survivors, and when he crossed to the rescue frequency I cautioned him to watch for 'intruders'.

By this time I was taxi-ing back to the area where we had landed and Captain Arnold was being assisted by airman Rodrigues in an effort to hang the jato [jet-assisted take-off] units. After a great deal of exertion they managed to get the port jato bottle into position but couldn't manage the bulky starboard one. Captain Arnold arrived at the flight deck and told me they were having trouble with the starboard bottle and would have to rest a while from their exertions. About this time our cover aircraft reported a formation of unidentified aeroplanes approaching; this seemed to stimulate Captain Arnold and with an oath he rushed back and swung that bottle into place unassisted.

As we approached the shoreline numerous natives could be seen running for their junk-type fishing boats which were tied up at anchor. We approached within a hundred yards to take full advantage of all the possible smoother water and the shoreline effect upon the sea. Take-off was made without incident, turning approximately 110 degrees to port during the initial run. This allowed full effective power on both engines by the time the aircraft straightened out on heading. Control and altitude response was obtained before firing the jato units. During the final run the aircraft was nursed over three major crests and then stayed airborne. The approaching formation was identified as USN Skyraiders and as we completed our take-off two of them broke formation and flew beside us. Needless to say we were greatly relieved. We set course for Hong Kong.

There had been some anxiety that the Chinese might send yet more aircraft to disrupt the rescue, but Canton air control said that civilian aircraft could help with survivors, while warning that all military planes should leave the area immediately. To the last part of that message Captain Woodyard in his Grumman Albatross returned the most perfunctory of acknowledgements. Later in the day he landed with the survivors at Kai Tak and taxied in watched by a great throng of people, some of whom had had relatives aboard HEU but as yet had no firm news of who had survived and who had not. In fact a passenger from Bangkok, Miss Rita Cheong, who was badly hurt in the crash, died on the rescue plane. A great cry of anguish went up when only eight survivors were taken off; next day newspaper reports of the outrage and pictures of Valerie Parrish, aged six, being carried down the steps of Captain Woodyard's plane started a furore that was not confined to the Colony, but spread to Westminster and Washington DC as well. 'C.P.A. Airliner Outrage. Wanton Attack Made Without Slightest Warning' was the *South China Morning Post*'s front page headline above Captain Phil Blown's account of what had happened. The United States denounced the 'brutal' Chinese attack on VR-HEU that had killed three Americans and wounded three others, and almost at once two American Skyraiders and one Corsair from the aircraft carrier *Philippine Sea* shot down two Chinese fighters off the China coast, Admiral Felix B. Stump, the Commander-in-Chief of the US Pacific Fleet having warned everybody that the crews of his ships and aircraft had orders to be 'quick on the trigger'. In London, Mr Anthony Eden told the House of Commons that the attack was 'savage and inexcusable' and the Opposition leader, Mr Clement Attlee, who most embarrassingly was to visit China the following month, repeated that it was 'absolutely inexcusable'. However, the heat was taken out of the situation somewhat by prompt expressions of regret from Peking and an immediate promise to pay compensation and damages. It was a handsome apology, contained in a letter to the British Government from the Chinese Vice-Foreign Minister, and it read:

> According to the report received by our military authorities from Hainan Island, patrol aircraft of the People's Republic of China, while carrying out patrol duties over Port Yulin on Hainan Island, encountered an aircraft of the Chiang Kai-shek gang in that area and fighting took place. Upon receiving this report, the Government of the People's Republic of China undertook an investigation through various channels which revealed that the aircraft involved was actually a British-owned transport aircraft, mistaken by our patrol aircraft as an aircraft of the Kuomintang gang on a mission to raid our military base at Port Yulin. The occurrence of this unfortunate incident was indeed entirely accidental.

The Central People's government of the People's Republic of China expresses its regret, and is taking appropriate measures in dealing with it; it extends its sympathy, concern and condolences to the dead and injured and to their relatives.

The letter also made reference to the 'easing of the international situation – through the recent Geneva Conference' which had restored peace (temporarily) to Indo-China; and that perhaps is the reason why the Chinese were so quick off the mark with their regrets. Another aspect of the international scene at that time may well have contributed to the 'unfortunate incident'. The Chinese letter referred to landings by Chiang's secret agents on the coast of China, including Hainan, to the dropping of subversive pamphlets, in fact to a general campaign of harassment 'to create tension in Asia'. Nerves were very much on edge. Remembrance of those half-forgotten times came back like a book read long ago as Phil Blown sat thirty years later under the blue gums near the sign saying 'Road's End'. Yes, the Chinese had reason to be nervous, he said—

'The Americans used to run up and down the China coast, you know, looking. And the Chinese sent up planes to watch 'em. A hornets' nest was being stirred up then from Taiwan, Swatow, all the way down to Haiphong nearly. The Yanks were dropping pamphlets in Chinese over southern China. General 'Wild Bill' Donovan, the founder of OSS, America's wartime spy outfit, was around there as ambassador in Bangkok and used to fly about in Curtiss Commandos of Civil Air Transport – CAT – the Nationalist Chinese line. The Chinese didn't like all that. They were irritated, bloody irritated, and had been for some time.'

I asked, 'Were you and VR-HEU a little bit too close to Hainan for safety?'

'Not really. We were well inside the international corridor. So it was they who encroached. And they thought, probably, that Cathay Pacific was CAT. And then they thought – "Ah, Donovan – there he is, the bastard."'

Mrs Blown came into the room with two more cans of beer. 'They wanted to kill us all,' Phil said. 'If there'd been no survivors the Chinese pilots would never have admitted to their action. But compensation was paid. What happened to the pilots, God knows!'

The morning of the attack, Bunty Blown had gone to work as usual at the Butterfield & Swire passenger department. 'I thought that's funny, no one's talking to me. So I asked Marie Bok, "What's up?" and she said, "Well, there's been a plane lost. The flight from Bangkok." Of course I knew Phil was on that flight.'

'What did you do?' I asked.

'I went to the insurance office,' she laughed. 'No, not really. We weren't insured for that sort of thing. But you know what Phil did later? He sent his watch to Switzerland, to the makers, complaining it had stopped at the time of the accident. Meant to be waterproof, after all. And he got a new one back!'

In a letter to London, J. A. Blackwood, then Chairman of Cathay in Hong Kong wrote, 'The behaviour of all concerned seems to have been in the highest tradition. Captain Blown's effort in the manner of ditching and the saving of personnel has aroused the admiration of the flying world here.' Blown was out and about, he added, with apparently only a cracked rib and a bruised nose. Cedric Carlton was not so mobile, with a sprained ankle and more serious bruising. Neither of them wanted special leave, and indeed they were both soon flying again.

When it came to handing out rewards, a pleasant element of humour crept into the exchange between Swires' senior executives. In the margin of Blackwood's letter someone in the London office has pencilled: 'Should we give them a memento?' and a note from Jock adds: 'I would like to but who to? A gold watch to Woodyear?' Replying, Blackwood suggested: 'I think it would be a good gesture if CPA gave Captain Woodyard (not Woodyear) some tangible recognition of their appreciation. I doubt if a conventional watch would be of use to a member of the services. I should have thought that a salver, suitably inscribed, could find a place in his home now, although Captain Woodyard personally might not see a great deal of it until he retires. I certainly cannot think of anything that an Air Force man would carry around with him.'

In the event, Captain Woodyard received the Distinguished Flying Cross from the US Air Force and the salver proposed by Blackwood. It was engraved:

> To Captain Jack Thompson Woodyard, USAF
> In grateful recognition of his gallantry in AS-16,
> No. AF 1009 off Hainan Island, 23/7/54.

Jock felt that instead of a company award, Blown and Carlton deserved something rather grander. Sure enough, dressed in their smartest shirt-sleeve order, the two heroes paraded about a year later before Hong Kong's Governor, Sir Alexander Grantham, and before numerous distinguished guests he presented them with the Queen's Commendation for Valuable Service in the Air.

'It was a little bit of paper signed by Winston Churchill,' Phil explained. 'Not a gong, more a sort of shield you can stick on your lapel.'

'Do you wear it?' I asked.

'Oh, no, never,' he said smiling.

Bunty laughed. 'And you can't put QC after your name, can you?'

'What did you get, Bunty? A kiss on the cheek from Sir Alexander?'

'Oh, just a handshake. He was a dear old man, Grantham.' She went into the bedroom to find the commendation.

Phil Blown, stocky and dependable, looking more Cagney than ever, and as if nothing more exciting had occurred in his life than a sprained wrist playing croquet, told me, 'I had one kidney torn away in that ditching. Yes, Ced and I were thrown forward very hard and then the deceleration tore the kidney away from its moorings. It took about a year to find out about it. They sewed it back eventually and I've been fine ever since.' But I was wondering why he wasn't dead.

Bunty couldn't find the Queen's Commendation badge after all. We walked out to the short drive that led to the Road's End sign. Jays and mynah birds screeched and whistled.

'We've got foxes out here,' Phil said, 'and wombats.'

'And six-foot snakes, parrots, cockatoos and nasty spiders,' Bunty added. 'I was relieved,' she went on, 'when Phil "swallowed the prop" [pilots' slang for 'retire'] in 1961. Flying took him away so much. We had a son to educate here.' We looked at the countryside beyond the trees. 'There'll be a four-lane highway here some day, but not for twenty years. That's how slowly things work in Australia.' Light rain was beginning to fall and Bunty held out a hand to catch the drops.

Strange to relate, the Hainan tragedy had a silver lining as far as Cathay Pacific's future was concerned. Dave Smith believes it was a 'turning point', that the tremendous publicity had the effect of a particularly good advertisement. The reason for that, of course, was the heroism. For a time Phil Blown's performance was one of the smaller wonders of the world.

As for the compensation promised by the Government of China, Cathay handed in a bill for £251,400 which the Chinese promptly paid to the British Government. Inexplicably, Cathay got only £175,000 on account, and the Foreign Office took until the following year to make the final payment. The 'brutal' Chinese had moved faster.

In operational terms, however, the loss of HEU came as a staggering blow. Fresh capital might be in the offing, but how could Cathay continue to operate for the next few weeks without planes – that was the urgent question. At this late hour, could the airline carry on with only two DC-3s?

Clearly not. A replacement for HEU had to be found without delay.

Luckily Jock, as we have seen, had found a new friend on his trip to Canada. 'HEU was shot down 24.7.54,' he noted in his diary, 'and we cabled Grant McConachie in Vancouver "We have no aeroplanes can you help us". He leased us a DC-4 Skymaster VH-HFF at once.' Jock Swire, Grant McConachie, Ivan Holyman and Sydney de Kantzow – as Jock had pondered earlier, they all fell for each other at first sight: adventurers in the same mould. Jock's character once more had saved a dangerous situation from deteriorating into a fatal one.

The new DC-4 arrived three weeks after the loss of HEU. Cathay first leased it, then bought it from McConachie's Canadian Pacific Airlines. It was not the most immaculate Skymaster in the world. Initial trouble caused grave concern to Jack Gething, Cathay's Chief Engineer, when one after the other three of its engines had to be replaced by HEU's spares. But soon it was standing up well to the eighty hours a week required of it.

But that was not enough; VH-HFF only took Cathay back to where things had been just before HEU's shooting down: on the point of acquiring a DC-6. Accordingly Ivan Holyman, passing through the United States in November, succeeded in buying from Pan American–Grace Airways in Miami the DC-6 on which Jock had set his sights. The price of US$1,225,000 included all spares, two spare Double Wasp engines and the training costs for two crews. Holyman was assisted in this purchase by Jack Gething and Captain Kenneth Steele. Steele flew the new DC-6 to Hong Kong with Phil Blown, now an international hero, as co-pilot. Also aboard were Engineer Jack Williams and Flight Hostess Vera Rosario, whom we saw earlier bouncing about serving tea and sandwiches over the Australian outback in the DC-3s flown by Syd's 'pirates' in CPA's earliest days. Jack and Vera had recently married.

142

CHAPTER 15

Even after the agonizing decision to acquire a DC-6 had been taken, Cathay still had to run very fast to keep up with the Joneses of aviation. While the heart-searching over Hong Kong Airways, the doubts of future profitability, the debate over whether to pack up or be bold and risk money on a bigger aircraft had been dragging on, the jet age had been approaching Hong Kong like a meandering but relentless typhoon – and suddenly it arrived.

On 12 September 1958, before an applauding audience of VIPs, Sir Robert Black, the Governor of Hong Kong, bundled his wife and daughters into a helicopter that promptly took off and ceremoniously severed a ribbon stretched across the impressive new runway at Kai Tak. It was 8,350 feet in length, long enough to accommodate any aeroplane flying or likely to fly in the foreseeable future. Chinese firecrackers sparked and fizzed in celebration of a new era and, as if to demonstrate the sort of future the new runway heralded, a four-engined BOAC Comet 4 jet took the Governor's party up for a bird's-eye view of the Colony. Cathay for its part could only launch an old DC-3 and the new DC-6. But thank heavens for the DC-6.

Perhaps past adventures, Burma, the takeover of HKA and the recital of other events in Cathay's young life have obscured its still puny size. Even by 1955 Captain Pat Moore, the Company's flamboyant Irish Operations Manager, was sending directives intended for his senior flying staff to no more than fifteen pilots, including his Flight Superintendent, Captain Ken Steele. They were: Captains Phil Blown, Pat Armstrong, Dave Smith, Geoff Leslie, John Carrington, Laurie King, G. D. A. Rignall, G. V. Renwick (he retired in 1956), John Warne, Chic Eather, Cedric Carlton, B. G. Hargreaves (who joined Qantas in 1965), L. J. Kloster (ditto) and Norman Marsh.

Even if you add eight or nine First Officers and a small handful of Radio Officers, Moore's Merry Men were still a relatively cosy band. Change was in the offing.

At the severing of that ceremonial ribbon by Sir Robert Black, the knell sounded for days like the one on which Ken Steele, piloting a DC-6 into Kai Tak in pelting rain and with no windscreen wipers, skidded blindly with brakes full on to stop against the fence round the RAF compound and heard his co-pilot murmur, 'Go through the fence, Ken. There's a hospital there.'* And for moments like the one when grand old Captain Pat Moore replied to someone's grouse that he was barely skimming the rocky hills between the Kowloon Police Station and the old Kai Tak runway: 'Well, I'm not hitting 'em, am I?' It seemed that a more grown-up world had suddenly arrived. A good thing in its way, but sad, like the loss of childhood. Actually the new runway had been opened prematurely, fifteen days before the formal ceremony, because a USAF Skymaster had gone up in smoke (no casualties) on the old one. So the first pilot to touch down on the 8,350-foot innovation was a Philippine Airlines captain called Manuel Conde, who burbled excitedly to reporters that it was 'beautiful, smooth and straight'. (It would have been strange if it had been anything else.) A year later Kai Tak took another step into the modern world. Cathay's DC-3 Nikki flew in after dark: Hong Kong's airport was declared open for night operations at last.

Cathay's DC-6 had attracted favourable attention when the company added it to its all-Douglas fleet. The Hong Kong press called the new aircraft 'sleek' and 'extremely smooth', and when, like the Skymaster, it began a direct, non-stop service between Hong Kong and Singapore, leaving the Colony at sunset and taking off from Singapore at around midnight, businessmen were delighted by its greater speed and the newly installed sleeping berths. An advertising slogan – 'Be specific . . . fly Cathay Pacific' – was invented (inspired no doubt by the 'Don't be vague . . . ask for Haig' ads) to promote the all-night service. It was nicknamed the 'Midnight Special' – although flight crews swiftly dubbed it the 'Midnight Horror' owning to the absence aboard of even elementary navigational aids, coupled with the exhausting all-night flying and the prevalence of thunderstorms.

Since the early days of the DC-4 the Cathay flights had caught the imagination of the itinerant Overseas Chinese – and for this H. H. Lee in Singapore can take much credit. 'Luckily,' he said later, 'with my CNAC experience in China I had very good connections. Before 1947 CNAC had

---

* Bob Smith was Flight Engineer. He claims his exact words were: 'If we'd gone through the fence at least we'd have been in the bloody hospital.' This was RAF Kai Tak's infirmary.

connected South China and Hong Kong. CPA had flown second-generation Chinese from the Straits Settlements to Hong Kong, and from there they visited their native villages. They were energetic in Malaya, and some got rich and went home to show off their nice suits or to get a bride, to build a house or a temple and then return to the Straits. For a time from 1949, Overseas Chinese still harboured the idea that China would be much the same – only a change of government, even if it is Communist. Well, of course, they were disappointed. But in the early days we tried to develop the Overseas Chinese trade.

'We could give lots of help to Chinese – some had no passports, only Certificates of Identity. There were forms to be filled in, permits, landing cards, customs forms, immigration forms – all in English. We helped with the language. I was always out at the airport helping our passengers. BOAC made people handle all these strange, unfamiliar matters themselves, and in a foreign language. BOAC's air hostesses were all English and English-speaking. We slowly built up our reputation as Asians. We had oriental food, hostesses speaking every Asian language. So even when BOAC introduced faster planes than us – they had Britannias when we had the DC-6, and later they had 707s when we had Electras – Chinese and other Asian passengers were happy to take a longer time flying with us. We were better known to them. We flew the merchants whose goods travelled in our ships all through the region. Then in 1960 tourism began in quite a big way, too.'

Beavering away in the Ocean Building office or speeding back and forth to Singapore Airport, Lee was often encouraged, as so many other Cathay employees were, by the sight of the formidable though avuncular figure of Jock Swire dropping in for a visit. 'His suitcase was always tied up with string,' he told me.

This airline appealed to Asian governments and national airlines for an even more basic reason than those which H. H. Lee mentioned. Paul Jurgensen, a Danish ex-fighter pilot, a hard-headed veteran of the Biafran war and a down-to-earth character who became Cathay's South East Asian Regional Manager in the 1980s, believes that because of Jock's strict and perhaps old-fashioned standards of straight dealing, the airline became particularly well respected in Singapore from the word go. 'We were considered upright and honest – and in Prime Minister Lee Kuan Yew's rather puritanical "rugged society" state that is appreciated.' At first even Jurgensen, before he joined Cathay, thought 'the Swire business was weird'. He found it hard to grasp that, with them, a handshake really was final. 'Such a thing,' he believes, 'is not only honest, it is *unique*. Particularly,' he glowers, 'when you consider that the airline industry is a bunch of pirates!'

After Lee's technically go-ahead little island split with Malaysia in 1965, Singapore created its own excellent airline; relations with Cathay, which might have been strained by competition, remained extremely cordial.

Meanwhile, Captain Bob Howell (with Lyell Louttit) took the first DC-6 charter to London, flying into Gatwick on a drizzly Saturday in November and expecting to be met by Jock Swire in person. Instead, in the freezing wind, a Cathay secretary sweetly handed him a note that read, 'Welcome, Captain Howell – You should know better than to arrive at 3.30 on a Saturday during the fox-hunting season!'

The DC-6B that joined the Cathay fleet soon after was a sort of milestone – the first brand-new aircraft bought direct from the manufacturer. It was equipped with radar, and both planes usefully filled a gap and attracted passengers. The DC-6B did more – it pioneered the Hong Kong–Taipei–Tokyo route newly acquired after HKA's absorption into Cathay. But the DC-6s were already something of an anachronism – the new Kai Tak runway and the symbolic presence of the Comet showed that. A Brave New World had arrived, and with Pan Am's transatlantic crossing by 707 jet the time had come to switch to something more up-to-date than piston engines.

That did not mean that little Cathay should rush headlong into the world of pure jets. Propjets were quite a new phenomenon and modern enough for now. But which ones? Dave Smith said later, 'There was always a patriotic compulsion to buy British aircraft. But the fact was British aircraft didn't suit us. We had to have a plane that could hold fuel in case of emergency – say, flying Bangkok to Hong Kong, there had to be the possibility of diverting to Manila. We looked at the British Comet 4, but it still hadn't been cleared for civilian flying, and it had a record then that the public rather shied away from (though, of course, BOAC flew them again quite successfully). So we chose the Lockheed Electras – American planes. Two of them, in fact.'

Don Delaney, an experienced engineer, was quite sure the Electras were a much better choice than the British alternative, the short-range Vickers Viscounts and Vanguards. 'Electras flew like dreams,' he said, 'and handled like fighters.'

Dave Smith who was later to become the company's Operations Manager, brought Cathay's first Electra into a perfect landing at Kai Tak on 14 April 1959 after the 8,500-mile flight from Burbank, California, in under twenty-six hours. 'A most forgiving aircraft,' he thought. The Electra entered service ten days later. With her spacious interior arranged to accommodate sixty-six Economy and twelve First Class passengers on the

Hong Kong–Bangkok–Singapore route, her turbines smooth and quiet with a top speed of 450mph, she gave Far Eastern passengers their first taste of a fast, luxurious flight and became an immediate favourite. The second Electra flew into Kai Tak three months later with Phil Blown, hero of Hainan Island, at the controls. They were the first two such planes built at Burbank, and all at once the Cathay fleet had reached an impressive level both in quality and numbers of aircraft: one DC-3, one DC-4, one DC-6, one DC-6B, and two Electras.

In quick succession, and with much flourish and fanfare from the press of the entire region, Cathay opened up three more major routes with their smart new planes – one of the Electras inaugurated a regular weekly service to Tokyo; the DC-6B started a bi-weekly service to Calcutta; and, most thrilling of all, the second Electra kicked off a new service to Sydney – the fastest of any airline by more than seven hours. Each of these inaugural flights was a wonderful party. Cathay Pacific's Chairman, Bill Knowles, and Duncan Bluck, now Cathay's young and dynamic Commercial Manager, scattered invitations to as many important people from the countries involved – politicians, show business stars, journalists and big businessmen – as they could safely load aboard, and with the collaboration of Jo Cheng, the company's Hostess Supervisor, made sure they were pampered unmercifully.

In spite of these successes, on 18 February 1960 Jock Swire was moved to write a deeply troubled appraisal of Cathay's situation. To have achieved Cathay's first regular scheduled service Down South in the footsteps of Syd and Roy by breaking a record added a spectacular feather in the Company's cap, but it also represented a break out from the regional image Jock was convinced was the right one and which Cathay had created for itself and adhered to up to now, and from this sprang trouble.

Australia had its own national airline, Qantas, one of the giant international flag-carriers, and its directors were a very suspicious bunch who looked askance at ambitious upstarts like Cathay if they began to show signs of getting too big for their boots. Even though, as everyone knew, Cathay Pacific was the British-owned airline designated by Her Majesty's Government to fly the Hong Kong–Sydney route and therefore fully entitled to do so, it looked to some people in Qantas almost like a marauding raid into private territory. Australian hostility was further increased by the fact that a project to charter a Qantas Super Constellation aircraft to Malayan Airways for use on their Singapore–Hong Kong run was being bitterly opposed by Cathay, on the grounds that once Qantas had its foot in that door with its own Superconnie – no matter in whose name the plane was flying – it would never withdraw it. The Hong Kong–Singapore service was Cathay's bread and butter: no one at Butterfield & Swire was prepared to sit back and watch the crafty Aussies worm their way by stealth into a trade that, though a mere sideshow to an intercontinental airline like Qantas, was of vital importance to the existence of Cathay.

This time Jock's sudden anxiety for the future was unlike earlier bursts of soul-searching. Now the question was not 'To be or not to be?' but 'Where are we going – and why?' No one, since the influx of new capital and the modernization of the fleet, had talked any more of 'liquidation', of packing up Air and fleeing back to shipping. As Don Delaney put it later, 'Cathay took off with the Electras. It was sink or swim after that.' And to continue swimming two new elements had, all of a sudden, to be taken into account. These were, first, the hostility of Qantas and, second, the arrival in the Far East of the age of the pure jet, a good deal quicker than expected. These two elements combined to discomfort a Cathay Pacific still lacking somewhat in self-confidence.

Cathay had proudly started their swift, smooth Electra service to Sydney on 23 July 1959. Five months later Duncan Bluck reported to Jock that Qantas had responded with *their* Sydney–Hong Kong Electra service – and Qantas flew three times a week to Cathay's once.

'We must now compete,' Bluck warned, 'with a well-established operator with three times our frequency and with identical equipment.' That was one development. Bluck signalled sombre indications of another: 'I understand Jardines have been asked to prepare for the handling of Qantas's Boeing 707s in Hong Kong by June 1960.' Duncan Bluck had already reported that Pan-American was starting to fly 707s four times a week to Europe via Bangkok and Tokyo, two important Cathay 'ports', and Jock had pencilled his comment in the report's margin: 'This might hurt us quite a lot.' Now if Qantas was to introduce pure jet Boeing 707s – planes much bigger and faster than Cathay's propjet Electras – between Sydney and Hong Kong. . . .

With more than its new Australian route gravely at risk, Cathay now launched a strenuous diplomatic effort to woo Qantas into a much more friendly frame of mind. There wasn't much time – Qantas was the first to get American jets, and was already crossing the Pacific in 707s and flying them to London on the 'Kangaroo Route' too. In a meeting in Sydney with Qantas's Vice-Chairman Bill Taylor, its Chief Executive C. O. Turner, and Commercial Manager A. F. Foster, John Browne, CPA's Managing

Director in Hong Kong, spelled out Cathay's ideas on cooperation rather than confrontation. He said that a Qantas jet service to Hong Kong would have serious consequences on Cathay's business and that, as Qantas and Cathay were the only operators on the Hong Kong–Sydney route, the continued use of Electras would result in a sounder economic return than to have a race for speed.

Cedric Turner replied for Qantas. According to John Browne, he was both 'offensive and evasive'. He had already publicly stated that Qantas would do its damnedest to 'run Cathay off the Sydney route', a remark that got back to Jock Swire who told friends that Qantas's hatred for Cathay appeared to be 'quite psychotic'. All Turner would say to Browne was that Qantas must have jets in the Far East, but that for technical reasons they were unlikely to be operational to Hong Kong until 1962. However, he added that if equipment became available Qantas would certainly introduce the 707s earlier than that. He carelessly brushed away Browne's suggestion that Qantas and Cathay should agree on pooling, or sharing, the Hong Kong–Sydney route.

Turner certainly seemed to have set his mind on the destruction of Cathay's attempts to expand southwards, even though Cathay had every legal right to be there. Turner was an odd bird. A clever, even brilliant, operator, he treated Qantas's founder-President Hudson Fysh, at this late period in Fysh's life, as if he were a superannuated fuddy-duddy who should have retired a decade before. He could be outrageously outspoken, after a few drinks too many. 'He had extraordinary habits,' says someone who worked with him in Qantas. 'He'd slump at dinner, his head half an inch from his plate. The drill was to ignore this if you could, because after an hour or so, he'd look up, rub his nose and go on as if nothing had happened.'

The task of interpreting whether or not Qantas was really ready to come to terms with Cathay was complicated by conflicting reassurances from Turner's colleagues on the Qantas Board, who spent a good deal of time trying to cover up for this 'ruthless and egotistical individual', as one Cathay director described Turner. Bill Taylor might soothe John Browne by telling him that Turner had no business to express publicly a desire to 'run Cathay out', that it was not the policy of the Qantas Board to do any such thing. A Qantas director who was also a well-known aviator, Robert Law-Smith, confirmed this, privately assuring another Cathay emissary that 'the Board tells Cedric Turner what to do', not vice versa. Yet what was one to make of another statement by Taylor that such a view was 'strictly for the birds'. Or of the strongly expressed opinion of yet another senior Qantas man who insisted with startling conviction, 'Turner is the real power. Qantas is spelt

T-U-R-N-E-R.' Significantly, whatever they thought of Cedric Turner, none of these Qantas directors would go so far as to agree to a pooling arrangement for the Hong Kong–Sydney route; nor did they promise that Qantas would keep its 707 jets off that route.

Law-Smith, intentionally or not, probably put his finger on one important cause of Turner's rooted antagonism for Cathay when he told Browne that he wouldn't trust Reg Ansett of ANA 'across the room' – Ansett who had succeeded Ivan Holyman on the Board of Cathay. When he was not upcountry shooting crocodiles, Ansett was formidably ambitious, regarded by everyone in Qantas as all set to take any opportunity to spread abroad at Qantas's expense. Because of the ANA shareholding in Cathay, Law-Smith confessed that no one much trusted Cathay either. When Browne protested that Butterfield & Swire ran its own business even if people like Ansett and BOAC had money in Cathay, Law-Smith shrugged, almost pityingly, that air business was getting 'too big and tough for shipping people' – a thought that had worried Jock in the past.

Ambitious or not, Ansett for his part told Browne that he considered Bill Taylor and Robert Law-Smith 'straight and fair'. The hope persisted in Hong Kong and London that Qantas would restrict its use of Boeing 707s to their Sydney–Manila–Tokyo run (on which it was fighting off over-the-Pole competition from a KLM pure jet service) and leave the Electras, with which Cathay could compete, flying between Sydney and Hong Kong.

But Cedric Turner got his way. It was not his habit to announce his intentions in advance – Duncan Bluck had complained bitterly that, whereas Cathay always had the courtesy to inform Qantas of its intentions (for example, to add a second flight each week to Sydney), it only learned of any new Qantas move after the event and from press reports. As late as 29 August 1961, after lunching with Bluck at the Hong Kong Club, Jock noted in his diary, 'I am disturbed to discover how nebulous and unsubstantiated the rumour that Qantas are putting Boeings on HK–Sydney apparently is. We *must* know definitely what their intention is.' He didn't have to wait long.

In November Qantas replaced its Electras on the Hong Kong run with the far superior Boeing 707s. That was the end of Cathay. The same month Chic Eather flew the last Cathay Electra out of Sydney. Des Cooper, who moved to Cathay in Sydney from Qantas, thinks 'It was a terrible blow when Qantas's 707s drove us off the route. But we actually made a very small effort in Sydney – although most of the Hong Kong to Sydney trade was generated from there. We had one little office – me and a secretary. Chester Yen, Cathay's Sales Manager and Bluck's No. 2, tried to talk that delightful chap

Bill Knowles into having a full-time ticketing office in Sydney. But no.' Cathay Pacific leased their rights to the route to BOAC, and the Company was not to return to the Australian route for thirteen years.

The Qantas–Cathay bitterness did not last. Jock even envisaged a possible association with the Australian airline and contemplated giving a seat on Cathay's Board to Bob Law-Smith, whom he found 'a really delightful chap. Pleasant and interesting.'

With the experience of the tussle with Qantas in mind, Jock thought it was high time for Cathay to clear its head and take a cool, steady look at the future. 'We have now reached yet another crossroads in the history of Cathay,' he wrote. As he saw it, Cathay had two choices. It could go on expanding and keeping pace with the equipment used by the major trunk lines with all their subsidies and government support. Alternatively it could get back to 'our proper regional function' of giving the best possible service with the best possible aircraft – plus, when aircraft were available, long-range chartering.

The first choice was the path that Jock personally mistrusted, and he thought he saw Cathay drifting down it. He had warned constantly against expansion and would continue to do so for many years to come, believing that trying to keep up with the Big Boys of aviation would undoubtedly require capital far beyond Swires' means and would eventually lead to losing control of the company – to (say) BOAC, Qantas or ANA – in the search for that capital. He rejected the argument that the whole trend of modern life was for combines to get bigger and bigger and that the little man could never survive this irreversible trend. 'We are not the "little man",' he snorted. 'And we have got powerful friends.' Even so, it would be no good just barging blindly ahead and increasing the number of flights on the Sydney and Tokyo runs, for instance, with all the necessary groundwork, unless Cathay was prepared to face up to the natural consequences of doing so.

The second, however, was comfortably within Cathay's own limited but slightly increased resources. It would enable Swires to retain the Company's independence and the family's control of it. It might conceivably avoid the need to switch to those expensive pure jets: if Cathay could hold on for four or five years, the big trunk lines with their superjets would to some extent be overflying Cathay's area, and for that reason would be only too pleased to have Cathay keeping the regional pot boiling below them.

Jock had thought about how Cathay's regional routes might be pruned and improved. 'We might sacrifice Hong Kong/Sydney *and* Hong

Kong/Tokyo. We might abandon Calcutta and exploit Borneo a good deal more, as also perhaps Jakarta. The stopping service Taipeh/Okinawa/Korea and Japan is regional and perhaps worth retaining. Hong Kong/Singapore must at all costs be maintained.' For all this it would be essential for the next four or five years to have the best equipment in the region – though not in the world. The two Electras should be able to hold their own for that long.

Whither Cathay Pacific? Small, regional, cosy – or big-time, inter-continental, de luxe? Who in the early sixties would have enjoyed making that decision?

'It seems to me,' Jock ended, 'that no time should be lost in making up our minds which of these two roads our long-range policy should follow.'

There were already discernible differences of opinion on the expansion issue, in both Swires and Cathay. Roughly, the pro-expansion lobby consisted of Bill Knowles and Duncan Bluck, and the anti-expansionists were Jock and John Browne. John Bremridge, Cathay's Managing Director, held a position somewhere in the middle, though tending towards Jock-like caution. Browne, Bremridge and Bluck – the three Bs – are key figures in this story; they dominated Cathay's management through the sixties, seventies and into the eighties, taking over direction of the Company one after the other like runners in a relay race.

As a purely regional line Cathay had on the whole done well. The Company's (and Jock Swire's) attitude to the big airlines had been placatory – 'We're not competing with you. We'll feed you passengers from Singapore, Bangkok and elsewhere, and take over and look after the passengers you deliver to Hong Kong. We'll help each other.' Admittedly, there were political problems in this sensitive post-colonial time: the Cultural Revolution shut down China; when General Ne Win came to power in Burma, traffic more or less ceased and Cathay had to close down there; the Vietnam War closed down Hanoi and Haiphong. On the other hand, Duncan Bluck was proved right over Japan and Taiwan; he had predicted their 'miraculous' economic recovery, and the advent of tourism there. It was easy to play for safety and 'think regional' – but only as long as Bluck was not around. He had exciting ambitions, for himself and for the Company. He was a gadfly; the sting under the Company's tail.

'An aviation genius,' Jock had said of him when Bluck was still a young and rising star in the early sixties. A wise man, Jock. Bluck knew Japan well, having served three years there in CNCo's shipping offices in Tokyo, Kobe and Yokohama. He had seen the hopelessness of Japan under the post-war American occupation: Japanese businessmen could only travel abroad at the stern whim of General MacArthur; thousands of American servicemen who came for occupation duty and went home on leave only travelled in American aircraft. There was no profit for Cathay in that. But Duncan Bluck, perhaps before anyone at Cathay Pacific, foresaw the Japanese recovery – the 'economic miracle'. When the signs were right he helped to launch Cathay's one DC-6B and two Electras at Japan, and the Company saw its trade there blossom spectacularly. This success, its parallel in Taiwan, and the influx of American and other tourists into the East made up in the sixties for a good deal of frustration earlier on. And besides, there was always the good, dependable Manila route.

But Duncan Bluck was thinking bigger than that. He gave Jock a sturdy nudge towards global expansionism in a report he wrote after a five-week tour of the United States and Canada in February and March 1961. It made very good reading, according to Jock's old buddy John Scott, and it certainly made important recommendations. Bluck pointed out the vast amount of business immediately available in the United States, leave alone the potential business. (He got to specifics: while he was actually in the Los Angeles office of Ed Sullivan, Cathay's American sales agent, a mere four phone calls had netted HK$140,000-worth of business right there and then.) Bluck said that Cathay's services just had not been brought to the attention of American tour operators; if Cathay would flaunt itself a little on the West Coast, who knew? The sky could be the limit. Get a good full-time salesman, Bluck said, to work with Ed Sullivan, who was himself exceptionally well known and liked in the American travel business. Apart from anything else, San Francisco and Los Angeles (and Vancouver up the coast in Canada) harboured the largest Chinese populations outside Asia.

Bluck was not saying that Cathay should start flying to America's West Coast – at least, not yet. He was merely drawing Jock's attention to the gold mine that all those potential passengers – Chinese or non-Chinese – could represent once someone told them that Cathay Pacific Airways not only existed, but was hopefully looking their way.

It was a razor-edge time of 'Shall-we-shan't-we?' Jock was right to urge his managers to hurry up and decide on the best way ahead. But it turned out that any such decision had to be postponed. For, when Cathay Pacific seemed about to soar at last, in America two Lockheed Electras lost their wings in flight.

CHAPTER 16

The first man in at the death of Braniff International Airways Flight 542 was a farmer, Mr Richard White. The wreckage fell on his land, not far from Buffalo, Texas, in the middle of the night. He told Federal investigators it seemed as if suddenly the entire sky was on fire, and then that unearthly light faded 'as if a monstrous Roman candle had spent itself'. There was a noise like thunder and strange sounds came out of the sky – shrill whistles in different keys. White and his wife stood on their porch hugging each other in terror as heavy metal objects crashed about them. Next there was a fearful silence. A wetness fell from the air that was like rain but was not rain because it smelled like kerosene: jet-engine fuel. White ran barefoot to his vegetable patch. It was littered with pieces of what looked like aluminium. The rudder of an aircraft hung in a tree near the pigpen. On it red lettering said: 'Fly Braniff'. White didn't recognize it, but he was looking at the remains of a Lockheed L-188: an Electra. And two Electras were the pride and spearhead of Cathay Pacific's little fleet.

So on 29 September 1959 began one of the most tragic yet inspiring stories in modern aviation history. It has been grippingly told in its complex entirety by Robert J. Serling in his book *The Electra Story*, published in 1963. Here it is only possible to give an outline of the disasters, of their investigation, of Lockheed's brilliant recovery and of the impact of the tragedy on the upward progress of Cathay Pacific Airways. At once an army of investigators from the Federal Government's Civil Aviation Board descended on the White farm, and certain things were soon established. Flight 542 had been carrying a crew of six and twenty-eight passengers. Captain Wilson Stone, the pilot, was highly experienced, with 28,135 flying hours behind him. Admittedly only forty-nine of them had been in Electras, but as Cathay's Laurie King said later, the Electra was 'really easy flying; really easy. That is, provided you listened to the Lockheed pilots and didn't fly it as if you were flying a DC-3 or a DC-4.' Captain Stone would not have flown 542 anything but correctly.

From two huge barrels full of small pieces of metal the experts tried to find out what had happened. There had been – all witnesses agreed – a quick, vivid flash and then a reddish fireball. A meticulous search over a very wide area revealed sections of the left wing and bits of Nos 1 and 2 engines far from the nose crater. From this it was deduced that the left wing had snapped off. Had the explosion destroyed the wing – or had there been a wing rupture and then fire resulting from the igniting of spilled fuel? Sabotage was ruled out: there had been no emergency messages from the crew. Might the captain have put the plane into a violent manoeuvre to avoid a collision with another aircraft? The Federal Aviation Agency could trace no aircraft anywhere near. It was baffling.

Yet the investigators uncovered two interesting facts. First, marks showed that the No. 1 engine propeller had been wobbling as much as 35 degrees out of the norm; it was a key clue, but no one thought much of it at the time.

The second fact had a Sherlock Holmesian property about it. Many of the farmers in the area of the crash remarked that 'Every coon dog for miles started howling' at about the time of the explosion or just before it. That seemed to mean that something was causing a shriek or whine on an unusual sound frequency. What kind of sound? What could be the cause? There was no answer. After a great deal of brain-racking and meticulous investigation of the site and the remains, the accident looked like joining the list of unsolved crashes.

Then, on 17 March 1960, approaching Tell City, Indiana, in clear weather at 18,000 feet and at 400mph, an Electra of Northwest Airlines suddenly burst into a black cloud of smoke. It emerged from the cloud minus its right and most of its left wing: the fuselage dived almost vertically to earth, where it dug itself a smoking crater forty-foot wide. Northwest Airlines Flight 710 had on board thirty-three men, twenty-one women, eight children and one infant, all bound for Miami. The aircraft's pilot, Captain Edgar E. LaParle, had been with NWA since 1937 and had flown 27,523 hours with them. The Electra in which he died had flown less than 1,800 hours and only the week before had undergone a major inspection.

This time the scene of the crash was one of almost unimaginable horror. Rescue workers, masked and gloved, delved about in that steaming hole to find the fuselage and its contents crushed into a mass of molten metal; the fuselage itself was no more than a third of its original length. It was something of a miracle that as many as seven of the sixty-three bodies could be identified. An army chaplain from Fort Knox nearby and the Tell City coroner, as well as local health authorities, were so distressed by what they saw from the lip of the cauldron that the order was given for bulldozers to cover up the hole and everything in it without more ado, and for a commemorative stone to be placed over this communal grave. But for the Civil Aviation Board – and Lockheed – it was a duty to do everything possible to unravel the mystery underlying both this crash and the earlier one of Braniff Flight 542, and the CAB was obliged to obtain a restraining order from the Governor of Indiana to prevent the bulldozers getting to work.

The consequent investigation was astounding in its thoroughness. As before, CAB investigators moved in like ants, collecting, marking, plotting the scattered wreckage as hundreds of soldiers supported by helicopters scoured a twenty-five square-mile area. This time the investigators had some extremely valuable help – two US Air Force jet-bomber pilots had been flying in the vicinity of Flight 710's path at the same time, and now they reported that without warning they had hit clear-air turbulence so severe that they were bounced out of their seats. So Flight 710 had met a jet stream at 18,000 feet moving at something in excess of 100mph and at 90 degrees to its flight path. It was, as Robert Serling says, as if the Electra, travelling at 400mph, 'had bounced into an aerial ditch – a jarring collision of metal and wind in which the metal had come off second best'.

But clear-air turbulence was nothing new. So why had an Electra – a modern aircraft that in terms of structural strength actually exceeded the very high standards set by the Federal Government – been wrecked by it? Whatever the answer was, ninety-seven people had been killed in two aircraft of the same make, and a nationwide furore broke over Lockheed's bewildered head. Pilots, engineers, CAB investigators and Congressmen felt that Electras should be removed – temporarily at least – from passenger service. And the only government official with the power to take such a step was the head of the Federal Aviation Agency, ex-Air Force General Elwood R. Quesada, commonly known as Pete.

A former fighter pilot, Quesada was considered by many to be too autocratic: he was stocky, tetchy, and suffered fools not at all. It was a time, however, when most people thought air violations had increased to a point beyond a joke and that civil air regulations needed 'a tough cop'. In Quesada they got one. With his most senior assistants he visited that terrible crater near Tell City. They had already begun forming theories – considering the 'severe turbulence' reports of the Air Force pilots – as to what might have happened. But the dire decision – whether or not to ground every Electra in the world for the foreseeable future – had to be taken.

One of Quesada's top colleagues had an idea: instead of grounding them, why not put the Electras under a speed restriction? His reasoning was as follows. The Electra was the fastest prop-driven airliner ever to fly, and as a result it was taking its conventional, straight wings into speeds not far from those of the pure jets, the wings of which were swept back to absorb subsonic turbulence. The Northwest Airlines plane at least had hit turbulence at high speed. Placing speed restrictions on the Electras during intensive investigation would have the effect of adding strength to their wings. Lockheed's engineers agreed. So did Quesada.

The FAA first ordered speed restrictions three days after the Tell City crash, but strident calls for total grounding were not diminished by that. It was a brave thing for Pete Quesada to oblige Electra crews to keep their speed down from 373mph to 259mph (roughly the speed of a DC-6 or a Constellation) but to let them keep flying. He was taking a risk – a calculated risk for sure, but a fearful one. 'If another one goes down,' said an FAA official quoted by Serling, 'Pete might as well be on it.' Quesada himself told Serling later, 'You're damn right I was worried. I knew one more crash and I was finished.'

CAB officials returning to Washington from Tell City refused to travel in Electras; a fact which in itself could have put the kibosh on the Electras if it had leaked to the press. And the proponents of grounding had an impressive point: the first Electra had lost its wings from an unknown structural cause in level flight and in calm weather, with no turbulence in the vicinity. If there was a third and similar crash the Electra would be finished for ever, its reputation smashed beyond what even a grounding order could do – better a wrecked schedule and lost dollars than another crash and more deaths. Sick jokes began to be bandied about: 'Seen the new aviation play – *Mourning Becomes the Electra?*' and 'Read the new Electra book, *Look Ma, No Wings*'? Inevitably, the rumour was put around: 'It's a fact Lockheed paid Quesada $50,000 not to ground the Electra.'

Nevertheless Lockheed did have friends in an unlikely quarter. As the almost superhuman effort to determine the cause of the accidents (code-named Operation LEAP) got under way at Lockheed's plant at Burbank, California, even the company's fiercest rivals, Boeing and Douglas, sent aerodynamic specialists to help. Two hundred and fifty of Lockheed's own engineers went on three shifts a day, seven days a week; some worked an eighty-four-hour week. The California Institute of Technology lent additional computers; the National Aeronautics and Space Administration (NASA) made available the huge wind tunnel at Langley Field, Virginia. In laboratories, in wind tunnels, in hair-raising test flights, Lockheed started driving an Electra wing to destruction: a complete wing with its engines were subjected to the most powerful twists and shakes that America's best aviation engineers and most courageous and skilful test pilots could contrive. It was an awe-inspiring joint effort by the major airline manufacturers and operators. As the search went on, Electra pilots across the country voted by overwhelming majorities to continue flying the aircraft (under the FAA speed restriction), even while the cause of the crashes remained unknown. Cathay's Laurie King was flying them on a regular schedule at the time: 'We had the speed restriction and we were flying only by hand. They suspected the autopilot for a while. I think we knew it had something to do with wing oscillation. We inspected every day for wing fatigue. We were pretty philosophical about it.'

Wing oscillation – a severe 'flutter' on a wing – could destroy a plane, everyone knew that, but the Electra had wings as flutter-proof as any in the world. In tests the wings survived, but attention focused on where and how the engines were mounted on those wings, on the strength of their mounts and struts – that was where, it appeared, something was very seriously wrong. On the Braniff aircraft marks had shown that the No. 1 propeller had wobbled very considerably. It was the sound of this – the shriek of a supersonic propeller gone haywire on a wing that was shaking itself to death – that had set all those Texan 'coon dogs' howling. For the Lockheed examiners now realized that not only had propellers wobbled – the entire engine had wobbled on its nacelles or wing fixtures, and these violent oscillations had twisted the wing itself in an unstoppable gyroscopic seizure. Unstoppable because the oscillations, occurring at the same frequency, fed on each other and *in less than thirty seconds* reached a degree of violence and speed that snapped off the wing. In the case of Braniff, perhaps an earlier 'hard landing' had weakened the engine mounting; in the case of the NWA Electra, the impact of turbulence on the weakened engine-mounts simply hastened the self-destruction of the wings.

The enormous effort had paid off; now it was time for major surgery. The stiffness of the nacelles was almost doubled, the rear engine mounts strengthened with heavier metal. Braces were added, and wing-ribs relocated to increase their resistance to twisting stresses. Altogether Lockheed would have to call in the 136 Electras being operated by seven domestic and six foreign airlines, including Cathay. The cost was estimated at about $24 million, which proved to be accurate. Once again, Lockheed's test pilots took to the air to see how far the newly modified Electras could be pushed in adverse conditions. The tests must have been unbelievably dramatic. Electras were dived at speeds up to 418mph, having been deliberately weakened to simulate structural failure. Unusual flight loads were flown in turbulent weather to record critical strains in the wings and fuselage. Whatever the test pilots did, there was now no sign of oscillation, flutter, whirl or whatever you liked to call it. The modification programme on each aircraft took about twenty-five days and on 5 January 1961, fifteen months after the Braniff disaster, the FAA announced its approval of the programme and removed the speed restriction on any Electra so modified. Pete Quesada could sleep peacefully at last.

Like the other dozen affected airlines, Cathay had had to grit its teeth and improvise. Jock instructed John Browne to make it his top priority 'to see what can be done to brace ourselves to meet the critical period while the FAA restrictions are in force, followed by the lay-up time for modification'. December–January 1960 was the time allotted to Cathay by Lockheed – not too long to wait, Cathay's directors thought, although greater delay would be bad for the crews' morale. At the same time, to fill the gap while the two Electras were in Burbank – particularly on the then still operating Sydney run – Cathay chartered a Britannia turbo-prop from BOAC for £4,000 a week plus £75 per flying hour.

Captains Phil Blown and Pat Armstrong flew the Cathay Electras to Burbank, where Don Delaney was waiting to supervise the modification. Chic Eather, who flew one of the duly modified Electras back to Hong Kong, had this to say about them: 'Pilots considered the Electra a wonderful aeroplane. The modifications had returned the type to its full speed potential and they were a credit to the family name of Lockheed. The Electra rebuilt its somewhat tarnished reputation to one of maximum reliability.' Laurie King, flying an Electra out of Sydney for Hong Kong, had the unnerving experience of a severe lightning strike on the nose radome. The electrical charge hit just in front of the co-pilot and left the aircraft near No. 2 engine. The radar antenna jammed, and on the descent to Darwin the radome collapsed completely. King simply reduced speed and landed safely. His views of the skyworthiness of the Electras match those of Chic Eather.

Naturally the Electra affair had been a bad moment for Cathay, and one made still grimmer with the discovery by Gething, Delaney and HAECO's engineers of serious corrosion – a growth of 'green slime' – in the inboard fuel tanks of both Electras. Don Delaney explains: 'It was a sort of fungus on the tank floor, an algae not unlike seaweed – it was caused by a chemical reaction between the fuel and the aluminium metal in the structure. If left it would have eaten its way through the tank and the wing skins. Luckily for the survival of Cathay the corrosion was discovered before and not after a disaster. Lockheed dealt with it: during the modification operation at Burbank they put an additive into the fuel to prevent algae.

The Cathay Electras had returned from Burbank with new lettering – the two words CATHAY PACIFIC in bold, clean capitals replaced for ever the old-fashioned sprawl of 'Cathay Pacific Airways'. But should the planes themselves be renamed? Duncan Bluck had been disturbed by the adverse reaction to the Electra, particularly in the eastern United States while he was there: 'Our agents made it very clear to me that although they appreciated the merits of the modified Electra they had great difficulty in selling it to the public.' Should the modified Electras be called something new – like 'Electra Mark III' or 'Electra 400'? At least two American airlines did follow this course. But Bill Knowles decided that Cathay's ads would contain, for a while, the reassuring words 'fully modified to FAA requirements', and that was all. In fact, in Asia the flying public's aversion to the Electras had been relatively mild throughout the restriction. In any case, even in America, after a few months passengers were boarding them as confidently as they had before the disasters.

Duncan Bluck's report from America also carried an urgent message. Faster aircraft were coming in on many routes, he said. Let there be no beating about the bush, the jet age had arrived. However much one admired the Electras, one had to admit that their carrying capacity was definitely on the low side. In a series of notes entitled 'Planning', Bluck took cautious but convincing issue with Jock on future policy:

'It has been suggested that it is possible that there would be a future for CPA if they were to concentrate on their secondary routes on which they could operate second class equipment, and withdraw from the highly competitive primary routes. In my opinion no such future exists, as the secondary routes will progressively disappear.' Cathay would then be left with slower, cramped and outdated aircraft trying to combat competition on secondary routes that had become primary routes with several airlines operating modern aircraft on them. Qantas's 707s had driven Cathay's Electras off the Golden Road to Australia. Let Jock banish his doubts – Bluck believed Cathay could find a way to finance a more up-to-date fleet – and would soon positively need to do so.

His views were heeded. At this point in his diaries and memos one notices

Jock beginning to muse much more positively on the subject of jet engines, if not yet on territorial expansion. Boeing 720s, Convair 880s and British VC-10s and Comet 4s become a gleam in Jock Swire's eye, rather as Betsy and CPA had been a gleam in Roy Farrell's and Sydney de Kantzow's eyes twenty years before.

PART THREE

DREAMS FULFILLED

CHAPTER 17

The 1960s represented a change of life for Jock Swire's airline. The Jet Age had inescapably arrived, and there was to be no more time-wasting debate in London or Hong Kong about Cathay's future direction.

An announcement from Cathay's Chairman, Bill Knowles, made no bones about it. 'Our traffic has been sliding towards our jet competitors,' he glumly told his Board in January 1962 – revenue had fallen well below any previous reasonable estimate, only partly owing to the absence of the two Electras flown to Burbank for modification. The chartered BOAC Britannia that stood in for them had meant a reduction in the number of Cathay's flights, and although, when the Electras rejoined the fleet, they settled down very well, they were already *dépassés*.

The Company needed a jet – but which? The Boeing 707 and the Douglas DC-8s were too large for Cathay; the British Comet 4 had had a bad press. But an American firm, General Dynamics Corporation of San Diego, California, had developed an aircraft with a passenger-carrying capacity somewhere between the DC-8 and the Comet: the Convair 880 Jetliner. It was a good-looking jet with high, sweeping wings and a good turn of speed. Japan Air Lines had bought quite a few, and so had Civil Air Transport (CAT) of Taiwan, and the plane was popular with pilots, who called it a 'hot ship'. General Dynamics, being nevertheless somewhat worried about their ability to sell enough Convairs when worldwide demand was for larger and larger planes, were willing to make Cathay a generous offer: immediate delivery and quarterly payments over four years. Engines were offered over a five-year payment period; spares were available in Japan; and HAECO was equipped to service the aircraft. So the Convair it was to be, and seven captains, six first officers and five flight engineers were dispatched to San Diego for the necessary training. When they returned they would fly the new jet between Tokyo–Osaka–Taipei–Hong Kong–Bangkok and Singapore, and on the Hong Kong to Manila run.

The Company's first 880 was flown into Kai Tak from California on 2 April 1962 by Dave Smith, accompanied by Bob Smith, the 'hero' of the Moulmein pagoda incident, Jack Gething's Assistant Chief Engineer, Don Delaney, and Captain Norman Marsh who in time would succeed Dave Smith as Director of Flight Operations.

The Convair's inaugural arrival created great excitement. 'We are proud to have brought the Convair 880-22M Jet Service into being,' a half-page Cathay ad proclaimed in the *South China Morning Post*, signing off with the triumphant words 'Cathay Pacific – Hong Kong's Own Airline'. The *Post* ran a special 'Jet Age Supplement' full of expensive expressions of support and affection from Hong Kong-based companies. Rothman's King Size said: 'Congratulations to Cathay Pacific on the Inauguration of their Convair Jet Service.' Caltex announced their pride in being associated with Cathay Pacific and the inaugural flight of its Convair. Other pats on the back came from Shell, Pan Am, SAS (the Scandinavian airline), Nina Ricci, Haig whisky and Beefeater gin. The *Post*'s own headlines in the Supplement were equally gratifying – 'Cathay Pacific's New Fast Jet Makes Big Impact' – 'Exhaustive Testing of Convair Proves Stamina' – 'The Men Behind the CPA Aircraft'. One admiring article in particular drew attention to the new 'on-top-of-the-clouds' comfort, the tinted glass of the windows, the blue carpeting, the single-stroke chime that summoned the air hostesses – and the jet-age cuisine: kangaroo-tail soup, shark's fin, smorgasbord and the *pièce de résistance* of Cathay's 'flight-kitchen wizard' M. Matti: 'Omelette Surprise Alaska'.

A year later Jack Gething and Captain Ken Steele, architects of Cathay's transformation into an organization that could match flying and maintenance standards with any major airline, retired, to be succeeded by Don Delaney and Dave Smith as Engineering Director and Flight Operations Manager respectively. The rest of Cathay's senior echelon out at Kai Tak is shown in the chart opposite. Cathay's Chief Flight Engineer was W. B. Holyman, a nephew of Jock Swire's collaborator Ivan Holyman.

With the Company 'going jet' the first non-jet redundancy soon followed – Nikki, CPA's second DC-3 bought sixteen years before by Roy Farrell and Syd de Kantzow, was sold to Royal Air Laos for £22,320. The remaining senior citizens of the Cathay fleet – the DC-6, the DC-6B and the last DC-4 – were soon wheeled away into oblivion. By January 1963 the Cathay fleet consisted of one Convair 880 and the two modified Electras, with the Convair covering over 50 per cent of the Company's total passenger miles. A second Convair arrived in November 1964 in part exchange for an Electra. Still a third, bought from VIASA (Venezolana Internacionale de Aviacion

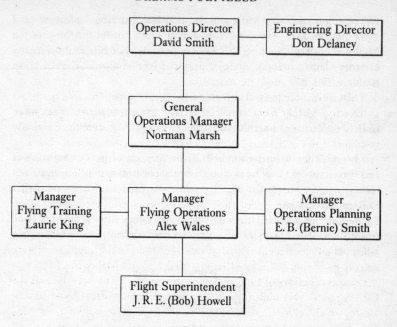

SA) for £1,348,000, followed in November 1965. Things moved fast. The remaining Electra was phased out: five more Convair 880s swelled the Cathay jet family in the next three years, and so within a mere five years – to Duncan Bluck's especial delight – the Company had suddenly become a single-type, all-jet airline. The passenger appeal of the sleek 880s was obvious. They would last into the 1970s.

Though the pilots loved the Convair, the technicians' view of the new aircraft was not, at first, solidly favourable. 'In fact, the 880 had the best airframe ever built,' Don Delaney remembers. 'But we had to make all sorts of changes elsewhere. For example, the 880 engine was initially the source of lots of trouble. It was a light engine that couldn't stand much punishment in the Far Eastern climate. But with the help of General Dynamics, TWA and Delta – they had Convairs, too – we modified it out of sight. And we changed the seats and the interior to accommodate 119 rather than 101 passengers.'

For a few Cathay pilots the Convairs' arrival meant the end of the road. Laurie King says, 'I loved the Convair – and I flew 7,000 hours in it. It was strong and stable. Of course we all had to get used to the swept wings of the jet. But once you got used to it you could cope with its temperament.' If indeed you *could* get used to it. For the truth was that some Cathay pilots of great experience in propeller-driven aircraft simply could not learn how to handle the swept-wing jets. 'The trouble lay,' King told me, 'in the extremely high nose-up attitude jets have to adopt on approach. Older pilots couldn't hack it.'

'Like silent film stars unable to adapt to the talkies?'

'Exactly.' Cathay's ex-Navy pilots, used to high-nosed attitudes when landing on carriers, made the transition to Convairs quicker than anybody else.

The only thing Laurie King had against the Convair was its high rate of fuel consumption. And, he says, they were noisy and smoky, trailing black fumes as if they were on fire. But that was nothing special – most jets did that in those early days.

One Convair chose to show an unaccustomed flash of temperament. The *South China Morning Post* on 7 July 1964 carried the following front-page headline:

FORCED LANDING AT KAI TAK
Nose Wheel Of C.P.A. Airliner Jams
No Casualties

In an accompanying picture 'Captain Lawrence King who brought the CPA jetliner to a safe landing' was to be seen walking away from it with a sombre expression through a crowd of admiring Chinese onlookers. Another showed Chic Eather, King's co-pilot, being embraced by his attractive Chinese wife.

Hundreds of people in the Airport Terminal Building [the newspaper said] watched tensely when the skipper of the aircraft, Capt. Lawrence King, radioed the Control Tower that he would attempt to land.

'The nose wheel mechanism jammed,' Laurie King said later. 'We dived and pulled G [trying to use gravity to free it]. We even tried to open the inspection window and ram in a crowbar to unjam the damn thing. No good, though. The cabin staff were briefed to go through their emergency landing procedures and I made a personal announcement informing the passengers of the exact situation. I emphasized that the touch-down would be normal until the speed reduced to about 80 knots and the nose contacted the runway, when they could expect some sensation of impact. I also told them to stay in their seats until the doors were opened and the emergency chutes were in position. All the passengers were strapped in and shown how to brace for impact.' Like an officer encouraging his men by strolling along the exposed parapet of a front-line trench, Chic Eather walked calmly through the cabin immediately before the landing to check the emergency procedures, and this in King's opinion did much to keep up the passengers' morale.

His conclusion was that it is of extreme importance to kill panic by preparing passengers for the imminent sequence of events – the odd noises and frightening motions during the various stages of impact. He avoided braking to soften the 'nose-down' contact with the runway, and so reduced the sparks. 'I daresay there were a few passengers praying. We were forty-five minutes up there, which is a pretty long time to wait for a tricky landing. Well, in the end I suppose it was pretty straightforward, really. The book tells you what to do. It was a thing that could happen to anybody.'

King's skill earned him a letter from Bill Knowles.

Our very best congratulations and most grateful thanks for extricating your aircraft so successfully from her grave and dangerous position last night. It was a magnificent piece of piloting, and it is evident that you and your crew's handling of the passengers before as well as during the actual landing won their complete confidence, and prevented any behaviour which might have added to the danger. The Board of Directors and Management all wish me to express their admiration and gratitude for the way you and your crew responded to the prolonged strain and the final climax.

At this time of major transition, the Company's leadership too faced changes. First, on 30 September 1964, Bill Knowles, who had been Cathay Pacific's Chairman since 1957, and a non-executive Chairman of the Hongkong and Shanghai Bank, had retired to become Vice-Chancellor of Hong Kong University, an unusual honour. When Knowles died in 1969, Jock, who had known him all his working life and was devoted to him, delivered a moving Address at a memorial service at All Hallows-by-the-Tower in London. He could hardly do justice, he said, to the memory of a man for whom he had had such a high regard for more than thirty years, for the last fifteen of which the two of them had hardly ever been out of touch. 'Although 10,000 miles apart,' Jock recalled sorrowfully, 'we might have been sitting in the same room.'

If in this story Bill Knowles has lurked rather in the shadows, his own diffidence is partly to blame. Even during his lifetime his important role as Swires' Taipan in Cathay's struggle for survival between 1957 and 1964 was a good deal masked by that extraordinary modesty. Knowles, Jock said, had always seemed a little puzzled by his own success. Yet he was a distinguished mathematician – a First at Cambridge – and an imposing presence. Photographs show a wide, substantial figure, feet set solidly on the ground, a fleshy face with eyebrows like black caterpillars and illuminated by a small but benevolent smile. Jock had come to think of Knowles as wise, kind and a rock of reliability, almost a second self.

The first duty of Knowles's successor, H. J. C. (John) Browne, was a happy one – he could announce to his Board at the beginning of 1965 that a dangerous corner had been safely turned. The increase in air traffic, he said, was already 'very pronounced'. During 1963–64 there had been a 26 per cent increase in the number of tourists visiting the Colony by air, and Cathay alone had carried well over half a million passengers in and out of Kai Tak – an increase of 14 per cent. Singapore and Bangkok were now served daily by jet. Most significantly of all, Browne announced the opening of three more Cathay offices in Japan which, with Taiwan, now accounted for 90 per cent of the Convairs' capacity with a service bumped up to fifteen flights a week. The Big Boom, the Japanese economic miracle long predicted by Duncan Bluck (and Browne himself), had materialized. The phoenix had risen from its ashes.

CHAPTER 18

At this satisfactory juncture a second retirement was announced: that of Jock Swire. It was as if a beloved monarch had abdicated, and the shock of the announcement was only slightly relieved by another that said he would stay on as Honorary President of Cathay Pacific Airways. His place on the Cathay Board was to be taken by his second son, Adrian, a doubly appropriate appointment since Adrian was an enthusiastic pilot in his own right, and his elder son, John, succeeded as Chairman of John Swire & Sons in London. Yet this was not the end of Jock. The soldierly figure with the trilby and the baggy suit, the battered briefcase and the suitcase held together with fraying rope would not disappear from the airports of the Far East. Far from it. As a sprightly septuagenarian, he had visited Bill Knowles in Hong Kong to take a look at the new Convair, pronouncing it 'a lovely aircraft and very quiet'. After a prolonged globetrot that included Australia and a call on General Dynamics at San Diego, he had noted in his diary:

> Reached London Airport as early as 4 p.m. and found a strike of porters and had to handle our own baggage, so got through very quick. Met by Adrian and home by 6 p.m. 35,000 miles in 18 different aeroplanes and slept in 26 different beds. . . . A very successful trip. I have put on 7lbs. and feel ten years younger.

Jock would continue to bound about the world until he was nearly ninety. Still, his retirement closed an era. To everyone in Swires and Cathay, even to Jock himself, it seemed a very long time since the day in 1914 when he had sailed into Hong Kong's wonderful harbour and first glimpsed from the deck of the Blue Funnel steamer the Peak and the sunlit, green hills of the New Territories rising into China. A long time, too, since his return from the Western Front to take Swire's staff under his wing and pen in his diary, 'The reason why B&S lack *esprit de corps* is because London are not sufficiently human or sufficiently acquainted with local colour. . . .' It had almost amounted to a manifesto.

Suddenly it was time to reflect on the nature of the man and on the meaning of Jock's leadership. Those who worked with him speak of Jock as a great man; but that does not mean he was free of all human failing. His son Adrian points to an angry, impatient side to his father that now and again erupted with Vesuvian effect. 'He didn't stand fools or malingerers gladly. He could be quite frightening – he gave his senior colleagues hell from time to time. But it was never his way to bully his juniors. He was not a bully. Ever.'

Mrs Joan Esnouf who was Jock's personal secretary and assistant for many years, including those of the Second World War and the Blitz, says of him: 'Terribly generous. Terribly impulsive. Terribly impatient.'

'Autocratic?'

'No-o-o. Not that. And not really frightening – he had this saving sense of humour, you see. He had a temper, yes, but if he was in the wrong he became very upset and would rush back into the room crying, "Oh, I'm so sorry. I'm so terribly sorry. Oh, dear. Excuse me." He was so human. I remember a little secretary, a new girl, said, "I'm so glad Mr Swire's back off holiday next week. It's like a dead office without him." He loved the family idea of Swires. When the wartime government rationed food he used to bring a bottle of milk from one of his own Jersey cows in his old attaché case, just for him and me. I expect you've heard about the attaché case. Its four corners were worn away and patched with leather. He loved that little case.'

In his time Jock *was* Cathay Pacific, just as Roy and Syd had been. He made Mrs Esnouf think of Mary Stuart and Calais: she almost believed they would find CPA written on his heart if the Company ever failed. A compulsive traveller on Cathay's behalf to his dying day, Jock was a compulsive worker (and writer) as well: everything went down into memos, official letters, private letters and that personal diary. However exhausting a day had been, Jock wrote up his impressions of it.

He'd say, 'I like getting things off my chest.' Striding up and down and fiddling with his watch-chain as if it were a string of worry beads, he'd dictate pages of letters to Hong Kong, sometimes long after everyone but he and Joan Esnouf had gone home. 'It was like talking to himself. If he wasn't satisified with the day's long telegrams to Hong Kong, he'd back them up with letters. He liked to record *everything*.'

While this book was in preparation I lost count of the number of former employees now retired in Australia, Britain, New Zealand, America or Hong Kong, who happily recalled meetings with Jock Swire in offices or on airfields, in aeroplanes or at Company parties, at which inevitably he had hailed them by name as if they had been his own nephews and nieces. The Cathay family feeling was unfailingly reinforced whenever Jock made an appearance. Of course, things have changed. Success has increased the tally of Cathay's employees to such a number that no living soul could put a name to all of them on sight. Even by the late 1960s, Cathay's staff totalled 1,372, of whom 109 were captains, first officers and flight engineers. Nowadays the total staff numbers some 9,000 with the cockpit crew figure getting on for 800, and still growing.

Everything one reads or hears of Jock Swire demonstrates his two greatest virtues – an inflexible dedication to straight dealing and an extraordinary humanity. People said that his handshake was every bit as good as a signed contract (not, by the way, something that could be said of many business leaders in Hong Kong's rough-and-tumble history). And as we have seen, his private diaries register the most homely details: that maddening stomach upset on the Yangtze River; the hat stolen in Shanghai; the crying need for some curtains and a kitchen range for the occupants of the Taikoo house in Hangkow.

Jock Swire's life is not the story of a superman who took a mangy little airline by the scruff of the neck and with splendid, unhesitating gestures raised it to enormous triumph. There were hesitations galore, and misjudgements, too. Adrift in the barely understood world of Air, a world composed of contending forces of terrific intensity, Jock thought quite seriously once or twice of giving up and returning to familiar earth, but he was not one to panic and he stuck it out. He too had his romantic side. In his cautious, old-fashioned English gentleman's way, he shared the vision of Roy Farrell and Sydney de Kantzow.

Now he was gone and a new generation came to the fore. Thirty-nine years old when he became Chairman, John took over Jock's traditional responsibility for the Company's staff, and the noticeably high quality of Swires' expatriate employees in the East (it is universally remarked upon) must owe a good deal to him. Twenty-one years later he too retired to be Honorary President, and Adrian inherited the Chairmanship.

Adrian was to have more direct dealings with Cathay Pacific than John. Born in 1932, he had joined Butterfield & Swire in the Far East at the age of twenty-four after Eton and University College, Oxford, and a spell in the Coldstream Guards. After five years learning the business in Hong Kong, Japan and Australia, he had returned to the directorship in London in 1961. Adrian Swire was well suited to aviation; he was born with a love of flying as others are born with a love of the sea. He had learned to fly as a very young man; joined the University Air Squadron at Oxford; and later enrolled in Hong Kong's Auxiliary Air Force. In 1969 he bought a private Spitfire Mark IX, which he kept for fifteen years, managing, he says proudly, 'to get it off the ground and down again regularly over that period without ever breaking anything.' Apart from his directorship of Cathay Pacific, he became Chairman of the China Navigation Co. in 1967, and fifteen years later this dedicated flyer was knighted for his services to British shipping.

The succession of Jock's two sons ensured continuity of the family feeling. It was not difficult for those who had known Jock to feel his spirit reborn in John and Adrian. John was not unlike the old man in appearance – a towering, rather military figure with an easy laugh. Adrian, though physically less a replica of his father and certainly less intimidating, shared all Jock's enthusiasm for travel, people and, of course, for Cathay Pacific Airways. Both brothers inherited their father's openness and his fondness for coming straight to the point. The Swire family's benevolently patriarchal control of its empire had been re-emphasized to the satisfaction of everyone in it.

What the airline now amounted to was well set out in an article written in 1968 from Hong Kong by Derek Davies for the *Financial Times* of London.

Size for size, the airline – Cathay Pacific Airways – must be one of the most successful commercial operations in aviation today. Yet it is a private company and has no Government subsidy. Thus, despite the decline in British influence in that area, a British airline plays a leading role throughout an area of the approximate size of North America and straddling 13 Asian countries. It is by far the largest regional carrier in the Far East. . . .

What is it that particularly attracts the passenger to Cathay Pacific? Partly the convenience and frequency of schedules. But in its cabin service the airline is no longer just British: it is international. About 35 per cent of the pilots are from the UK, 60 per cent from Australia and 5 per cent from New Zealand. Cabin service crews are drawn from all the main countries to which Cathay Pacific flies – Koreans, Japanese, Taiwanese, Filipinas, Hong Kong Chinese, Thais, Indians, Malaysians, and Singaporeans. All speak excellent English (mandatory for all staff) plus their own national language. Food, too, is international – everything from Malayan satay and tempura to steaks and lamb chops prepared under the control of highly trained Swiss chefs. Economy passengers also get a pre-meal cocktail, and wine with their meal. . . .

Derek Davies's article must have been a great boost to Cathay's image. Wine, cocktails and an international cuisine controlled by Swiss chefs! It was a long way from the DC-3 world of Vera Rosario, the world of bucket seats, coffee and sandwiches, and the horrendous bumps that made you feel you were in a high-speed elevator and spilled hot tea all over poor Jo Cheng.

Editors everywhere were suddenly paying attention to Cathay Pacific, this new-born phenomenon out of the East. 'Most remarkable,' an aviation correspondent, John Seekings, wrote in *Aeroplane*, 'Cathay's record has been achieved in the most highly competitive area in the world. Between Tokyo and Hong Kong, for instance, there are no fewer than fifteen carriers competing for services. Between Bangkok and Hong Kong, another key route, there are twelve carriers sharing the market.' What were the advantages, he asked, that enabled Cathay to be such a sudden success after a period of solid but unspectacular performance? He pinpointed several basic factors. First, the sheer attraction of Hong Kong as a tourist centre and as one of the few places in the world where very high-grade labour – skilled and energetic – is available relatively cheaply. Second, the region is one in which Swires have unique experience. Next, sound organization.

Then there was HAECO, now one of the major aircraft engineering companies in the world, employing 2,000, offering high-quality engineering at low prices to Cathay and the owners of the 1,500-odd aircraft which passed through its hangars each year. And finally there was Cathay's air catering service and Swire's share (with Jardine Matheson) in Hong Kong Air Terminal Services (HATS) which organized all the passenger-boarding and aircraft ground-handling at Kai Tak Airport.

The *Aeroplane* article made much of the quality of Cathay's flight crew recruits and the generous rates of pay, then £9,500 a year for a married Senior Captain with two children. Because of this, the article said, 600 pilots had applied recently for twenty vacancies. Allied to this, small aviation companies found it difficult as a rule to attract high-calibre management recruits, but Cathay was part of the much larger Swire group of companies, with 10,000 employees in a wide range of activities (trading, shipping, shipbuilding, property) in an exotic part of the world. If you joined Cathay, you signed up for the opportunities enjoyed by the whole group. Finally, *Aeroplane* said, and more important than any other factor, had been Jock Swire's early insistence on taking into management only the top class of graduates in the graduate-recruiting scheme he had set up way back in the 1920s. *Aeroplane* did Cathay no more than justice.

Yet no echo of this eulogy can be found in the office records of Cathay Pacific Airways or in Jock Swire's private diaries. There, self-congratulation is, and always has been, taboo. Even mildly hopeful predictions of the Company's future course are packed round with cautious phrases like 'with luck' or 'should things go well'. Success was never to be taken on trust, for Jock was a steadfast believer in the dangers of *hubris*, the overweening pride which, the Greeks thought, drew down sooner or later on human heads a terrible corrective from the gods. 'Pride goes before a fall' was a maxim no Swire employee needed to pin to his office wall. It was stamped on his brain from the day he joined.

Thus, typically, John Browne at this moment of early success: 'We have had successes. We must be wary of over-optimism for the future. Competition from the world's major airlines is hotting up. A new spaciousness is coming into air travel with 747 Boeing aircraft able to carry from 350 to 450 passengers looming in the early 1970s. Fares are dropping and we shall undoubtedly continue to have to fight every inch of the way.' Spoken like a true Swire man.

What a melancholy thing it is to have to record that Cathay Pacific Airways, having cast out *hubris* and standing at long last on a plateau of unaccustomed success, was hit by not one but two mishaps. The second of these was as great and as unmerited a tragedy as any that has struck any airline anywhere in the world.

CHAPTER 19

Senior First Officer Ian Steven was in the left-hand seat. Captain Ron Jackson-Smith sat on his right-hand with the young Flight Engineer, Ken Hickey, just behind him facing the flashing lights of his switchboard. It was a fine November morning and Steven taxied Convair VR-HFX away from Kai Tak's Terminal Building in the warm sunlight of Guy Fawkes' Day.

The flight was a full one: 116 passengers to Saigon, Bangkok and Calcutta, a good number of them South Korean engineers and merchant navy seamen and Vietnamese civilians. It was also a 'check', or monitoring, flight. That meant that the normal complement of two pilots, Steven and Jackson-Smith in this case, was increased by one, a Check Captain, Bob Howell, there to assess the performance of the other two – of the First Officer's suitability for promotion to Captain, and the Captain's suitability for appointment as Training Captain on the line. In these perfectly normal circumstances Steven was in control of the aircraft, Jackson-Smith occupied the co-pilot's seat, while Bob Howell breathed down both their necks from the 'jump seat', the spare seat behind the pilot. It is probably worth adding that, although this was a 'check' flight, all three men were fully qualified to fly Convairs.

At 10.30 a.m. the Control Tower signalled 'cleared for take-off'. Steven called to the Flight Engineer for maximum power and away she went. Everything normal. Faster . . . faster. . . . At 122 knots, well below take-off speed, the plane began to vibrate.

'This vibration increased', Steven said later, 'and became very severe; the whole aircraft was shaking.'

No one on the flight deck could tell what it meant, Steven couldn't control it and, to add to the bewilderment, Bob Howell thought he had heard a loud bang just as the vibrations started. Had a bird been sucked into an engine? The question was academic – the Convair had to attempt to rise into the air or stay on the runway and try to stop without hitting anything. The shaking was now so bad that the aircraft might not be able to fly, and Ian Steven had to make the split-second decision of a lifetime – and he made it. 'Aborting!' he yelled, and wrenched back the power levers and slammed on the brakes.

'I had my feet hard on those brakes and heard Bob Howell shouting, "Maximum brakes!"' Steven says. 'Trouble was the braking didn't seem normal. The aircraft just didn't decelerate. My God! I reached across for the reverse thrust levers, and yanked 'em right back.'

For all the effect it had he might just as well have combed his hair. The aircraft continued to speed ahead as in a nightmare. With her brakes fully applied – doubly applied in fact, since Steven could feel Jackson-Smith also pressing on the right-hand pedals – and reverse thrust from all engines, VR-HFX began to veer to the right. The end of the runway was getting closer by that time, and Steven, having applied full left rudder to counter the slew to the right and feeling no response from the rudder or nose wheel steering, could only brace his legs against the rudder pedals and his hands against the instrument coaming as the plane roared across the grass flanking the runway towards the waters of Kowloon Bay. Like a drowning man he saw a good many of his thirty-four years flash vividly through his mind in the fleeting moments before the Convair took the sea wall like a steeplechaser rising to a hurdle. Then she put her nose down, and dived into the harbour in a spectacular cloud of spray.

Ian Steven did not drown. Luckily for him, Ron Jackson-Smith and Ken Hickey, the fuselage cracked just behind the cockpit when it hit the water and, although the cockpit itself did submerge, the greater part of the plane's body stayed afloat. It lay there about eighty yards from the sea wall, like a lazy silver whale with a broken nose.

'The three of us in the cockpit were unhurt,' Steven says, 'and I saw Ken Hickey trying to open the cockpit door. The damned thing had jammed. We decided to abandon the aircraft by the sliding windows on the flight deck and they opened without any trouble. The water level was just below the left-side window and I virtually swam straight out once I'd seen the other two go out of the starboard one.'

Bob Howell had been between the two pilots, standing behind them.

'When I saw that the aircraft was unstoppable and heading across the grass strip for the Bay, I dived smartly out of the cabin and wedged myself between two seated little Chinese girls. I had no belt on of course, so I got bumped around a bit when we went over into the water. I remember one of the Chinese girls saying nervously, "I can't swim, Captain." At first many passengers had wanted to make for the rear door and shouted to Chief

Purser Chir to let them out. Well, if he had done so he'd have let the water in and then the plane's tail would have subsided and disaster would have been certain for those inside. So Chir urged them all to wait to get out the front way. He won an award for that.'

Despite his confident smile Bob Howell could swim no better than the little Chinese girl and found himself stuck half in, half out of the front passenger door – all Ian Steven saw as he swam up was Bob's bald head and an arm sticking out. Steven yanked the door open and 'the next thing, Bob was floating away and the two little Chinese girls who couldn't swim were sitting on my head'. Untangling themselves, they struggled to a rescue boat. Several were already there, thanks to an alert Traffic Control Officer who had sounded the crash alarm when he saw the plane going over the sea wall. Tugs and launches crowded round the long fuselage, and even the cross-harbour ferry boat *Man Shun* had swung off its course between Hong Kong Island and Yaumati to reach the port wing where many passengers were huddling, having escaped through the emergency exits. Others squeezed through cracks in the hull. Later, they all praised the cabin crew, composed on this occasion of Japanese and Thais as well as Hong Kong Chinese. One Korean seaman said the Cathay cabin girls were the heroines of the day. 'Most of the women passengers lost their heads and began shouting. The stewardesses did everything to bring order. If not, I don't think I'd be here.'

An American lady, Mrs Barrett, said that the plane was rushing along the runway at high speed when suddenly she felt a sharp braking that jolted the entire aircraft; then came a bump. 'We shot into the water. My husband quickly helped me unfasten my seat belt' and she followed fellow-passengers through the emergency exit onto the wing. A pretty Korean crooner on her way to entertain Allied troops in Vietnam wept for her missing passport. 'I hope this accident will not prevent me from doing my duty to the boys in Vietnam,' she moaned seductively. The press cameras flashed and she was soon comforted by reporters and discharged her duty in due course. As Duncan Bluck remembers it, an Indian passenger claimed that he had lost a bag crammed with thousands of dollars, his life savings, and demanded compensation double quick. Bluck arranged for divers to make a special search; but when they brought up the bag it contained nothing but a bundle of well-worn dhotis.

Of the 116 passengers and eleven crew aboard, eighty-two of the passengers and all the crew escaped unhurt, although thirty-three passengers were treated in hospital. Tragically one passenger, a Vietnamese woman, died at the moment of impact from a fractured skull.

How did this experience affect the crew? According to Ian Steven: 'I hadn't smoked for some time, but I must have had five or six cigarettes on the ferry taking us ashore. Going over the sea wall I had thought I was dead.' He didn't stay dead long. He was flying again almost at once, and as I write is still flying for Cathay as a Senior Captain on Boeing 747s, although talking of his retirement in Australia or New Zealand.

Still dripping from the wreck, Bob Howell telephoned his wife as soon as he got ashore. 'Good heavens, Bob,' she said, expecting him to be well on his way to Saigon. 'Where are you?' 'Oh, just having a swim.' But despite his light tone, he was as shocked as Ian Steven. As the plane swerved off onto the runway's grass verge and headed towards the harbour, he had heard himself silently screaming, 'This can't be ME!' For both men the great uncontrollable rush towards the Bay had seemed to go on for ever. Witnesses in the Kai Tak Control Tower could tell them that actually, from Steven's shout of 'Aborting!' to the sickening plunge into the harbour, a mere twenty-one seconds had elapsed.

The Convair had been seriously damaged. Crane barges had difficulty towing the wreck to the RAF slipway, and once there, in order to lift it ashore, a cable was slung around the fuselage. When winching began, it was found too late that part of the tail was embedded in the harbour mud and the cable cut through the fuselage like a wire through cheese. The aircraft was finally brought ashore in pieces while all four engines stayed on the bottom of the Bay. They too were recovered, badly damaged. But Convair 880 VR-HFX was a total wreck.

Over the signatures of John Bremridge, Managing Director; Dave Smith, Alec Wales, Don Delaney and R. J. Smith, Cathay's Training Manager, the Company's report blamed the accident mainly on the sudden shredding of the right-hand nose wheel tyre. Retreaded more than once, as was customary, the tyre had disintegrated causing the terrible shaking. With the nose wheel to all intents and purposes gone, Ian Steven lost his ability to steer with it, hence the uncontrollable swerve to the right. The Goodyear Company, the manufacturers of the tyre, stated in its report that it believed foreign objects on the runway – markers, lights and so on – might have torn the retread. The Cathay report recommended that retreading of nose wheel tyres should be more carefully monitored. Both reports completely exonerated the flying crew and congratulated the cabin staff for preventing panic and an even worse disaster.

Even so, it was a bad day for Cathay. For a time 'See the Bay with CPA' became a local joke. Worse, the Company had lost an aircraft when its fleet was already at full stretch, though it was some consolation that Don Delaney was able to salvage something financially from the wreck. 'We had a fantastic amount of spare parts from it,' he said, 'and the hull we sold quite well for scrap.'

The accident had come just as John Browne was preparing to announce the Company's acquisition of a HK$7.5 million (about £500,000) Convair simulator from Japan. This would reduce the need to use real and expensive aircraft for crew training and, of course, the risk of losing them. Now, thanks to Don Delaney's brilliant gift for improvisation, a number of bits and pieces from the carcase of poor Convair VR-HFX went into this new Japanese electronic wonder.

Delaney also had the presence of mind to rescue the Convair's registration plate. When Howell retired, Delaney presented it to him as a souvenir. Bob had it mounted on wood above the legend: 'The One He Swam Away From – VR-HFX 5.11.67', and it hangs on Bob's living room wall.

CHAPTER 20

The Kai Tak mishap had been caused by a few feet of worn rubber. It could have happened to anyone. Five years later a second Cathay Convair became the centre of a horror story embracing multiple death, mystery and the pursuit of an alleged mass murderer.

On 15 June 1972 a 'Top Urgent' message to Swires in London brought news of the airline's worst tragedy:

MUCH REGRET ADVISE CV880 REGISTRATION VR-HFZ INVOLVED MIDAIR COLLISION
ABOUT 0600 RPT 0600 WEST OF QUINON SOUTH VIETNAM WHILE ENROUTE FROM
BANGKOK TODAY UNDER COMMAND CAPTAIN NEIL MORISON. TOTAL 81
PASSENGERS CREW ON BOARD. BLUCK WILL PHONE.

Duncan Bluck had been out on his sailing boat that morning; it was lucky that a Cathay captain had seen him setting off and was able to find him and bring him back. Neither Bluck nor anyone else connected with Cathay Pacific would get much sleep for several days. A midair collision? Over Vietnam, too. That complicated things for the American war with North Vietnam was then at its height.

Next day came a follow-up message. Jock, John and Adrian Swire and Michael Fiennes, suffering mental agonies in London, learned that a Cathay investigation team flown from Hong Kong to South Vietnam the night before had already been lifted by American Army helicopters to the scene of the crash, far up in a remote, forested region of the Central Highlands near the town of Pleiku. The team was led by Captain Bernie Smith, Cathay's Operations Manager, and included Brian Thompson, the Chief Engineer, representatives of HAECO and of Hong Kong's Department of Civil Aviation, notably Cyril Wray, the Colony's Accident Inspector.

Peter Sharrock, Reuters' bureau chief in Saigon, was quickly onto the story and his first urgent dispatch quoted an American military spokesman as saying that the Convair had collided in midair with some unidentified aircraft, and that one of the two planes had fallen midway between Pleiku city and the port of Qui Nhon on a mountain range about 250 miles northeast of Saigon. The collision was merely presumed, although the spokesman added that no locally based military aircraft was listed as missing, and yet the theory did seem plausible since commercial airliners like Cathay's regularly flew across Vietnam at about 30,000 feet, an altitude sometimes favoured by the high-flying American B-52 bombers based on Guam. Nevertheless, nothing in the wreckage spotted so far bore the green and black colours of a B-52; the tail plane in the jungle was silver.

A dispatch from Agence France Presse added to the speculation, quoting a Vietnamese Government spokesman who said that the second plane had been a Nationalist Chinese C-46 military transport from Taiwan, not a B-52. The report added that uniformed Montagnard tribesmen (the friendly hill-people of central Vietnam) were poking about the wreckage in gas masks in appalling heat, while aviation experts tried to read some sort of message in the widely scattered bits and pieces. It even hinted that there might be some survivors.

Into this tortured uncertainty the *Hong Kong Standard* decided to jump with both feet. On 16 June a front page banner headline proclaimed 'CPA Ignored Air Warning', and in fine thumping vein went on: 'Cathay Pacific ignored three warnings – one by the Hong Kong Government – to stay out of the Vietnam air "corridor" that claimed the lives of eighty-one people yesterday.' It would be hard to imagine a more damaging allegation the day after such an accident, and it struck everyone at Cathay a second blow almost as devastating as the first. It came before any reliable facts were available, and it was wholly false. Duncan Bluck, after alerting Cathay's legal advisers, put out an emphatic rebuttal which in the circumstances he managed to keep remarkably calm.

Cathay Pacific have announced that there is no truth whatever in the report printed in the *Hong Kong Standard* to the effect that the airline had ignored warnings regarding designated airways.

Cathay Pacific have made it clear that the routing of their Convair 880 VR-HFZ on Thursday 15th June was through the international airway between Bangkok and Hong Kong used by the majority of carriers on that routing. Furthermore, a position report was received at the designated reporting point which was approximately four minutes prior to the accident and it is therefore known that the aircraft was on track and in communication with Saigon control.

The following day the *Standard* did an about-face. In a headline display on its front page, as eye-catching as the original calumny had been, the words 'Apology To Cathay Pacific Airways' were followed by 'The *Hong Kong Standard* acknowledges that our report was wholly inaccurate and regrets the false impression created by [it]. The *Standard* wishes to make it clear to its readers that Cathay Pacific Airways have at no time ignored any warnings or failed to accept any recommendations which are made in the interests of the safety and comfort of its passengers.'

The paper unreservedly acknowledged the untruth of its own reported slice of fiction and apologized to Cathay for permitting it to be published. It was a rapid and handsome apology and the *Standard* ran it for two days.

With that distressing distraction out of the way, all thoughts could turn to the search for survivors and to discovering the cause of the disaster. This was not easy. One of the first two Vietnamese helicopters to have found the wreckage was shot down next day by the Viet Cong or North Vietnamese Army units infesting the region, but despite the dangers and difficulties of the war zone Cyril Wray, Bernie Smith and their colleagues poked about the crash site in almost unbearable heat and humidity, charting and identifying the various bits and pieces. They soon reported that major parts of the wreckage could be removed to Saigon for closer examination by Vietnamese, American and Hong Kong experts, with accident investigators expected to arrive at any moment from Britain.

The first Cathay announcement of the disaster had spoken of eighty-one passengers and crew. There had actually been seventy-one passengers of a variety of nationalities, mostly Japanese, Thai and American. Two complete families had been on the Convair: at Bangkok seven members of an American family called Kenny had boarded together; and a Filipino civil servant, Norberto Fernandez, his wife, his niece and his five children were on their way home to Manila. 'There's a possibility of survivors,' the Saigon spokesman had said, but a telegram from Bernie Smith put paid to that hope: 'Returned from crash site definitely nil repeat nil survivors.' That dreadful message, according to Adrian Swire, left everyone in Swires' London office feeling almost intolerably remote and miserable; Joan Esnouf recalls seeing old Jock in tears. The Convair's Captain had been an Australian, Neil Morison, Fleet Captain of the 880s fleet and a friend of Adrian Swire from his Hong Kong Auxiliary Air Force days. First Officer Lachlan Mackenzie had flown 2,687 hours in Convairs and had been flying the aircraft under routine instruction from Morison. The right-hand seat had been occupied by First Officer Leslie Boyer and the Flight Engineer was Ken Hickey, one of the Cathay crew who had swum to safety from Convair VR-HFX after her plunge into Kowloon Bay. The Hong Kong Chinese cabin crew consisted of two pursers, Dicky Kong and William Yuen, and four hostesses – Winnie Chan, Ellen Cheng, Tammy Li and Florence Ng.

To the Vietnamese helicopter pilots who first spotted it, all that was left of the Convair, strewn across an area of wooded hillsides, must have looked like the debris of a monstrous paper-chase, but even so an initial close-up inspection of the crash site told the investigators a good deal. Before hitting the ground the aircraft had broken into three main parts: the nose (all that part ahead of the wing), the central fuselage (where the wings join it and the landing gear joins the wings), and the aft fuselage behind the wings. This last part had fallen vertically and been impaled on a tree. The force of the fall from the plane's normal flying altitude of 29,000 feet had compressed it into a mere six feet, crushing seats, galleys and overhead racks; on its right side there were distinct signs of scorching. A search round the wreckage showed that many passengers had been thrown out, although some were still strapped in their seats. The cockpit too was hideously crushed and virtually inaccessible. Bernie Smith spoke delicately of the 'unpleasant proximity of crew remains'.

Behind a protective cordon of American troops (the Viet Cong were close at hand), the investigating team concentrated on the landing gear beam situated where the wheels and wings join the fuselage, for there they found significant signs of structural failure. It was at this point that the idea of sabotage rather than collision first crept into their minds. It was too early to be sure of anything – structural failure, after all, could mean metal fatigue. However, when the suspect parts had been moved to Saigon and two British Government experts from the Accident Investigation Branch of Whitehall's Department of Trade and Industry had looked at them more closely, a still more significant discovery was made. A small crater was detected on the inside of the aircraft's skin where it was attached to the main landing gear beam; a crater, they decided, caused by an explosion of some sort of infernal device in the part of the cabin nearest the right wing. Such a device would certainly have fragmented, and some fragments would equally certainly have embedded themselves in the passengers and in the seats nearest to the explosion. Who had been in those seats? It became a matter of urgency to X-ray the remains of passengers known to have been seated in that area and, sure enough, metallic particles were found embedded in their limbs. Further tests confirmed that these particles were indeed fragments of a bomb.

Even while the tests were in progress, the joint Vietnamese–American–Hong Kong team ruled out the earliest hypothesis. The collision theory went by the board when it was found that without doubt there had been no movement of military or commercial aircraft in the region at the time of the crash. The other possibility considered, that of a SAM surface-to-air missile attack by the North Vietnamese, was also discounted because all the bomb fragments found on the Convair were of light metal whereas military missile fragments are large, heavy and thick. Furthermore, a missile is designed to shatter an aircraft over its entire length, and this had not happened to the Convair. Apart from that, once the warhead had exploded on contact with its target the body of any missile – a pretty hefty object – would have fallen very near the aircraft wreckage. A careful search revealed no such thing.

The state and positioning of the bodies, too, told their own story. The aft fuselage section contained fifteen bodies – two cabin attendants, the rest passengers: a purser was dressed in his in-flight meals service jacket; some of the passengers were in the aisle, others in the toilet area. Twenty feet from the wreckage a flight hostess lay in full uniform; she was wearing her serving apron. She was badly injured around the face, but her body had made only a shallow indentation in fairly soft ground, from which it was clear that she had fallen from the aircraft at a relatively low altitude. A little forward of the aircraft's nose the Second Purser, Dicky Kong, lay spreadeagled on his back, his face swollen but undamaged, the two-bar insignia on his shoulders confirming his identity. The nearby body of a male passenger in the clothes of a priest was easily identified as that of the only Irish passenger, a Father Cunningham. When the mangled cockpit was prised open, the first body to be recovered was that of Captain Morison, identifiable only by his epaulettes and by his build. Later, in the Saigon mortuary, the bodies of Leslie Boyer and Ken Hickey, too, were identified. Lachlan Mackenzie was missing (and was never found).

Because, when disaster struck, some passengers had had their seat belts fastened and some had not; because some evidently had been standing in the aisle; because all doors were locked and all life jackets stowed normally; because, as far as anyone could tell in the shambles of the cockpit, the crew had not donned their oxygen masks – for all these reasons, coupled with the readings taken from the aircraft's 'black box' flight recorder which was retrieved only slightly damaged, it was established to expert satisfaction that everyone aboard had been taken totally by surprise. Whatever had destroyed Cathay's Convair VR-HFX sixty-four minutes and two seconds after take-off from Bangkok's Don Muang Airport, the plane had been flying normally at the time.

One can assume from their dress that the pursers and hostesses were busy serving lunch when the end came. Without warning something had happened: the stricken aircraft had turned over on its back and broken up into quite large sections during its plunge to earth, shedding bodies as it fell. The best one can say is that certainly everyone – passengers and crew – lost consciousness in the massive decompression which followed the explosion.

What exactly had happened, so brutally, so suddenly? It was time for the bomb experts to give their opinion. Vernon Clancy, a distinguished British explosives expert and a veteran of ninety-six bomb investigations, cleared the air a bit more. In his confidential report to the Vietnamese Director of Civil Aviation, Saigon, he stated bluntly, 'There is firm evidence of an explosion of a substantial quantity of high explosive within the aircraft, probably within the cabin in way of the wing roots.' This 'firm evidence' expanded on the first report of a small crater in the aircraft's skin. By now a number of such craters, large and minute, had been found on the inner skin and near the No. 3 fuel tank. Within one of them partly fused fibres were visible, suggesting that a fragment had passed through the carpet in the passenger cabin.

Experiments with a typical high explosive in a thin metal container had produced very similar craters to those found in the Convair's wing roots and particles very like those recovered from the bodies. Clancy was unable to identify the explosive exactly, but he believed it was one with a high velocity of detonation, a military explosive, perhaps, or one used commercially for blasting. C-3 or C-4 high explosives, packing twenty times the power of TNT, could have done the trick; both looked like chewing gum and could be squeezed into any shape at all.

Meticulous examination of the wreckage coupled with Clancy's findings led Eric Newton, the British Civil Aviation Department's Chief Inspector of Accidents, to the following reconstruction of events. As Cathay's flight CX700 sped serenely from Thailand into South Vietnam, a bomb had exploded between rows nine and ten on the Convair's right side, blowing out a largish section of the right cabin wall over the wing, indicating that at least two kilograms had been used. At least one passenger and a seat or two had been sucked out of this big hole and whipped backwards to strike the right-hand stabilizer so violently that it broke off. At the same time escaping fuel from the punctured right-hand tank ignited and flames streamed back along the right-hand side of the fuselage. Without its right-hand stabilizer, the aircraft had pitched suddenly upwards with great force, yawed to the right and turned on its back. The explosion having severed the flying controls beneath the cabin floor, the crew had no hope of controlling these erratic, high-speed manoeuvres. In the sickening vertical plunge tail-first that followed, the aft fuselage began to separate from the wing; the rudder and all four engines separated (only No. 3 engine was recovered); the landing-gear went at about 10,000 feet; and the front section snapped off, too.

Eric Newton was quite sure that there had been an explosion between seat rows 9 and 10 on the right side; that meant on or under seats 10E or 10F. A check of Cathay's records showed that these two seats had been occupied – by a Miss Somwang Prompim and a Miss Somthaya Chaiyasuta, both of whom had boarded at Bangkok. Cathay's District Sales Manager in the Bangkok office, Mr Allan Chao, found that the two passengers had been booked to travel to Hong Kong by twenty-nine-year-old Police Lieutenant Somchai Chaiyasuta of the Police Aviation Division, stationed at Bangkok Airport. Chao further reported to his boss, Jock Campbell, Cathay's Manager for Thailand, that after the crash of CX700, officials of New Zealand Insurance and American International Assurance had telephoned him with some very interesting information: the former had sold a travel accident policy for 1 million baht (then about US$50,000) to a Miss S. Prompim, and the latter had sold two policies, one to Miss Prompim for 2 million baht and one to Miss Chaiyasuta for 100,000 baht. The beneficiary in each case was Lieutenant Somchai. Mr Chao went on:

> On Friday morning [16th June], Lt. Somchai and his sister came to our office to make necessary arrangements to proceed to Saigon [as next-of-kin]. The secretary to our Manager was taking care of him while I was sitting in my office. I heard him mention to the secretary something about insurance which brought to my attention [sic]. I then went out from my office to ask him where did he buy the insurance. He told me that he bought the policy at the airport before departure. I then asked how much did he buy. He said one million baht for his wife and one hundred thousand for his daughter. He did not mention any other policy with other company and I did not ask him any other question either.

When this news reached Duncan Bluck in Hong Kong he wrote to Swires in London: 'For your information there is one major suspect who is a lieutenant in the Thai police and who is at present in Saigon with some of the other next-of-kin. He is alleged to have insured his common law wife and daughter for a large sum. It is known that they had no hold baggage, and only one suitcase which was placed under the seat specifically requested by him for his common law wife.'

CHAPTER 21

Cathay Pacific now urgently called on their Chief Security Officer to begin a little snooping on his own in Bangkok. Geoffrey Binstead was a Far Eastern hand and a security operative of great experience whose long and adventurous career had started with the British Colonial Police in Palestine in the days before the British Mandate there came to its violent end in 1948. Much more recently he had formed his own security company in Hong Kong, a major undertaking with a staff of several hundred. Burly, handsome and tall, with wavy hair and blue eyes, Binstead was a 'character', indefatigable and fearless. He was also a jolly extrovert with a policeman's shrewdness born of decades of close-range contemplation of sinful humanity. There were, people said admiringly, no flies at all on Geoffrey Binstead.

He now embarked on what he was later to describe as 'a very weary and trying period'. He instantly made it his top priority to establish an excellent and amicable rapport with the Royal Thai Police officers who were investigating the case. And he was careful to keep the British Embassy informed of his progress, although the Ambassador, Sir Arthur de la Mare, made it very clear to him that 'if things went sour I collected the acid.'

Binstead picked up a titbit or two on a flying visit to Saigon. Mark Henniker-Major, Cathay's Assistant Sales Manager, and Patrick Tsai, the Deputy Sales Manager, were both there from Hong Kong and had been coping against odds with the stridently emotional next-of-kin of the crash victims. The large contingent of agitated Japanese was particularly vociferous and many of them were not – as they should have been – relatives of the deceased, but colleagues or even mere acquaintances. Seventeen Japanese crash victims lay in the mortuary, but something like 150 self-styled 'next-of-kin' aggressively milled about in the sticky heat of wartime Saigon, badgering Tsai and Henniker-Major with impossible demands.

Among other things they tried to insist that Tsai fly them at once and en masse to the crash site, ignoring his protestations that not being a five-star American general he was in no position to organize such a major expedition to a battle-zone or to guarantee anyone's safety once there. Eventually as a compromise, an American Army helicopter flew down from the site with a load of stones, branches and bits of debris which were handed out in Saigon as consoling mementoes for the bereaved.

The Thai next-of-kin, of course, included Lieutenant Somchai. Mark Henniker-Major recalled that Somchai had made himself memorable by claiming to be a police lieutenant-colonel and 'by always asking the same question – what had caused the crash? No other relative of the dead persons in Saigon to identify the bodies asked about the cause of the crash. And at that time we didn't know it.'

Meanwhile, in Hong Kong, Cathay had arranged for the names of the dead passengers and crew to be printed on the back of the order of service at the memorial service held at St John's Cathedral for everyone who had perished – the seven Kennys, the Fernandez family of eight, the Thais, Japanese and Hong Kong Chinese, Father Patrick Cunningham, the flying and cabin crews. John Swire was there to read the Lesson and even as John Browne walked slowly to the lectern to deliver the Address, in Bangkok Geoffrey Binstead was beginning, with his customary gusto, to cast around for a scent.

First, [he later reported] I questioned staff at the Bangkok Airport who were present at the check-in of Prompim and Somthaya. They remembered these two passengers well. At the time of check-in Somchai was there in police uniform and had made a special request for seats 10E and 10F. When he was informed that they were not available, and that seats 15E and 15F were allocated to his wife and daughter, he continued to demand that 10E and 10F be allocated to them.

Somchai had accompanied his wife and seven-year-old daughter into the Departure Hall at Don Muang airport and from there he had seen them onto the bus to the aircraft.

Then Somchai remained in the Departure Hall talking to a Cathay Pacific hostess and a Thai ground hostess. He was not seen to board the aircraft. I was informed at this time by Cathay's Station Superintendent that he [the Superintendent] had been called into the aircraft by the cabin staff as Prompim was demanding that she and Somthaya be given seats 10E and 10F, 'because they were seats they had wanted for a long time'. (This, although the seats' views were not at all ideal being blocked by the aircraft wings.) The Superintendent said he went aboard and asked a Japanese passenger who was sitting in 10E if he would move. The aircraft then took off.

It was also noticed that Somwang Prompim had considerable difficulty in completing the embarkation card. She did not speak English and appeared to have little education, something which hardly matched Somchai's claim that 'his wife' came from a well-to-do family from the north of Thailand and that she had been a mortgage broker for two or three years in Bangkok. In fact, police investigations showed that Somwang's parents were poor farmers and that they had last seen her seven years before when she had been setting off to find work in a restaurant in Bangkok. They had not heard of any marriage; they had never even heard of Somchai.

Perusing copies of the insurance policies acquired by the Thai police, Binstead wondered why, if Somwang Prompim was Somchai's wife, as he claimed on the policies, they did not have the same name. He was told that Lieutenant Somchai had explained that Somwang was his 'minor' or common law wife of two years. As for the seven-year-old girl, Somthaya, she was not the daughter of Somwang but of Somchai's first wife, a Filipina named Alice Villiagus. She had been at Adamson University in the Philippines when she met Somchai, at that time an engineering student there. The couple had divorced after a few years (Somchai's parents did not take to Alice) and Alice agreed to Somchai's request that their daughter should go to live with his parents in Thailand. Alice told Binstead she was most surprised to hear that Somchai had married Somwang. She also confirmed what the police already knew – that Somchai was something of a man-about-town, a familiar face in the better type of Bangkok night club. This last fact caught Binstead's attention because he had recently learned that Somwang Prompim, too, had been no stranger to late-night Bangkok.

Accordingly, Geoffrey Binstead bent his steps towards the bright lights.

I received information that Prompim had been a receptionist at the '24-Hour Café' in Siam Square, and that she had two friends known there as Tommy and Dang. I therefore went to this restaurant and inquired for these two females. They are hostesses whose company can be hired. From them I was able to verify that Prompim had worked there, was quite popular with customers and had become a close friend of Somchai, and that she had, to the best of their recollection, some six weeks previously gone to live with Somchai.

They also informed me that they had been told by Prompim that Somchai suggested they should go to Hong Kong and get married there and that he would pay the fare. To show his honest intention he would ask her to take his daughter to Hong Kong where they would be met by his mother who would arrange hotel accommodation and give her US$500 for spending money. He would join them within a few days.

Binstead dutifully reported this to his Thai police contact Colonel Term Snidvongse of the Crime Suppression Division, and to his assistant Major Charuk. Then he set off on another prowl. By what now seems to have been an amazing stroke of luck, at a place called the Café de Paris in Patpong Road, the most *mouvementé* of the Thai capital's raunchier thoroughfares, he struck gold.

I don't think the Café de Paris exists today. The Memphis Queen, Lucky Strike Disco, McCoy's (The Real Taste) on the corner of Silom Road, Fine Cat, Spot On, Pussy Galore or King's Castle (Go Go Girls. Hot Stuff Lovers) – any one of them and twenty others might once have been the Café de Paris. At any rate, it was there that Geoffrey Binstead found a hostess called Katharine who at once, when he confided that he was dealing with next-of-kin in the Cathay Pacific crash, cried, 'Oh, you should meet Sathinee!' Sathinee, said Katharine, had been offered money by a Thai policeman to take his child to Hong Kong.

'*Had been asked to take his child to Hong Kong?*' Binstead could hardly believe it.

'Yes. That's right.'

Sathinee was busy for the night, it seemed, but Binstead wasted no time. Very soon Katharine found herself round the corner at the Narai Hotel in Silom Road, where Binstead was staying, and deep in conversation with Colonel Term and Major Charuk. Next evening she returned to the Café de Paris with Binstead to search for Sathinee. They found her and so Sathinee, too, joined Binstead, Colonel Term and Major Charuk at the Narai Hotel, quickly confirming her story of the policeman's offer. She was later to repeat the story in the Criminal Court, where – sheltering coyly behind dark glasses – she prettily described how Somchai had promised her 30,000 baht (US$1,700) if she would accompany his seven-year-old daughter on a shopping spree in Hong Kong. He wanted her to act as though she was married to him so that he could dodge a marriage his mother, then in Hong Kong, had arranged for him. It would be strictly a 'marriage of convenience', he assured her: she could 'divorce' him the minute the mission had been completed. He explained that this simple trick would net him a cool million baht in inheritance money. How about it? Sathinee thought of the money. Well, why not? But a little later she thought better of it.

'Why?' asked Binstead.

'Well, when we left the café he wouldn't pay his taxi driver. He shouted that he was "Number One police" and that he did not have to pay. So, well, I thought, if he was *that* stingy. . . .'

To test him she asked him to give her an advance on the deal of 5,000 baht, and when he refused she said flatly that it was no dice. Later, she said, when she read about the crash and the deaths of Somwang and Somthaya on their way to Hong Kong, apparently in circumstances strikingly similar to those suggested to her by Somchai, she sat up thinking, 'There, but for the Grace of God. . . .' She was scared. Particularly when very soon a man she knew to be one of Somchai's friends came sidling up to her in the Café de Paris one night and snarled in her ear, 'Don't say anything. Just keep quiet. See?' She did see, and when she told Binstead's police friends about it, Colonel Term spirited her away to another room at the Narai Hotel, and later on to the grander Dusit Thani. From then on the police provided her with pocket money and protection as befitted a key witness.

On 31 August 1972 Somchai was arrested, stripped of his police rank and charged with premeditated mass murder and sabotage.

The trial of Somchai Chaiyasuta began on 11 May 1973 and lasted for over a year. At his first appearance, before the Criminal Court panel of three judges and without benefit of jury, Somchai pleaded not guilty. 'The neatly-dressed defendant,' an English-language Bangkok newspaper said, 'who stands accused of a crime which could make him one of the worst mass murderers in history, looked nervous and ill-tempered. But he appeared to get a grip on himself after getting his shoulder patted by defence counsel.' Somchai's own father, a successful Bangkok lawyer, led the defence.

Everyone needed to get a grip on themselves, for the trial generated great and universal emotion. For a time some observers, particularly (but not only) from outside Thailand, had been inclined to think that the Thai Government would find it impossible to accept the bomb theory – it was a matter of 'face'. The government of that time ruled as a virtual dictatorship (it was to be overthrown in 1976 as a result of violent student riots) and its leaders took umbrage at rumours that a Thai – and a Thai policeman, at that – could have done such a terrible thing. Furthermore, the idea that a bomb could be smuggled on board an international flight from Bangkok's airport seemed an outrageous slur on what Thai ministers, especially the powerful Deputy Prime Minister and Interior Minister, General Prapas Charusthien, claimed to regard as impregnable security arrangements. It appeared to him to be a dastardly attempt by unscrupulous foreign aviation interests to destroy the international status of Thailand's major airport. Equally, for the Thai man-in-the-street – who is undoubtedly one of the world's proudest human beings – it went wholly against the grain to believe that a Thai father would deliberately destroy his own daughter, for whatever reason. No Thai would ever do such a thing! These attitudes changed as the trial progressed, worn down by the weight of expert evidence from the likes of Eric Newton and Vernon Clancy as well as the evidence against Somchai gathered by the Thai police investigators. Geoffrey Binstead thought very highly of these officers' ability and appreciated their determination to preserve the good name of the Royal Police Force by insisting that everything be brought into the open.

As the trial progressed it was alleged that Somchai had hidden his bomb in a cosmetics case he had given to Somwang which she carried aboard the Convair 880. A Thai official from the Embassy in Saigon told the court that when the bodies were being identified by next-of-kin, Somchai kept telling him, 'I don't care about the bodies, but I would like to have the case.' Police had discovered in Somchai's house four cosmetics boxes similar, if not identical, to the one Somwang had been seen carrying onto the plane; strange holes had been drilled in two of them. Somchai later told the court that these holes were to accommodate a wire (perhaps an aerial) and an earphone for a walkie-talkie. He intended to carry the walkie-talkie in one of the boxes, he said. Or perhaps he might fit a camera into it. When the prosecutor asked him what kind of pictures he liked to take with the camera, Somchai said he had not yet decided.

It was also alleged that Somchai had taken a course in explosives during an official training visit to the Netherlands. While on the subject of Somchai's knowledge of and interest in explosives (the prosecution made quite a lot of this), a Thai police pilot was brought in to testify that, on a course at an aviation training centre at Hua Hin in southern Thailand, he had given Somchai a cake of C-4 high explosive. He'd got the C-4 from a friend, he told the three judges, but hadn't really wanted it – on leaving the course he had passed it on to Somchai, who later told him he had used the C-4 to 'blow up fish'. A Thai master-sergeant at Hua Hin testified that Somchai had actually asked him where the best place was to place a bomb in an aircraft. 'Somewhere near the wings,' he was told.

Heads craned (according to the press) when the pretty night club hostess, Sathinee Somphithak, tripped into the witness box. She told a hushed court how Somchai had tried to bribe her to take his daughter to Hong Kong, and why – thank God – she had refused.

Of extreme importance was the evidence of Wesley A. Neep. A former chief of the US Army Mortuary in Saigon, he testified that between 1966 and 1972 he had identified more than 30,000 bodies of American servicemen at the Saigon mortuary, and assured the judges that in his twenty-six years of experience he had never made a wrong identification. In this case he admitted he had had his work cut out. It had been necessary to use a process of meticulous elimination to identify Somwang's body. Hers was a difficult case, he said, because there were no teeth, no hands for fingerprinting and the facial half of the skull was missing. So were her legs below the knee, although her body was scarcely touched. In fact, Wesley Neep told the court, the injuries were typical of a boobytrap or grenade victim. Enlarging on this, a Thai police ballistics expert theorized that Somwang had been sitting with the bomb at her feet. She might have been reading. Or she might have bent down to open her case and so triggered the bomb.

The condition of the wreckage was vouched for by Cyril Wray for Hong Kong's DCA, who also confirmed that Somwang's corpse was 'peppered with foreign bodies'. As for the cause of the disaster, Eric Newton derided a suggestion by Somchai's lawyers that the plane could suddenly have stalled, gone into a vertical dive and disintegrated. 'I have to assume,' he said, 'that the pilot would be able to gain control of the aircraft in the event of a stall and continue to fly perfectly safely.' He similarly parried a second suggestion from the defence that the plane might have crashed because a bird had been sucked into an engine. 'To my knowledge,' he said firmly, 'there is no big bird that flies over Thailand or Vietnam at an altitude of 29,000 feet.'

The trial dragged on. In all, the prosecution called sixty-seven witnesses. Waiting to be called to give evidence, Vernon Clancy, the accident investigator from London, was obliged to hang around Bangkok for nearly two months, increasingly worried by the thought of all the work piling up on his desk in England. There were delays while the interpreters struggled to gear their inadequate linguistic skills to cope with the technical evidence. On one exceptionally stuffy morning the strain proved too much for one of them and he passed out. People rushed to stretch him out on the prosecution's desk. His tie was loosened, his jacket removed. Someone held smelling salts under his nose. It took more than half an hour of determined fanning before he was able to stand up. He was told to go home and the hearing was adjourned for a couple of days. But at last, on 30 May 1974, Somchai stood before the crowded court in chains, his eyes hidden behind wrap-around dark glasses, and heard Judge Chitti, the Deputy Director of the Criminal Court, deliver the two-and-a-half-hour summing-up.

Judge Chitti started by pointing out, first, that Somchai was not badly off and, second, that he said he loved his daughter. He could not therefore be said to suffer from the family or financial problems attributed to him by the prosecution. Somwang was not a prostitute, as Colonel Term had alleged, for if she had been, Somchai, who came from a respectable family, would not have accepted her as his common law wife. On the question of the bombing itself, the judge felt that it was not sufficiently proven that Somchai had taken an explosives course in the Netherlands, and the court also found it unlikely that the police pilot at Hua Hin who said he had given Somchai the cake of C-4 had actually done so. 'Why didn't he use it himself?' the judge wanted to know. 'Why did he deliberately give it to Somchai?'

As for the Café de Paris hostess, Sathinee Somphithak, she alleged that Somchai had offered her a free trip to Hong Kong and 30,000 baht as part of a phoney marriage deal, but Somchai had stated from the witness box that he had never set eyes on Sathinee until she pointed him out in a police line-up. Anyway, the court could not believe Somchai had made Sathinee such an offer because he had arranged already for Somwang to go to Hong Kong. That lack of belief took care of Sathinee's further allegation that after the air crash she had been threatened with death by one of Somchai's friends.

Moving on to the cosmetics case said to have been carried on board the Convair by Somwang, the judge said, 'If there had been explosives in it, the case would have weighed about five kilograms and given Somwang cause to suspect what was in it.' It was also most unlikely, he added, that Customs officials would have missed checking such a heavy item, particularly if it had had holes drilled in it as alleged by the prosecution. True, expert foreign witnesses had stated that they had found 'foreign bodies' in Somwang's body, but why were no fragments of the case found in it?' The judge made no mention of Somwang's (and Somchai's) insistence that she and Somthaya be given seats 10E and 10F over the wing.

The long-awaited verdict caused a sensation. 'Not guilty. Somchai to be held in custody pending an appeal.' As the words fell into the room, sweating, shouting spectators stood on tables and chairs in a hubbub of applause amid the blinding explosions of flashbulbs. Somchai, who had stood to attention during the long summing-up, his face expressionless, now managed a tight little smile. 'I'm very happy because I am innocent,' was all he said, and he took off his dark glasses for the photographers. His triumphant father and defence counsel, Sont Chaiyasuta, added, 'I'm pleased to have won the case. He's not only my son, he's my client.'

The prosecutor, Foi Malikhao, had already made up his mind to appeal and he did so a few days later. But he had no better luck the second time round. More emotion, more tension, and when at last the final act was played out, two more weary years had dragged by and the appeal judges had discovered new reasons not to convict Somchai. One was the idea that, because the aircraft had broken into three pieces, there might have been more than one bomb on board. The judges were also impressed by the fact that, after learning of the crash, Somchai had left for Saigon immediately without notifying his boss. This, the judges said, proved the impressive power of Somchai's family feeling – his natural anxiety for the fate of his wife and daughter had clearly transcended his fear of disciplinary punishment for having gone absent without leave. Furthermore, the judges considered that if Somchai had really sabotaged the plane he would have tried to vanish into the blue instead of returning to work. (How, having skedaddled, he would ever have managed to collect the insurance money, presumably the sole object of the alleged exercise, the judges did not explain.)

At the end of everything, his shackles removed at last, Somchai walked from the Central Military Appeals Court a free man. Outside, he handed a local reporter a written statement which said, 'Thank God that the Court of Justice still exists in Thailand. . . . For those who have tried to insult me, God says "Forgive and forget", and that's what I aim to do.' He was given back his police rank and in later years was to be promoted two grades. He took the insurance companies to court one by one and by 1978 had received the millions of baht for which, six years before, he had insured Somwang and little Somthaya.

The perpetrator of the mid air bomb explosion was never brought to justice. After Somchai's acquittal no other suspect was ever considered, leave alone pursued. The crux of the matter was this: that despite the heavy weight of the prosecution's evidence against Somchai, the crucial parts of it were entirely circumstantial – and in Thai law circumstantial evidence alone is not enough to convict. Had anyone *actually seen* Somchai placing a bomb in the plane? Who had *seen* the explosives allegedly hidden in Somwang's cosmetics case? The answer to both questions was – no one.

The outcome of the trial left anger and bitterness. Many Thais were delighted to see Lieutenant Somchai acquitted, but many more thought justice had been thwarted – on orders from General Prapas, or somebody. Friends of Thailand feared that the acquittal had harmed the country more than the affair itself. To this day senior Thai police officers who knew Somchai have strong doubts about his story, and there have always been those who felt not merely doubtful about his innocence but positive of his guilt; there were even some who played for a while with the idea of vengeance – of paying a 'hit-man' to knock him off. A well-born Thai woman in Bangkok, quite close to the affair, expressed what I suppose is one typically Thai view of it: 'If it's true about Somchai's guilt, he will be unhappy for ever. How can you live after having killed eighty-one people?'

Thailand, one of the most beautiful countries in the world, with an ancient and unshakeable culture, easily survived this dismal affair. It is a self-confident place of temples and palaces and its semi-divine king rules a strong-minded people of unmatchable charm. Since 1972 Don Muang Airport has been enlarged and modernized out of all recognition, and today it is as safe and efficient as any airport anywhere. In fact it has become a mecca for tourists and, day in day out, thousands of flights – including Cathay's – take off or land there without mishap.

I visited Geoffrey Binstead recently. The genial tracker is living now in happy retirement with his Thai wife (he met her during the investigation) among the green peaks and clear fresh Pyrenean air of Andorra. Talking about the case, he voices the British policeman's philosophy as well as anyone could: 'Well – you win one, you lose one.'

As for Somchai, after resigning with the rank of Police Colonel, he went to the United States in 1983. Two years later he returned to Thailand with cancer of the kidney and died after two weeks, aged forty-three.

CHAPTER 22

The Vietnam nightmare failed to put passengers off either Cathay Pacific or its Convairs. On the contrary. Despite the worst disaster in Cathay's history, 1972 turned out to be the best financial year the Company had ever had. Expansion had been the policy of John Bremridge and his directors before the Convair disaster, and that policy remained unchanged. Consequently the Company needed a new and larger aircraft. Boeing's 747 (the Jumbo) sprang instantly to mind, but for little Cathay the size and expense of this giant were intimidating. The Boeing 707 was a handier size, so that was chosen instead. Cathay's first four 707s came cheap at US$30 million as a result of a deal with Northwest Orient Airlines of Minneapolis, and HAECO smartened them up with a 'wide-body' interior design. By 1 January 1973 Cathay's fleet numbered eleven, including seven Convairs. To go with the 707s the Company bought an electronic wonder appropriate to this new era of mechanical wizardry – a 707 flight simulator, to be installed at Kai Tak. Made by the Japanese firm Mitsubishi, it gave anyone sitting in it an unearthly impression of utter reality and its 'brain' could be programmed to reproduce with equal reality the night scenes of twelve international airports. Soaring, rocking, plunging and banking in response to its controls, it was an ideal training machine, removing the risky necessity of checking pilots in actual flight, using no fuel and saving much money. Indeed the simulator even made money for the Company; when it was joined later by more advanced replicas of TriStars and 747s, Cathay, when not using them, rented them out to other airlines for considerable profit. Jock Swire, reappearing in Hong Kong, found time to play with the new toys.

Bernie Smith has just taken over from Norman Marsh as Operations Director. Captain Howell and he took me round the Engineering side and I saw the latest Boeing 707 and drove the 707 simulator. The lecture rooms for training and flying staff are most marvellously equipped with every modern service, internal tv and other stunts.

When in 1974 Cathay's 707 fleet increased to twelve it was deemed time to revive the Company's Hong Kong–Sydney service that had been so rudely interrupted thirteen years before, when Cathay's Electras had battled to Sydney via Manila and Darwin and been chased off the route by the Qantas 707s. On 21 October a Cathay 707 re-inaugurated the service, and now there was no objection from Qantas. As his diary shows, only old Jock refused to be too enthusiastic about this.

I am still just as apprehensive as to the wisdom of CPA's extension to Australia as I was all those years ago. I am sure they will get tied up with Australian politics and pilots' Trade Union nonsense. . . .

Nor was his enthusiasm uplifted by a bad first flight to Sydney. It left Kai Tak at 9 p.m. and

the service was quite appalling. They did not start serving dinner until nearly 11 and didn't turn off the lights until 12.15. Breakfast was even worse. They started at 4 by pouring out the coffee, then gave us rolls and butter and marmalade, then fruit (by which time the coffee was cold) and did not produce the eggs for quite half an hour after serving the coffee. The staff just mooched about in a sort of coma. If they go on like this there will be no passengers in a month.

Luckily things picked up on his return flight to Hong Kong:

The best air hostess (called Aro) I have ever known on any flight. The service and timing of the meals were superb. What a difference. Possibly they overdid the drinks and one well-known Sydney drunk became quite impossible (a Welshman with a lovely voice). He and a Nansen whose father was a great explorer had to be strapped into the cockpit for a lot of the time. To see Aro, a tiny little Japanese girl, deal with them was a masterpiece. . . .

Despite Jock's forebodings the Australia service was back for good. This time there was a proper office and a serious effort to spread the good news far and wide of Cathay's return in strength. Cathay had recently discovered – rather late in the day – the value of publicity. Duncan Bluck was its initiator, as he was initiator of so much else. 'Well, we had to do something about it,' he said later. Some time before the resumption of the Sydney run he had looked around for a suitable advertising agency, and chose an Australian company, Fortune Advertising. Ken Landell-Jones, head of Fortune and a highly successful Sydney publicist, recalls their first meeting:

'There was this English bloke Duncan Bluck, clipped-voiced, unsmiling.

He threw a few sketches for a Cathay advertising campaign on my table. I said, "They're no good. They're childish. We'd be the laughing stock." I sent for my Art Director. He agreed with me. I said to Bluck, "When are you going back to Hong Kong?" He said, "Next day." Well, we worked all night and – believe me – we gave him his new ads the next morning. Duncan examined them one by one – "Yep . . . yep . . . yep. . . ." He liked 'em. We were hired! I never met a man who'd take a decision so quickly.'

One result of Landell-Jones's recruitment was the early Cathay theme – 'The Best of Both Worlds', referring to the Company's combination of ultra-reliable British and Australian pilots up front and superlatively beautiful Asian air hostesses in the cabin. It was a most seductive formula. For now, in striking half- and full-page ads, dependable-looking pilots and bewitching hostesses smiled up at the reader over the words 'We know you'll like us,' beside copy that had an unaccustomed glow:

> Today Cathay Pacific, Hong Kong's beautiful airline, starts an exclusive service from and to Hong Kong. Three times weekly we'll jet you to Hong Kong. From there to thirteen beautiful cities. Our experienced, reliable pilots and engineers are Australian and British. The best in the business. Our cabin staff are Asia's finest. Our food and wine superb. Our service – out of this world.

Landell-Jones was also responsible for the addition to the livery of each aircraft of the Taikoo logo – the house flag in red, white and blue that decorates Cathay planes to this day as it has always advertised CNCo on the funnels of Swires' ships. One thing Ken found out relatively early on was the parsimonious aspect of Jock Swire's character. No great sums of money were going to be spent on his publicity efforts, he could see that. 'Jock was a real Englishman,' he said. 'I met him in London first, he was wearing his tweeds, of course. He took me out to a lunch of cottage pie and a pint of beer in the Stock Exchange Club or somewhere (it cost about fifty pence, I know that). There seemed to be only one bottle in the office, a bottle of sherry and he and his old friend, John Scott, took it in turns to buy it. "Your bottle next time, Scott," Jock said.'

By the time Cathay's 707s resumed the Sydney service another Australian live wire, Keith Sillett, had joined the Company as Marketing Manager, and with him and Landell-Jones at work Cathay returned to Australia with a bang, to be welcomed with rapture Down Under. So many Cathay pilots were Australians it was like a homecoming. The newspapers published photographs of a Cathay flight crew, all of whom were Australians: First Officer H. F. Dyball of Sydney, Captain B. J. Wightman of Lismore and

Flight Engineer P. D. Dunn of Sydney. Although not Australian himself, the man who actually piloted Cathay's inaugural flight into Sydney, Captain Len Cowper, was much interviewed.

> Captain Len Cowper is a pilot with his head in the jet age but his heart in the world of fabric, wire and wood of old aircraft [the *Sydney Morning Herald* said]. When he is not flying the big Boeing at speeds of up to 880km/h at an altitude of 14,700 metres, Captain Cowper relaxes behind the stick of a 31-year-old Boeing Stearman biplane.
>
> 'Flying the Boeing is like driving a limousine,' Captain Cowper said yesterday. 'The Stearman is a fun machine. It is like going for a ride in a red-hot. . . .'

One of the Company's 'stars', when he retired a few years later he liked to boast that he had flown every type of Cathay aircraft since the DC-3 except the Catalina.

A new slogan – 'Fly Hong Kong's discovery airline' – put a dash of adventure into Cathay's appeal. Its sales desks in the office at the corner of Hunter and O'Connell Streets were dominated by a big mural depicting Hong Kong harbour at night, painted, it was announced, by a Lebanese artist called Haider Hamaoui in six hours. Then Ken and Keith had another brainwave. Jim Macdougall, one of Australia's best-known and respected daily newspaper columnists and a humorist to boot, was on the point of retirement. 'What about a Cathay column?' Landell-Jones asked him over a drink. Macdougall was all for it and Ken swiftly negotiated prime space for a column in editorial type on page three of *The Australian*. All these years later the light-hearted Jim Macdougall column still runs on its merry way, informing thousands of readers of all sorts of goings-on in the Australian world of Cathay. A breezy court circular announcing the comings and goings in Cathay's aircraft of what Macdougall refers to as 'high achievers – kings, princes, presidents, potentates, people of fame and credit in a vast range of human activity', the column brings an extra touch of personality to the airline. Apart from this, Keith Sillett can take credit for a number of publicity gimmicks including Cathay sponsorships of professional golf, tennis and other sporting events in Hong Kong. Far and away the most popular of these, though it owed its inception more to Jock Campbell than to Sillett, is the annual international seven-a-side rugby football tournament played in the Happy Valley stadium. It attracts competitors from France to Fiji and Korea to Sri Lanka, and is growing in popularity each year.

At first three days weekly, Cathay's Australian service eventually became a daily one. And there was a further expansion. Urged on by Duncan Bluck,

Cathay introduced a three-day-a-week 707 service to the Arabian Gulf, first to Bahrain and later to Dubai as well. This too proved extremely profitable. The Gulf – thanks to oil – had become one of the world's fastest growing trade areas. Even the poorest Arabs wore gold watches, rings and bracelets, many drove large cars and all of them shunned manual work like the plague. Asian labourers were thus much in demand and Cathay flew in thousands of them, mostly from Taiwan and Korea.

The 707s on their swept-back wings had sped Cathay into the wider world. Success fed ambition and in next to no time the Company's thoughts turned towards a genuine wide-bodied, intercontinental aircraft – ideally, the eye-popping jumbo-sized Boeing 747, undoubtedly the Aircraft of the Age. The trouble was that the Jumbos were designed to carry about 450 passengers, and several airlines, including Cathay, were not sure that they could fill these monsters. There were, however, two other wide-bodied aircraft coming onto the market then with a 300-passenger capacity: the Douglas DC-10 and the Lockheed TriStar, both three-engined aircraft. The DC-10 was powered by engines made by the American firm, General Electric; the TriStar's engines came from Rolls-Royce. There seemed little to choose between them, so a team from Cathay set out for America to investigate at close quarters. They arrived at a time of desperate competition between Douglas and Lockheed with the big, long-range DC-10 well out ahead – in fact, already flying. Lockheed had also produced a superb aircraft – indeed the TriStar was something of a technical miracle – but was lagging behind Douglas in production and therefore in sales.

The Cathay team returned to Hong Kong with their recommendations and, in accordance with them, on 29 January 1974 John Bremridge and his directors unanimously agreed to go for the Douglas DC-10. And that normally would have been that.

But something quite unexpected occurred.

It had been agreed to defer for thirty-six hours any announcement of the Board's decision in favour of the DC-10 to allow time for the British Government to be informed of it. This was an unusual procedure; but the involvement of Rolls-Royce with the TriStar had created a special circumstance. For Rolls-Royce just then was in crisis. Swires in London had an idea that the official reaction to their choice of the rival DC-10 with American engines might be . . . adverse. And adverse it was. So adverse in fact that the Minister responsible, Michael Heseltine, was moved to telephone in person to request the earliest possible meeting with John

Swire, Adrian being away in Hong Kong. When they met, the handsome and youthful-looking Minister was plainly upset and made no attempt to hide it. He felt let down, he said, by Cathay's decision – indeed he had been 'flabbergasted' by its suddenness. Why had he not been given a chance to bring pressure to bear on Lockheed to give Cathay a better deal? Or 'to have a word' with Rolls-Royce, who were admittedly going through rather a difficult patch but who could no doubt be prevailed upon by government to provide cast-iron guarantees of all-out technical support in the future? As John Swire later reported, there was no table-pounding at the meeting; there was more sorrow on the Minister's part than anger. Actually, calmly fingering his Brigade of Guards tie, Mr Heseltine was all 'urbanity and sweet reasonableness'. He simply made it very plain indeed that he and his advisers needed an answer to one question: 'Why, oh why – with nothing to choose between the two aircraft – had Cathay come down unanimously in Douglas's favour?'

As everyone in Swires to do with aviation was in Hong Kong, John Swire was able to fall back on his genuine lack of technical knowledge, while admitting that, of course, all other things being equal, Cathay would have preferred an aircraft with a British component. At this Heseltine nodded and smiled. 'Just so,' he said, 'yes.' But, he went on, commercial decisions had to be made in their totality. Nevertheless, the British Government was very concerned to look after the interests of both Cathay Pacific *and* Rolls-Royce. 'It would be much less embarrassing for me' – he smiled again – 'if those two interests had dovetailed.' The Minister kept his most telling point to the last. Walking Swire to the lift, Heseltine gently slipped a final word into his ear: 'I should perhaps tell you that one of my embarrassments is persuading other Asian airlines to buy British equipment at a time when one of the most successful operators in the area – British, at that – has gone elsewhere.' He hoped Cathay would hold up their final decision to give him time to encourage Rolls-Royce to improve the package they and Lockheed were jointly offering.

John Swire drove away from the meeting with his brain buzzing. For a Minister to take such a keen personal interest in these matters was most unusual. Cathay Pacific had been making its own decisions about buying aircraft for over twenty years, and this was the first time Her Majesty's Government had intervened. Was Cathay being officially leaned on? John Swire had not been quite sure, but a further meeting with Sir Peter Thornton, Permanent Secretary at the Department of Trade and Industry, clarified things no end. Sir Peter spelled it out: the deteriorating British balance of payments; the need to keep workers working at Rolls-Royce; the desirability of giving an encouraging lead to the other airlines in South East Asia (excluding China) at that very moment undecided whether to order the TriStar or the DC-10 – these were all pressing British concerns. Of course, Sir Peter hastened to add, HMG would not be putting pressure on Cathay Pacific if it did not believe the TriStar was a good aircraft, but as it was, the Government hoped – indeed expected – that Cathay 'would take all these British concerns into account'.

Cathay's interpretation of all this was that a 'patriotic' decision in favour of the TriStar and Rolls-Royce would ensure, for any plans Cathay Pacific might have in the future, a sympathetic attitude from the Department of Trade and Industry, the British Government's aviation 'overlord'. So Cathay and Lockheed went back into negotiation, and the upshot was that Lockheed undertook to provide an improved aircraft at a cheaper price, thus achieving a considerable edge over Douglas. For its part, Rolls-Royce promised to keep producing the excellent RB211-22B engine and to come up with an even better one very shortly.

A blatant appeal to patriotism on the one hand; a commercial need for the best plane on the other – that had been Cathay's dilemma and it appeared to have been resolved. Slightly shaken but with a good conscience, the Company went ahead and ordered two long-range TriStars with an option on two more. The first Cathay TriStar, VR-HHK, arrived from Palmdale, California, at Kai Tak on 2 September 1975, flown in by Bernie Smith and Laurie King to be officially welcomed by Hong Kong's Governor, Sir Murray Maclehose, and the Hong Kong police band. VR-HHK and VR-HHL, brought into service two months later, are flying with Cathay to this day. Both of them began their life on the Hong Kong–Taipei–Tokyo, Hong Kong–Singapore–Jakarta and Hong Kong–Manila routes, and were an instant triumph, hugely popular since passengers loved the new wide bodies, and therefore very profitable.

The TriStars' arrival coincided very neatly with a boom in Asian air travel, and thus it was that at the end of 1978 John Bremridge was able to announce to the Board an operating profit six times larger than that of the year before. By May 1979 the Cathay fleet consisted of eight 300-seat TriStars and eight 707s, a tremendous increase in both traffic and capacity. TriStars have undoubtedly proved their worth despite the strange circumstances surrounding their acquisition, and with their sophisticated technology are set to survive alongside the magnificent 747s well into the 1990s.

Rolls-Royce kept its word. Few in aviation would deny that Rolls-Royce is producing the most advanced and most efficient commercial jet engine in the world. Cathay flies them on every single one of its aircraft, 747s as well as TriStars, and intends to keep on flying them in all the aircraft (such as the ultra-long-range 747-400s) it has a mind to buy in the foreseeable future.

Is there a moral to this tale of two aircraft – the DC-10 and the TriStar? Perhaps it is that on its own, as Nurse Cavell said, patriotism is not enough, but that if it comes coupled with the best possible deal – well, that's a different matter.

Quite aside from the ministerial goings-on in London, later in the year the Lockheed TriStar became the subject of a worldwide business scandal that touched Hong Kong and – for one sad and embarrassing moment – touched Cathay itself.

Captain Bernie Smith had been a member of the Cathay team that toured America to choose between the DC-10 and the TriStar and had brought Cathay's first TriStar to Kai Tak. When the *South China Morning Post* reporter approached him he said, between sips of champagne, 'It's a beautiful plane to fly. It's much nicer to handle than the Boeing 707 and it has the most modern navigation system in the world!' Later Smith had appeared in Cathay advertisements for the new TriStar service, describing the aircraft as 'the most intelligent aircraft I've ever flown'. It was an impressive testimonial because Bernie Smith, one of Cathay's best-liked senior captains, had a long and distinguished record that went back beyond his twenty-two years with Cathay Pacific to service with RAF Fighter Command.

But five months after his welcome from the Governor, Bernie Smith, in disgrace, boarded a late-night Pan American flight to Bangkok, making for his villa in the south of France, never to return. All that was known – it was spread across the front pages of the world's best newspapers – was that a Senate Sub-Committee in Washington had heard evidence from Mr Carl Kotchian, the Vice-Chairman of Lockheed, of a campaign of bribery that was startling in its global scope.

With the aim of winning the sales war between Lockheed and Douglas, a struggle which had threatened to bankrupt one or even both of them, Lockheed had started handing out 'monetary inducements' and 'kickbacks' to helpful friends in high places from Sweden to Japan. The Prime Minister of Japan, Mr Kakuei Tanaka, for example, was alleged to have accepted US$7 million in bribes to ensure that All Nippon Airways bought TriStar. When the scandal broke, Mr Kotchian, coming clean, pointed his finger in all sorts of interesting directions, even at Cathay. 'A British agent living in

France', he said, had 'received US$80,000 for payment to Cathay Pacific officials'.

Decisive as always, Duncan Bluck launched an immediate no-names-spared investigation. Who was this 'agent'? Who were these 'Cathay officials'? After a long talk with a chastened Kotchian, Bluck issued a terse statement.

> It is now clear that a payment of US$80,000 was made by Lockheed Aircraft Corporation in November 1974 to Captain E. B. Smith, Director of Flight Operations of Cathay Pacific Airways, as a payment to him in assisting Lockheed Aircraft Corporation in their efforts to sell Lockheed TriStar aircraft throughout this area, to airlines other than Cathay Pacific.
>
> There are no other payments involved.
>
> Captain Smith has resigned from Cathay Pacific with effect from 10th February.

For Bernie it was a pathetic come-uppance. The Hong Kong press printed sad pictures of him in happier times: a small, trim, fair-haired man, proudly wearing a captain's four gold rings on each sleeve, posed smiling in front of the first TriStar at Kai Tak and before a fine company house in Kowloon Tong – the scene, friends remembered regretfully, of many swinging parties. Colleagues had had respect for Bernie, recalling his extraordinary services to Cathay. In June 1972, John Browne had circulated to everyone in the Company a letter welcoming Smith back from his hazardous investigations into the Convair disaster in Vietnam: 'I would particularly like to record our appreciation for the extremely hard work in very unpleasant circumstances which has been carried out by Captain E. B. Smith and his investigating team.' The phrase 'unpleasant circumstances' was an understatement – the Vietnamese experience had not only involved more than one sortie into an active war zone amid acute danger and discomfort, but considerable frustration due to the rather less than all-out cooperation from the Vietnamese authorities in Saigon. For that Bernie Smith deserved a medal for valour and diplomacy. As it was, everything ended with a humiliating resignation, a handsome pension forfeited and a midnight flight into oblivion.

CHAPTER 23

In the minds of some senior people in Cathay Pacific the fight for the London route and the name of Mr Leonard Bebchick will be for ever linked. It was the pursuit of licences to fly the Golden Route from Hong Kong to London that threw them together. The legal struggle, first before Hong Kong's Air Transport Licensing Authority and then the United Kingdom's Civil Aviation Authority, was grim, long drawn-out and for Cathay, at first, disastrous. But Mr Bebchick, although brilliantly representing British Caledonian, one of Cathay's rivals, consciously or unconsciously brought to it a welcome degree of comic relief. Or so a reading of the transcripts seems to reveal.

The situation before the CAA hearings began was as follows. Further expansion for Cathay in the eighties could only lead in one direction: to London. To land there would be a crowning achievement, surely not the final extension of the Company's network but certainly a very special one: it would be a sort of homecoming for the Hong Kong airline with the Union Jack on its tail. The airline already flew to Bahrain, a most valuable stopping-point almost halfway along the route from Hong Kong to Britain. Now it was time to go the whole hog and apply for the necessary licences from Hong Kong and London.

The important London–Hong Kong–London route had long been a British Airways monopoly: BA could operate as many flights as they liked, and they already flew ten a week. But it was universally agreed that lack of competition had spoilt BA; by taking the route for granted, the company had come to neglect it. Its punctuality record was appalling. Its aircraft regularly stopped at two or three points en route, including Bombay and Delhi, where time and again there were long delays with angry passengers stuck for hours in the dust and heat. In increasing numbers, businessmen, tourists and other travellers were fleeing the British flag-carrier for the better services provided by foreigners – Lufthansa, Swissair or Singapore International Airlines. Why not another British carrier?

In December 1979 Cathay took the first step towards challenging BA's monopoly by applying to the Hong Kong Air Transport Licensing Authority (ATLA) for a licence to fly to London. The Company did not apply alone. British Caledonian (BCal), an independently owned British airline with Scottish connections, was also energetically in the running, and so was the famous price-cutting boss of Laker Airways' transatlantic Skytrain operation, the ebullient Sir Freddie Laker. Cathay, BCal, Laker – the three applications were to be considered together.

Cathay had hoped to be the sole new licensee in addition to BA: to the Company's management it seemed that one British airline from each end of the route seemed a realistic proposition. BA had accepted the inevitable and started to make room for a competitor, lopping three flights off its weekly ten, so Cathay saw an opportunity to make up the complement with three of their own, building up in time to many more. BCal could not agree to that – to do so risked being squeezed out of the running completely, and furthermore the BCal Board, claiming to believe that BA had dropped the three flights expressly for Cathay to pick up, began to cry 'Collusion!' There would be no difficulty in all three airlines flying the route, BCal argued. But not Freddie Laker. None of them wanted Freddie Laker. Reality forbade any reciprocal attempt by BCal to press for Cathay's total exclusion from the licence, for their investigations in the run-up to the ATLA hearings swiftly revealed the extraordinary pro-Cathay sentiment in Hong Kong. Ranging from the Governor to any Hong Kong Chinese with an interest in flying, it represented a popular and undeniable force that could not be ignored.

ATLA was an *ad hoc* group of individuals who – with the exception of the Chairman, Judge Ross Penlington – had little or no professional knowledge of aviation: they heard the evidence and deliberated, and the result of those first deliberations was an odd one. Perhaps partly to allay BCal's loudly expressed suspicions of collusion, ATLA's members decided to grant BCal a licence to operate four flights a week and a licence to Cathay for only three.

The lop-sided decision came as a shock to Cathay. The Company (and Hong Kong generally) genuinely believed that BA's seven flights, BCal's four and Cathay's three, in addition to other carriers, would create a glut of air services even on a route on which extraordinary growth was expected. Nevertheless, ATLA was of the opinion that only the option of a new daily service would provide really testing competition for BA, and this was initially not going to be offered by Cathay's own suggested three flights a week. As for poor Sir Freddie, ATLA gave him the bum's rush: he got no licence at all.

But this was not the end of the story. Application for any route was a twin hurdle, for licences had to come from both ends – in this case from Britain's Civil Aviation Authority as well as from Hong Kong's ATLA.

The Civil Aviation Authority – Mr R. Colegate (Chairman), Captain E. W. Lowden (Member) and Miss G. M. E. White (Adviser) – met on 13 December 1979 and on five subsequent days at Civil Aviation House near the Strand in London to hear the various applications and submissions. The hearings were suspended over the Christmas holiday period and resumed for three days towards the end of January 1980. It was going to be a long haul.

British Caledonian was, of course, represented by Mr L. N. Bebchick. A diminutive and bald-headed man with all the bounce of a brand-new tennis ball, Leonard Bebchick was a self-confident, voluble American lawyer, a Director and Joint Company Secretary of BCal. Briefed by Peter Martin, who led for Cathay, Peter Bowsher QC appeared for the Company. British Airways had retained the services of an immensely tall and sardonic counsel, J. T. C. Philipson, who used his golden locks, his spectacles and his haughty manner to the historic maximum. Sir Freddie Laker, an accomplished self-advocate and still in there fighting, had a second voice in another American lawyer, R. M. Beckman. Sir Freddie on his own account often introduced some welcome light relief.

It was for Mr Bebchick to kick off. For a start, and for the benefit of the Authority, he rehearsed a number of facts, including notably that the present BA service was totally inadequate, with 53 per cent of its flights on this route arriving three hours late. He also stressed that BCal continued to support a 'three carrier regime', a sharing of the route among the three British companies. Cathay would be incapable of going it alone, he maintained. Their proposed three services a week were inadequate, and anyway their recently acquired Boeing 747's very high break-even passenger load factor would make it uneconomical. As for Laker, Mr Bebchick dismissed him briefly and completely – his proposal for cheap mass flying was utterly unrealistic.

Peter Bowsher reiterated Cathay's suggestion in favour of two airlines, not three, with equality of opportunity from both ends of the route. Cathay already had one 747-200B and was expecting delivery of three others which would give them the capacity they needed. He pointed out that Cathay was naturally supported by the government and people of Hong Kong because, as a local carrier, it would be extremely responsive to the demands of that market. The 'eastern-ness' of Cathay – the image of it as 'Hong Kong's airline' – was again expounded by Duncan Bluck when he took the stand. Cathay, he emphasized, had a long history of profitable operation in and out of the Colony; it had a large network of routes in the Far East and from these it could feed traffic into the London–Hong Kong service. As for the 747 being the right, or wrong, aircraft, Bluck said that for one thing customers preferred the 747 over the DC-10 and 'We certainly don't accept that a smaller aircraft [the DC-10] with 270 seats is better suited for a long haul route than a 747 with 408 seats. After all, it is long-term development of the route that is important.' Bob Dewar, a skilled accountant and Cathay's doughty Director of Airline Operations, and Richard Stirland, the Company's bright young Planning Manager, developed these arguments in their turn. As for Laker, Stirland pooh-poohed the notion that hordes of Chinese with itchy feet were lurking in the bushes, waiting impatiently for cheap tickets to romantic places like London. Hong Kong passengers were mostly businessmen, government servants, officials: there was no mass market there for Laker-style Skytrains. As for holiday group tours to Hong Kong – Hong Kong was not Miami.

Mr Bowsher weighed in again. Let it not be forgotten, he said, that Cathay had made a considerable and patriotic contribution to the British aerospace industry and would by 1982 be the only Rolls-Royce-powered airline of its size in the world. And of course the 747 was eminently suited to the route: its greater number of seats would also help relieve the expected overcrowding on the runway at Kai Tak Airport. But despite the projected extra demand for flights, he too dismissed the Laker application as unrealistic.

Naturally, Sir Freddie was not going to be swept under the rug like that. He stoutly maintained that Hong Kong might indeed become another Miami. He would offer a daily service – a comfortable, one-stop service. He would develop low-cost tours from both ends of the route. He would cater, above all, for 'the many, many forgotten men and women at the bottom end of the market'.

The CAA hearings seemed set to last forever, frequently bogged down in tedious niggling over largely hypothetical figures. It was lucky for everybody present that their number included characters like the peekily abrasive Mr Bebchick and the ebullient Sir Freddie, both of whom demonstrated a public persona that, in another day and age, might have assured them a future in the music-halls. Laker's confident predictions of a boom at the 'bottom end of the market' and his plans for cheap fares prompted Peter Bowsher to say that his rock-bottom fares would only appeal to those who didn't mind what they sat on. He started to elaborate: 'You could go on wooden seats' – when an indignant interruption from Laker's American counsel, Mr Beckman, silenced him. 'This room,' protested Mr Beckman, 'is full of press writing down what Mr Bowsher is saying and the statement regarding wooden seats is untrue. . . . It is scandalous and very damaging to us.' Presumably he feared the next day's newspapers would come out with headlines like 'Freddie Laker To Use Wooden Seats in Skytrain, QC alleges'. Mr Beckman was calmed by a word of support from Mr Colegate: 'Let me say that I have sat in a seat in one of Laker's DC-10s and it was quite comfortable.' Not wood at all. . . .

At one point Sir Freddie sought to draw a conclusion from his estimate of future passengers and revenue, excusing the vagueness of it by saying, 'Surely we are entitled even in these rather formal proceedings to have a little bit of latitude and do a bit of generalizing?' Mr Philipson, for BA, suavely reassured him: 'Generalizing, Sir Freddie, is something which I would never seek to persuade you away from.' On another occasion, Sir Freddie exploded with, 'If you pull all the feathers out of a bird it will not fly!' But Sir Freddie came over as a good sport. It was he who closed the proceedings for the Christmas recess by booming 'A very happy Christmas and a healthy 1980' to one and all.

BCal's Mr Bebchick, adroit and very American, seems to have had a high old time of it. Even when flippantly referred to as 'Mr Dabchick' – an ornithological put-down which produced some laughter in court – he rose serenely above such mockery. At other times he engaged in exchanges reminiscent of those famous satires of courtroom proceedings chronicled by the late lamented J. B. Morton ('Beachcomber') in the old *Daily Express* of London – especially those proceedings that involved the imaginary Mr Justice Cocklecarrot and the fictional barrister, Prodnose.
Thus:

Philipson (sardonically from his great height, to the Chairman):
    'Mr Bebchick really does not understand the point of my cross-examination.'

Bebchick: 'I wish you would stop saying that I do not understand you. I am quite intelligent. I do not think that these snide references get you anywhere and it is rather unprofessional of counsel.'

Chairman: 'It could be a case of *post hoc, ergo propter hoc*.'

(Prodnose: 'Well, precisely, m'lud.')

Mr Beckman, the other American, fared no better than Philipson. He and

Bebchick complemented each other physically: Bebchick short almost to vanishing point, Beckman thin, tall and dark.

Bebchick: 'I do not take Laker as serious. I am sure Sir Freddie takes himself very seriously.'

Beckman: '. . . Do you think this is a laughing matter?'

Bebchick: 'Yes, I consider your case to be a laughing matter. . . . I love Sir Freddie as a human being and he loves me, too, but when you approach a market like Hong Kong and put in a submission that says it's going to be like Los Angeles, and Sir Freddie tells us with great conviction that he personally will ensure that the market grows from 200,000 to 475,000 in one year, then I think it is a joke. I think it is a farce. I do not take it seriously. I'm sure *he* does, and I know *you* do, Mr Beckman. But Freddie Laker can be wrong. We all make mistakes. He has made a bad mistake here and if I choose to say it is a joke, that is what I choose to say. I do not view it as a serious proposal. I just do not.'

One up to Mr Bebchick.

As time passed, the drama of the scene seemed to Richard Stirland to take possession of Messrs Bebchick and Beckman. Their gestures became sweepingly histrionic, the room filled with echoes reminiscent of Perry Mason exhorting invisible juries to dispatch wife-slayers to the hot seat. Bebchick strode up and down, dragging yards of wire behind him and declaiming into the sort of hand-held microphone favoured by nightclub entertainers. Sonorous phrases like 'Let this court bear solemn witness' and 'May the record show . . .' might have become the flamboyant rhetorical norm of these quite straightforward hearings had not Mr Colegate put a stop to it. When Mr Bebchick protested that Mr Beckman had produced an unexpected document with an unseemly lack of advance warning he got a brush-off which prompted the following exchange.

Beckman (sadly): 'Poor Mr Bebchick. . . .'

Bebchick: 'I think the record should be clear. . . .'

Chairman: 'Mr Bebchick and Mr Beckman, this hearing has not yet become a television serial, although it seems in imminent danger of becoming a serial without the television. . . . Let us just get on with things. Let us take a break for five minutes while we all cool down and then let us carry on.'

When one evening Mr Bebchick said he would pop his 'final question' to a long-suffering witness, BA's Philipson muttered, 'I hope it will not be a leading one.'

To this Bebchick remarked: 'A leading question is one which requires the witness to answer yes or no. That is the American definition.'

The weary Chairman groaned: 'Perhaps we could do with more of those questions! Mr Bebchick, if I have understood the American way of life and terminology correctly, we are eighteen minutes into the "happy hour".'

These rhetorical high jinks were the leavening in hearings that were at bottom very weighty. At the end of it all the CAA's decision was awaited with bated breath and very few smiles. When it came, on 17 March 1980, ATLA's decision was overturned. British Caledonian was the only one of the three airlines to be granted a licence to fly between Hong Kong and London.

Laker was ruled out because the CAA doubted that Sir Freddie's 'forgotten men' existed at all, at any rate in significant numbers. 'As far as Hong Kong is concerned there is no significant charter market from which scheduled services can divert traffic.' The CAA also doubted Laker's 'ebullient forecast' of massive holiday traffic. Hong Kong was *not* Miami or Los Angeles. 'The Authority must regretfully regard the "forgotten man" as a myth; there is certainly no evidence that he is waiting hopefully for the opportunity to travel between London and Hong Kong.'

But why did the CAA choose BCal over Cathay?

It is worth quoting the report's relevant paragraph in full because the answer, in retrospect, is a very odd one indeed.

> Given its conclusion that the route will stand only one additional operator, the Authority is faced with the unenviable task of choosing between Cathay and BCal. . . . The conclusion is that Hong Kong and the public would best be served by granting the licence to BCal, whose aircraft size is better tailored to the needs of the route at its present stage of development. The Authority fully understands the desire of the Hong Kong Government for Cathay to be licensed. There would be some advantage in the route's being developed by a carrier based at the Hong Kong end. Cathay is well placed to develop Asian traffic from its Far East network and it already has the advantage of rights between Hong Kong and Bahrain. However, the Authority does not consider that these advantages outweigh the disadvantage that Cathay could not satisfy the needs of the market as well with its 747s as BCal could with its DC-10s.

The next paragraph surmised that political considerations influenced Hong Kong's ATLA to grant Cathay a licence rather than 'the harsh logic of the economic analysis'. It went even further than that, implicitly warning the Secretary of State for Trade that, should he overturn this decision of the CAA (it was in his power, and his alone, to do so), he would be saying in effect that 'it was more important to give Cathay Pacific a place in the sun than to provide the service which is clearly better for the travelling public'. No wonder Duncan Bluck's copy of the report at this point is splattered with angry exclamation marks and one ferociously scribbled word – '*Rubbish!*'

The news of Cathay's rejection fell like a stun-grenade among the Company's directors and employees alike. Mike Hardy, the present Director of Flight Operations, was in Hong Kong waiting at a traffic light. His wife, in another car, was alongside. Their car radios were tuned to the news and the CAA decision was announced at that moment. They sat there dismayed and unbelieving, staring at each other through their car windows. The lights changed and they still sat there. 'Cars were hooting impatiently,' Mike says. 'Drivers were shouting at us. But we had heard the news. We just couldn't believe it. BCal had got the London route. We were nowhere. Impossible!'

In Manila, in the flat of Duncan Pring, Cathay's Philippines representative, guests were assembling for a small dinner party. His wife was pouring drinks. A telephone rang and Duncan went to answer it. He came back with an expression of doom on his face. Cathay refused! It was as if all the lights in the flat had gone out.

Cathay Pacific lost no time in preparing an appeal to the then British Minister of Trade, John Nott, and Duncan Bluck called a press conference in Hong Kong to tell journalists that the basis of the Company's appeal against this 'extraordinary' CAA decision would be public preference for Cathay's 747s and the desire of Hong Kong people to see Hong Kong-based Cathay on the route: 'We are not appealing on the legality of the matter, but rather on the morality of it,' he said.

It seemed clear to Bluck, to Adrian Swire and other Cathay directors, that the CAA decision was based essentially on the dubious premise that the smaller DC-10 was a more suitable aircraft for the route than the Jumbo 747. They hoped the Colony's Governor, Sir Murray Maclehose, would share their outrage and mobilize the Foreign Office in London (and Lord Carrington, the Foreign Minister) behind Cathay's case. Cathay had been insulted – treated by Colegate's CAA like 'a 2nd XI colonial airline striving unjustifiably to force its way into the profitable long-haul UK-based preserve of pukka U.K. independents'. It would now be necessary to mount a wide press campaign in Hong Kong, to gain support from local Chinese administrative bodies and so on. 'Inevitably and sadly' – there one hears the patriotic voice of Swire – 'this campaign would have to follow the perfidious Albion line.'

It must have seemed like perfidious Albion indeed. At the headquarters of John Swire & Sons, Mr Heseltine's smiling intervention over the TriStars on behalf of Rolls-Royce and the TriStar had not been forgotten. A joint telex from Adrian, Bluck and Bremridge to Michael Miles, Managing Director in Hong Kong, ended with these words:

> We have now reached the ludicrous situation where the U.K., having leaned on Cathay to prevent it buying the DC-10, is now proposing to richly reward BCal purely for having done so.

It was not in the least surprising that this theme recurred in a letter from Adrian to Bluck a little later as they waited on tenterhooks for John Nott's decision on Cathay's appeal. If the decision went against them, 'We must react very quickly and positively if we are to extract the maximum from an injustice of this kind.' Among other things, they should demand an immediate meeting with John Nott. The purpose of such a meeting would be – partly – 'to put on record that, in our view, HMG had let us down/double-crossed us on a very fundamental matter, and that this double-dealing gravely undermines our faith for the future in HMG's evenhandedness. . . .' The fundamental matter referred to was, of course, the pressures that had been brought to bear 'to make us change our DC-10 order to the Rolls-Royce-powered Lockheed 1011'.

The result of the appeal was expected in June 1980. Meanwhile speculation and backstairs activity carried on apace.

On the adverse side, Duncan Bluck reported that certain people in BA were now in a bloody-minded mood and making it clear that they would do their best 'to run us off the London route' if Nott did allow them on it. On the other hand Michael Miles, invited to dine *à trois* with a local friend and John Nott in Hong Kong on a visit, reported that Nott was 'very relaxed' and spoke sympathetically of 'Cathay's natural claims' to the route. Nott also struck Miles – as he struck numerous others – as a man of very independent mind. He was well briefed, too, and obviously had a good grasp of Cathay's problems. That sounded just what everyone in Cathay wanted to hear.

Popular support for Cathay in Hong Kong gathered momentum. Everyone who was anyone wrote in to call for the overturn of the CAA's 'outrageous decision'. That included the Chinese press. For example, *Wah Kiu Yat Po*:

> The CAA considered BCal's DC-10s to be more suitable for the route than Cathay's 747s. Such reasons are incomprehensible since BA which is at present monopolising the route is also using 747s. We can predict that about half the would-be passengers on the Hong Kong–London route will be orientals and it is only justifiable that Cathay, as an *experienced airline*

servicing Asian countries should be granted the licence. . . . A majority of passengers would certainly pick Cathay as their first choice. So the CAA's worry about the shortage in passenger demand is unjustified.

The Hon. O. V. Cheung in the Legislative Council had this to say:

Cathay was encouraged to buy UK equipment. They specified their 747s should be powered by Rolls Royce engines. So far they have invested £70 million in Rolls Royce engines to that end and plan to invest £10 million a year on other equipment in furtherance of reciprocity. . . .

And a columnist in *Sing Tao Jih Pao* wrote under the headline 'Hong Kong Loses Face' something much stronger, something that underlined in thick black strokes of the pen how much Cathay Pacific and the Hong Kong Chinese population had come together:

I vaguely remember an anecdote in Dr Lin Yu-tang's book. It went like this: one day in the 19th century, a Chinese ambassador was walking in his clumsy padded quilt coat on a street in Washington, D.C., and coming across a swaggering American who asked, 'What the hell are you? Japanese? Chinese? or Siamese?'

The Chinese Ambassador replied coldly, 'What are you anyway? A monkey? An ass or a Yankee?'

This of course, happened in the age of gunboat diplomacy when China was generally regarded as a colony, or simply a geographical term instead of a sovereign state. The Chinese were then treated as hordes or coolies next only to dogs which were prohibited to enter public parks in the international settlement of Shanghai.

In this century, we may be sure that apart from sarcasm, mockery and animosity, this kind of thing could not have happened. But when the news of Cathay Pacific Airways being rejected to operate the Hong Kong–London route came, the people of Hong Kong had the same feeling as that of the Chinese Ambassador a century ago. Ironically, the British Civil Aviation Authority is probably not aware of the extent to which the self-respect of Hong Kong Chinese was hurt. Despite the fact that CPA is being operated by British, Hong Kong people long regarded CPA as their own airline. It's well-run, providing good services, making profit every year and gaining 'face' for Hong Kong, and it's the envy of many.

The predominant Chinese community here has reasons to feel being betrayed and discarded. They take the rejection on as an unfair treatment and even an insult. To the Hong Kong Chinese, nothing could be more 'face-losing' than having their own Hong Kong airline being denied the right to operate Hong Kong's own route. Hong Kong has always looked upon U.K. as the 'mother' country. Now the Civil Aviation Authority's decision to turn down CPA is an eye-opener. It is clear that this 'mother' not only fails in her duty but is – with a slight association of idea – so obnoxious that she could be prosecuted for maltreating her child. It is indeed sad to see that U.K. is so down and out as to have to protect herself against her own colony – a most humiliating page in the annals of Britain. It is a shame that she had to stoop so low as to take an action that would have been denounced in the 19th century. In fact, there is and will be plenty of room for both CPA and British Caledonian. The U.K. CAA could have taken a leaf out of Confucius' teaching and dealt with the matter in the principle of 'giving others that you want for yourself'. At any rate, one cannot very well say 'this is the finest hour of Britain'. U.K. CAA's decision is as unfair to Hong Kong as it is unworthy of Britain.

There was lots more from elsewhere – all in the same outraged vein.

The time and the agony dragged on. Then, on 17 June, during a joyful Hong Kong Association Dragon Boat dinner chaired by John Swire (on tenterhooks) at the Dorchester Hotel in London, the Minister made a witty speech. In the course of it, Mr Nott announced that he would overturn the CAA ruling. Cathay Pacific, Laker Airways as well as BCal were to be licensed to join BA on the Hong Kong route. The Minister gave several reasons for his decision. In his view the Authority had been unduly dismissive of the possibility of substantial new traffic being generated by a wider choice of services. He did not himself altogether dismiss, for example, the possibility of 'many, many forgotten men and women at the bottom end of the market'. Anyway, a wider choice of carrier was obviously what users of the route, having suffered under the BA monopoly, should be given. Particularly gratifying – it made John Browne at his table at the Dorchester snatch gleefully for the champagne and John Swire mentally tear up a biting indictment of Westminster's perfidy that he had prepared in case Cathay was rejected – was the fact that Mr Nott found it quite unreasonable that a second airline based in Britain had been granted exclusive rights to fly the Hong Kong route when there was an airline with a Union Jack on its tail – Cathay – in that territory very willing and very able to participate. After that John Swire's dignified speech was a purr of satisfaction and relief. A serious obstacle to Hong Kong–UK trade was now removed, he said.

While the champagne corks flew and the cheers of the carousing Hong Kongers jingled the chandeliers of the Dorchester, back in Hong Kong and well into the early morning Duncan Bluck held a jubilant press conference. None of the apparent injustice of earlier decisions mattered now. He broke out champagne for the blurry-eyed journalists and, raising his glass, announced that Cathay would start flying to London three times a week from 16 July. He thanked all sections of the Hong Kong community for their support, and then went down to help Cathay staff slap brand-new posters onto the ticket office windows. It was as if he had known in advance what the Minister's verdict would be: by first light those posters were already proclaiming to all who passed by: 'CATHAY PACIFIC TO LONDON'.

It was a famous effort. And Cathay's outstanding technical ability was soon on display when the Company actually 'went into Air' to London *ahead of* BCal. Furthermore, to confound the very basis of the CAA ruling, only a year later Cathay began a daily service between London and Hong Kong using the very planes – the Jumbo 747s – that the CAA had pooh-poohed as too big for the route.

On 16 July 1980, as the Hong Kong police band played once more, VR-HIA – Cathay's second 747 – left Kai Tak for Bahrain, flown by Captain Len Cowper. At Bahrain Captain Geoff Gratwick took over. Duncan Bluck was aboard, and Stewart John, Cathay's Director of Engineering, and David Bell, head of Public Relations. So was another Cathay pilot, Tony Dady, who was going home on sick leave. He had glimpsed Duncan Bluck in Hong Kong shortly after the CAA rejection of Cathay's application and Bluck had grimly assured him, 'BCal are not going to get away with this.' For Dady, Bluck was the personification of Cathay Pacific. Now, as the 747 headed on its triumphant way to London, he watched Bluck across the aisle quietly sipping his whisky and soda as if nothing much had happened, as if there had not been a famous victory. As the plane's wheels touched the ground at Gatwick, the passengers applauded and Bluck got up and made a characteristically deadpan announcement on the Jumbo's loudspeaker system – 'Welcome to London. We have worked hard for this.' No one knew better how hard.

Adrian Swire's Spitfire was waiting at Gatwick to lead VR-HIA across the tarmac to the terminal building. There was a Chinese ceremonial dragon dance, a town crier ringing his bell, and several television teams. John Dick, Cathay's Commercial Manager after Duncan Bluck, had emerged from retirement to serve as Traffic Manager, and after a while his Scottish impatience got the better of him. 'Can you move this bloody circus on?' he demanded of David Bell. 'I've got to get this bloody machine turned round and on its way back to Hong Kong.'

An old man with a soldierly bearing, in an old trilby and an old overcoat, had stood peering out from the terminal's big windows. Eighty-seven years of age, how can Jock Swire have believed his eyes? DC-4s, DC-6s, Electras, Convairs, they had all come and gone. But this monster with the Cathay 'green-and-white sandwich' tail and the familiar Taikoo logo – what was it doing here, so far from home, so far from Kowloon's Lion Rock, from the green hills that rise towards China behind Stonecutters Island and the Lei Yue Mun Gap? Did this great aircraft, this Swire leviathan, beached so serenely here in Sussex, symbolize victory – or was it a mistake? No, surely not a mistake. He had seen so many changes since that first meeting with Syd and Roy – was it really thirty-two years ago? He had got used to them all. He would get used to this one too in time.

CHAPTER 24

On 23 September 1983 Betsy came home to roost like some immortal bird out of legend. Cathay Pacific had sold her in 1955, and now retrieved her at last so that she could spend the rest of her life in Hong Kong, her home.

What had happened to Farrell and de Kantzow's pet during the long years of obscurity? She had lived pretty rough since Cathay had sold her in 1955; she had gone then to the Sydney-based W. R. Carpenter & Sons. She had lost her Cathay logo and red lettering, been repainted in the colours of Mandated Airlines, and had spent the next twenty years or so bouncing about over the jungles and mountain ranges of wildest New Guinea. In 1973 she was bought by a young Australian airline called Bush Pilots Airways and transferred to the relative tranquillity of Queensland. There, in yet another livery (white upper fuselage; dark blue stripe at window level; yellow tail), she spent ten years carrying essential cargo to the outback – food supplies, building material, mining equipment and the like.

Eight years later, Cathay's Martin Willing, the indefatigable historian of the Company's flying machines, discovered that Cathay's first aircraft was still flying and indeed was the only one of Cathay's fleet of DC-3s in existence. Betsy happened to be up for sale, so Cathay bought her back. What a long time she had been away! It was time for her to be led out to grass: she had earned a permanent retirement in familiar surroundings. Now she would go back where she belonged, and in Kowloon's new Museum of Science and Technology become a noble monument to Hong Kong's airline pioneers.

On 18 September 1983 Betsy waited at Kingsford-Smith Airport, Sydney, to take off on her long flight home. A Cathay 747 stood next to her; the two of them side-by-side before they both headed down the runway en route to Hong Kong, Betsy leading if only for a moment or two. An excited crowd included Company staff and many Cathay veterans, the oldest of them Captain Pat Moore who had been shot at by Karen rebels while flying

221

Betsy in the 'Burma Campaign'. Now eighty years old, posing for photographers under Betsy's nose in a white beard and his old Cathay officer's gold-braided cap, and supporting himself with a stick, he looked as much like a retired sea captain as a grand old flyer of Cathay Pacific.

'It was a choking moment,' Jim Macdougall recalls. 'An incredible sight, really. A warm day and sunny; not a cloud in the sky; hardly a stir of air. There they were – Betsy decked out once more in her out-of-date style of red lettering and the old CPA logo with the yellow map of the Far East and South East Asia, and the giant Cathay 747. Then the two of them moved off, little Betsy, the fragile little thing, with the great roaring of the monstrous giant behind her. The little one revving and trembling and the 747 rushing after her. We watched from the observation lounge. Pat Moore was wiping his eyes and there was total silence except for our choking. Betsy took five days of flying to reach Hong Kong. The 747 took eight hours.'

Betsy was flown by an Air Queensland pilot, Reg Perkins, and the flight took in stops at Coolangatta in Queensland (first day), Cairns, then Wewak in New Guinea (second day), Davao in the Philippines (third day) and Manila (fourth day). Betsy's interior was the same un-upholstered military khaki it had been during her war years, although a few modern instruments had been added. At Manila Adrian Swire was waiting with Cathay Pacific's Director of Flight Operations, Brian Wightman, and flew Betsy on the last leg to Hong Kong. Before they took off two retired Cathay engineers, Felix Manguerra and Ricardo Dominguez, pointed excitedly to a skin repair they had carried out on Betsy in 1949. Adrian wrote later:

> According to my log book, the Manila/Hong Kong flight took 6 hours 20 mins, with take-off at 06.15 hours and arrival at Kai Tak at 12.35 hours. . . . I was at the controls for the whole of the last period. It was a beautiful clear sunny day, and we flew at around 1,000 feet along the south of Hong Kong Island and then, with permission of Kai Tak control, within the Western Harbour and Port Shelter. The final approach and landing at Kai Tak was made from the Kowloon end past the chequerboard, and happily I managed a smooth touch down. . . . Australian pilots aboard, all from Queensland, were amused to see that even in the heat the reception committee were wearing formal dark suits and ties.

Duncan Bluck was there, the Hong Kong police band playing 'Those Magnificent Men In Their Flying Machines', and a splendid array of Cathay cabin attendants in uniforms of the past from bush jackets to miniskirts. Cathay's Managing Director, Michael Miles, cut a cake decorated with a replica of Betsy in icing sugar, specially baked by Cathay's chefs. It was a pity Jock Swire was not there. He had died earlier that year.

A year later I visited Betsy at her temporary resting place in a HAECO hangar at Kai Tak. Martin Willing went with me and I took some notes:

Huge hangar at HAECO you feel you could make a movie in. A notice on a wall that says 'Keep Your Hangar Clean' in large red letters. Betsy crouches beside a long-range TriStar with Chinese engineers all over her, painting United Airlines colours. She is like some great sleek beast (pig? armadillo?) being manicured and groomed by a Lilliputian army of beauticians. Next door is a Gulf Air TriStar with men crawling inside her engines while other men in white overalls open little doors in her mighty tail section and delve about like surgeons probing a giant's insides.

With all this activity around her, little Betsy points her nose to the hangar roof, almost snootily. She gleams there in her aluminium armour – though she could do with a good rub down, it seems to me. The Union Jack on her tail looks fresh, so does the old registration – VR-HDB. Betsy has two large outward-opening doors – these C-47s were freighters not supply droppers. You couldn't open these doors in flight. Supply doors opened inwards, or you took them off altogether. Martin says: 'They're the sort of ramshackle door you might have designed, Gavin. Thrown together, eh? Of course these planes were made in the hell of a hurry. The US Air Force wanted them at once.'

Inside, the wooden floor is painted drab military green. There's a loo in the rear – wooden seat and lid – and behind that an open door reveals what looks like piano strings controlling the rudder and elevators. A document on a holder on a bulkhead says 4423 – which means Betsy is the 4423rd plane ever made by Douglas. I have to duck and squeeze into the cockpit which is grey except for two red levers that raise the undergear and two white ball-like knobs that control the pitch (the angle of the propeller blades). The pilots' seats are the old bucket type – very comfortable – and Martin thinks they are the original ones. The control column bar in the right-hand seat branches awkwardly out from the right across a tall man's knees (like mine) and restricts them very comfortably. The windscreen wipers are oddly stubby. You can lean out of the windows; the cockpit windows slide back.

It is impossible not to think of the old days even not having seen them. From ancient photographs of Kai Tak I can imagine a field with grass patches and puddles of rain. A tower like a prison watchtower . . . a windsock . . . a tiny runway . . . low ridges beyond. . . . And those slow, old propeller-driven aircraft. A senior Cathay Engineer, Ken Barnes, has told me, 'Often after several hours of flying from Sydney to Hong Kong, I've groaned to myself "God, how many more hours?" But then I think Betsy would only have reached Brisbane by now – and we're already over the South China Sea.'

With Chinese mechanics looking on, I sit in Betsy's cockpit and Martin takes my picture. I feel I am sitting in an ancient monument as exciting as Noah's Ark or the throne of a pharaoh.

It is time to take a last look at Cathay Pacific, the airline that Roy and Syd built all those years ago.

Perhaps there should have been more in this history about errant individuals, unseemly incidents, all the bric-à-brac of gossip. I doubt it. If there is one sense in which Cathay is no different from other airlines it is that its history contains the usual quota of drunken pilots (not many), seducers of air hostesses and company wives (rather more), and the like. One or two people have suggested that a few early cases of gold smuggling on the part of pilots and air hostesses were actually an important part of Cathay's history. Of course that is not true. The smuggling incidents took place decades ago, involved very few people (and nobody in management), and were irrelevant to the main story of Cathay's struggle for success, and above all, banal.

On the other hand, more needs to be said about the Hong Kong Chinese contribution to that success. That *is* relevant. I have mentioned H. H. Lee, for years CPA's manager at Singapore who in the early days spent many hours at the airport helping Chinese passengers ignorant of English with the baffling rituals of immigration and customs. Recently I visited Chester Yen in Vancouver, where he has lived in retirement since 1972. Chester joined Butterfield & Swire in Shanghai in 1933, and became Cathay's Chinese Sales Manager in 1952 at about the time Sydney de Kantzow retired. He looked after Chinese passengers coming from Amoy – labourers and migrants mostly. 'There were delays at the airport and you had to go out there to help the passengers or they'd go and fly with someone else. In the old days most passengers were Chinese and they came to feel Cathay cared for them.'

Because he was a much respected figure in the Chinese world of Hong Kong, Chester Yen was responsible for recruiting Chinese into Cathay's staff. In 1961 he brought in Patrick Tsai. He says: 'We had to take great care of the Chinese commercial agents, too; in fact we had to spend days and nights with them, entertaining them. Speaking to them in Chinese, of course. I had air timetables printed in Chinese. And I made sure Chinese newspaper reporters were well entertained, too. We gave them Chinese meals and so on.'

In San Francisco I found the Company's first Purser, Marcel Lin, born in Mauritius. He had started flying with Cathay on the Hong Kong–Bangkok–Rangoon run in DC-4s.

'Did you enjoy it?'

– 'Oh, yes.' His face lit up. 'DC-4s were so reliable. We had a wonderful time.'

He had risen to Assistant Supervisor of Cabin Attendants when Jo Cheng was Supervisor. In 1954 Marcel had set up Cathay's first 'charm school' for its oriental air hostesses, and he is convinced that Cathay's oriental cabin crews continue to contribute enormously to the airline's success now that Cathay flies to those great Chinese population centres, Vancouver and San Francisco.

As for the engineering side of things, Stewart John believes the Chinese were, and are indispensable: 'Without HAECO's enthusiasm and pride in work – the Chinese "work ethic", call it that if you like – Cathay would be nothing. Strong words, but I mean it. HAECO is the envy of the world. Do you know HAECO has about four and a half thousand people working at Kai Tak and of those only about seventy or eighty are expatriates? Chinese are coming to the top in very senior positions.' He pointed to a name on a list on his table. 'Take P. K. Chan – he's running a small army of sheet metal workers, painters, upholsterers, carpenters. An exceptional man, a real dynamo. And there are so many more. . . . Believe me, our Cathay engineers are the most professional going – highly skilled and totally trained by us.'

John himself is a 'real dynamo' from the Rhondda Valley in South Wales. A gigantic, genial figure with a voice and laugh mighty enough to stagger the most experienced Welsh choirmaster, he never seems to stop moving or talking. In Hong Kong I have seen him driving through the night exchanging technicalities on the car telephone to his men at Kai Tak. Despite the hour, he was keeping 'a finger on the pulse'.

'Well, Gavin, you've got to keep a finger on the pulse. You've got to keep up the best commercial standards and operational standards. Good aircrews must have the best service – it's no good giving a fantastic driver a car if the door falls off when he comes to get into it.'

Stewart John's office at Kai Tak is just about big enough to contain a large painting of his hero, the Father of the Jet Engine, Sir Frank Whittle (whose son is a Cathay pilot), a good-sized desk and Stewart John himself. He starts and finishes his day on the telephone. 'Every evening before bed – *every* evening, mind – I call the shift superintendent at Kai Tak. He's a chap running several hundred engineers – Chinese or European or a mixture. I discuss the incoming defects, things that'll need doing when an incoming Cathay plane arrives. We know what these are because they'll have been computered in already. At seven in the morning I'll call again to see what he's got through during the night – any problems, like. Once a day *wherever* I am I call into my office or to my excellent deputy director, Roland Fairfield, who's been with me for years. Just checking.'

He grins: 'Perhaps it's wrong to interfere. But you have to keep the finger on the pulse, don't you?'

In 1987 Cathay was voted 'Airline of the Year' by *Air Transport World*, a much respected aviation magazine based in Washington, DC. Cathay will soon be flying a new longer-range Boeing (the Boeing 747-400) and flies to America and Canada as well as several cities in Europe. By 1991, at the present rate of recruitment, Cathay Pacific should have about a thousand pilots.

How has an airline with such a small colonial base achieved its present size without subsidy or government participation? Air is a notoriously hazardous business; one in which small private airlines like British Eagle, Laker, Continental and Braniff have foundered; and one in which even major world airlines like Pan Am and BOAC have suffered appalling losses. What was the unusual characteristic of the local soil which enabled the little Cathay plant to grow so vigorously? Adrian Swire has attempted to answer this question:

> The first point, of course, has to be Hong Kong itself. The airline is based there – clearly a very advantageous base. Think of its geographical position within the Far East; its participation in the economic growth of the whole Pacific Basin; plus all the characteristics which have made the City State of Hong Kong itself such a success story. These are: no exchange controls, low taxation, rule of law, pragmatism at all levels, no governmental corruption, realistic unions, laissez-faire economy, availability of Chinese management skills, and the overall high productivity of the place. Incidentally, you should not think that cheap labour was one of the key factors – indeed, Cathay Pacific's pilots include the highest paid British pilots in the world.

Cathay's lack of a government to provide a financial umbrella could have been fatal. In Hong Kong the umbrella was there in another guise – the personal relationship between Swires and the Hongkong Bank was just as good. The Bank were 30 per cent shareholders; they came up with the loans and gave copper-bottomed guarantees when Cathay was buying new aircraft. 'I cannot overemphasize,' Adrian says, 'the importance of the link we have had with the Hongkong Bank. A line of credit for many millions of dollars could be arranged on trust by a simple phone call.'

Cathay's later history endorses the view Derek Davies had expressed in the sixties: that Cathay benefited uniquely by being part of the old-established Swire empire. Swire managers knew the area and its agents – for example, the fact that Swires had been involved in Japan since the 1860s was particularly valuable to the airline. The Company was not considered there as upstarts.

Adrian believes, 'The management pattern – often Oxbridge, traditional, commercial, flexible – avoided the common postwar fallacy that airlines could only be run by retired air force officers.' The current Managing Director of Cathay, Peter Sutch, is an illustration of the interchangeability of Swires' managers: he, like Michael Miles, Duncan Bluck and John Browne before him, started his life with Swires in the shipping division.

Cathay can be unorthodox. A Company article of faith, for example, is that an airline should employ the minimum number of aircraft types. The ever-active brain of Duncan Bluck invented a phrase to encapsulate a policy that stems from this belief – 'the intelligent misuse of aircraft'. This means, in essence, a policy of using (or 'mis-using') the same type of aircraft on widely differing routes – a 747, say, on the long Vancouver route one day and on the very short Manila route the next – the object being to maximize the passenger load and minimize the amount of time the aircraft spends on the ground.

Even with its unique advantages of place and history, Cathay did not soar effortlessly from the rag trade of Shanghai to the riches of contemporary Hong Kong steered by a breed of supermen plucked from the dreaming spires of grand English universities. Not the least ingredient in this adventure was the mood of Hong Kong itself, an impatient, money-fixated place of refugees and exiles determined to pull themselves out of the rubble of the Japanese occupation.

What next? Hong Kong will become part of the People's Republic of China in 1997. According to the Sino–British Joint Declaration of 1984, the Colony will become a Special Administrative Region of China. There will be One State but two Systems: in China, communism; in Hong Kong, a capitalist dispensation very similar to the present one, though without a British Governor. The hope is that the Chinese of Beijing will see that their overriding interest lies in making sure that Hong Kong remains a thriving financial centre, a producer of the hard currency they so much desire and need. Swires say they have confidence in post-1997 Hong Kong; they intend to demonstrate that faith by continuing to invest there. This presupposes a belief that the Beijing Government mean what they say – that they want Hong Kong to prosper; that the Chinese genuinely appreciate that it can only do so as an international city; that they will allow Cathay to keep its international management. For if they don't the Company could wither on the vine.

It has recently acquired a new director, Larry Yung, the son of the chairman of the China International Trade and Investment Corporation (CITIC), the Chinese government's main commercial arm and since January 1987 a 12.5 per cent shareholder in the company. A guarded optimism rules the Cathay boardroom, as it usually has. Duncan Bluck points to Cathay's own huge investment in aircraft and in training, and the Swire companies' investment in luxury hotels, in two new apartment blocks, a new Coca Cola factory, a new paint factory. . . .

Naturally, growth has loosened the family ties within Cathay Pacific. 'It's getting today so that you don't know your First Officer or your Flight Engineer,' Ian Steven tells me. Duncan Bluck still greets most of the Company's recruits as they join. Peter Sutch is a youngish man of extraordinary warmth and energy. He takes an obvious delight in mixing informally with Cathay's employees, however grand or however humble they may be. He continually bobs up on the flight decks of whatever planes he happens to be flying in – cheerful, encouraging, more like a friend than a Managing Director – and the crews are delighted to see him. Still, the airway is no longer the cosy organization Jock knew. In the Hong Kong takeover of 1997, Adrian Swire confronts a hurdle bigger by far than anything that has come before. With a bold expression, he says, 'Cathay Pacific is established. I believe that it will grow as Hong Kong's scheduled carrier in the post-1997 era. *J'y suis, j'y reste.*'

TAKE-OFF

A nice mid-morning at Kai Tak: dry and bright under fairly high cloud. In a few minutes CX800, waiting on the apron, will leave for Vancouver and San Francisco.

In the grey eyrie of the cockpit the First Officer, John Williams, says, 'It must be three months since I did a Vancouver trip. It's been all London or Frankfurt.'

'Nice change, eh?' Peter Jerdan, the Captain, replies.

Jerdan's Australian voice is as calm and as cheerful as usual. As calm as it had been a month or two earlier when we had sat in the cockpit of the 747 simulator at four in the morning and he put the electronic marvel through its paces. He had dive-bombed Kowloon, shot the Jumbo over neon-lit Nathan Road with the speed of a flying saucer, and over Stonecutters Island thrown her into the sort of tight, heart-stopping turns I associated with a jet fighter, not a 747. He had turned the dignified Jumbo into a sort of airborne performing flea, and the plane's warning systems had reacted in outrage. Urgent mechanical voices in the cockpit barked, 'Too low! Too low!' and 'Terrain! Terrain!' Sirens wailed, hooters hee-hawed, lights flashed. Quite right too. But we were alone and in a building, and only there can you see what amazing things a 747 can do if you ask it politely. That morning Jerdan had even allowed me to take the captain's left-hand seat to steer the Jumbo onto the simulated Kai Tak runway, to rev up those mighty engines, to roar them down the narrow path of lights, and to heave the 300 or 400 tons of her into the night air with my own hands. Like lifting a block of flats off the ground, he'd said. It was extremely real and much better than any electronic game in an arcade – I'd managed to take off twice without dumping the whole caboodle into Kowloon Bay. 'Pretty good, Gav,' Peter Jerdan had grinned when we rocked to a stop, and I had thought so, too. Maybe I could start a new career.

Now, at 11.35 on an April morning, Jerdan sits in the left-hand seat, adjusting its height so that his eyes are level with a mark on the bulkhead nearest them: twenty-five feet above the ground. John Williams is on his right and Flight Engineer Martin leans forward between them from his position facing the banks of switches. An all-Australian crew.

The blue plastic coffee mugs with the dregs of instant coffee have been laid aside. A Chinese air hostess has appeared in the cockpit with a tray of cold towels like snow-white spring rolls, handed them out with a small pair of tongs, and taken them away again.

Now the ritual murmur of check question and answer between the Flight Engineer and the pilots comes to an end with the Engineer confirming: 'Checks complete.'

Then the Captain: 'Doors all closed?'

'Closed.'

Jerdan says: 'Start Four.' Martin brings the engines to life one by one, beginning with No. Four, and needles on the dials in front of us begin to jump. A smell of aviation fuel fills the cockpit, faint and not unpleasant. Ten hours forty-five minutes non-stop flying time to Vancouver requires 123 tons of fuel to burn on the way, a load which, with 326 passengers and their luggage aboard means that in a few moments Jerdan will be launching a 358-ton missile at the Lei Yue Mun Gap at an angle of 13 degrees.

He talks to the control tower asking for permission to taxi, gets it and releases the brakes. Set free, the plane rolls softly forward. Infinitely slowly we creep towards the thirty-foot Marlboro sign behind the boundary fence at the corner of Concorde Road and the turning to the Harbour Tunnel. Just in front of us, a pale blue Korean Airlines monster skims in over the drab tenements of Kowloon City, smoothly touches its undercarriage onto the runway in a puff of bluish smoke, runs on, swings left off the runway and begins the slow trundle back to the passenger terminal.

Jerdan says, 'Take-off checks.' Flaps? Stabilizer trim? Fuel set for take-off? Cabin crew alerted? Yes . . . yes . . . yes. We lumber on, then swing left to point down the runway's centre line. Jerdan presses down on the foot pedals to align our nose with long white arrows that point to the far end of the slender bay-bound causeway – about 11,000 feet away but to me more like 100 yards.

Adjust headsets. Check seat belts. Ready to roll.

The world stands still. . . .

Roll.

'Max thrust.' Leaning forward, Jerdan presses all four throttle levers forward as far as they will go. The metal shell trembles, begins to bump rhythmically, to sway. The runway flows towards us like a moving belt, faster and faster. In a moment or two we are eating it up at an amazing rate. I have an impression of the water on either side of us, grey and cold, but there's no time to look at it. A barge dumping rubble comes level and is instantly snatched away. Watch the centre line! 155 knots – 178mph. . . .

'V.1.,' the First Officer says distinctly, telling Jerdan our take-off speed is near. The water at the end of the runway is very near too.

'V.R.' R for rotate, meaning lift the nose so that the aircraft tilts upwards on the axis of its landing gear. Jerdan's hands grasp the black 'horns' of the control column near the top and pull back firmly and evenly several inches, perhaps nine. He feels no resistance – a gentle easing is all it takes to lift a block of flats with wings and a tail moving at 190mph. Our nose tilts: 10 degrees, then 13 degrees. Wheels off the ground, the great body begins to shake – but only for a moment, and then there is only the rush of air and a steady soaring.

'V.2.' 210mph now; the long finger of the runway has fallen swiftly away below us. I see objects like toys in the water: barges; a floating crane; a hoarding advertising cement.

'Gear up.'

The wheels retract with a tortured metallic groan like an ogre in pain. In the morning air, lifting, caressing, cradling, the plane is alive as a ship entering the open sea is alive when the immeasurable power of the ocean takes hold of her hull, changing as it enters its special element. Non-existent while we were on the ground, the air as we rise in it becomes as palpable as water, thickening as we thrust up through it into an almost solid substance.

To the left I can see half a hillside hacked away; the soft ridges of the New Territories; the islands of China. Then we are climbing through cloud.

Jerdan says: 'With our weight it'll take us about thirty minutes to get up to 29,000 feet. That's under 1,000 feet a minute.'

In the cloud CX800 is a blind white fish. Cloud-shadows flicker round the grey womb of the cockpit, across the crisp white shirts of the impassive men staring ahead into the fog with narrowed eyes or at their dials. Any minute . . . any minute . . . we shall burst out into the infinite sunshine. Now! In the sudden liberating explosion of light, the great white, green and silver flying fish gives a joyful spring. Sunlight showers over us. Everything is smooth and weightless.

'What about it?' Peter Jerdan speaks to me over his shoulder. 'Pretty good, eh?'

The sky all around us is clear, blue and full of promise. I loosen my seat belt. I might as well relax. There is still a long way to go.

Chairmen
of John Swire & Sons Ltd since 1946

Swire, John Kidston 1946–66

Swire, John Anthony 1966–87

Swire, Adrian Christopher 1987–

The Swire Hong Kong Taipans since 1941

Charles Collingwood Roberts, 1941–48; 1951

Eric Guard Price, 1949–50

John Arthur Blackwood, 1951–57

William Charles Goodard Knowles, 1957–64

Herbert John Charles Browne, 1 October 1964–30 April 1973

John Henry Bremridge, 20 May 1973–31 December 1980

Duncan Robert Yorke Bluck, 1 January 1981–31 March 1984
   Managing Director, CPA, 18 January 1971–1 January 1979
   Deputy Chairman, 1 January 1979–1 January 1981

Henry Michael Pearson Miles, 1 April 1984–31 May 1988
   Managing Director, CPA, 1 January 1979–31 January 1984
   Deputy Chairman, 1 January 1984–1 April 1984

David Anthony Gledhill, 1 June 1988
   Deputy Chairman, April 1984–31 May 1988

APPENDIX II

Engineering Department and Flight Operations Staff

Engineering Department

J. T. Gething, Chief Engineer, December 1950–April 1963

D. S. Delaney, Chief Engineer, 11 April 1963–August 1966
Engineering Manager, 6 September 1966–October 1969
Engineering Director, 21 October 1969–April 1980

S. M. John, Deputy Engineering Director, April 1977–May 1980
Engineering Director, May 1980–

Flight Operations

S. de Kantzow, R. (Dick) Hunt, R. P. Tissandier, C. F. (Pat) Moore,
September 1946–December 1957

K. W. Steele, Operations Manager, 1957–December 1963

D. Smith, Operations Manager, December 1963–November 1971

N. J. Marsh, Operations Manager, November 1971–November 1973

E. B. Smith, Operations Manager, November 1973–February 1976

J. R. E. Howell, Flight Operations Director, February 1976–
December 1977

B. J. Wightman, Flight Operations Director, January 1978–March 1986

M. J. Hardy, Flight Operations Director, April 1986–

APPENDIX III

The Growth of an Airline

Year	Aircraft at end of year	Destinations	Port	Pax	Cargo (Kgs)
1946	2 DC-3 (C47)	HKG-MNL-SHA-SYD (Charter operation)	4	3,000	15,000
1947	2 Catalinas 7 DC-3	HKG-BKK-MCO-MNL-RGN-SIN (+ Asian & Australian charter)	6	8,000	30,000
1948	1 Catalina 7 DC-3	HKG-BKK-MCO-MNL-RGN-SIN (+ Worldwide charter)	6	9,000	40,000
1949	5 DC-3, 1 DC-4	HKG-BKK-MCO-MNL-RGN-SIN	6	9,345	156,788
1950	4 DC-3 1 DC-4	HKG-BKK-CCU-HNO-HPH-JES-LBU-MNL-RGN-SDK-SGN-SIN	12	(50) 12,460 (51) 12,053	312,024 609,342
1951-54	2 DC-3 1 DC-4	HKG-BKK-CCU-HNO-HPH-JES-LBU-MNL-RGN-SDK-SGN-SIN	12	(52) 14,464 (53) 17,707 (54) 18,655	526,299 454,617 523,798
1955	2 DC-3, 1 DC-4, 1 DC-6	HKG-BKK-CCU-LBU-MNL-RGN-SGN-SIN	8	30,854	457,873
1956-57	1 DC-3, 1 DC-4, 1 DC-6	HKG-BKK-CCU-KCH-KUL-LBU-MNL-PNH-RGN-SGN-SIN-VTE	12	(56) 42,417 (57) 41,653	546,011 577,744
1958	1 DC-3, 1 DC-4, 1 DC-6 1 DC-6B	HKG-BKK-CCU-KCH-KUL-LBU-MNL-PNH-RGN-SGN-SIN-VTE	12	49,044	560,174

Year	Aircraft	Route			
1959	1 DC-3, 1 DC-4, 1 DC-6B, 2 Electras	HKG-BKK-CCU-DRW-KCH-KUL-LBU-MNL-PNH-RGN-SGN-SIN-SYD-TPE-TYO-VTE	16	68,929	769,487
1960	1 DC-3, 1 DC-4, 1 DC-6B, 2 Electras	HKG-BKK-BTN-CCU-DRW-KCH-KUL-LBU-MNL-OSA-PNH-RGN-SEL-SGN-SIN-SYD-TPE-TYO-VTE	19	99,645	1,038,447
1961	1 DC-3, 1 DC-4, 1 DC-6B, 2 Electras	HKN-BKK-BTN-CCU-DRW-JES-JKT-KUL-MNL-OSA-PNH-RGN-SEL-SGN-SIN-SYD-TPE-TYO-VTE	19	112,500	1,189,068
1962	1 DC-4, 1 DC-6, 1 DC-6B, 2 Electras 1 CV880	HKG-BKK-BTN-CCU-JES-JKT-KUL-MNL-OSA-PNH-RGN-SEL-SGN-SIN-TPE-TYO-VTE	17	143,271	1,489,108
1963	2 Electras, 1 CV880	HKG-BKK-BTN-CCU-JES-JKT-KUL-MNL-OSA-PNH-RGN-SEL-SGN-SIN-TPE-TYO-VTE	17	170,304	1,839,164
1964	2 Electras, 1 CV880	HKG-BKK-BTN-CCU-JES-JKT-KUL-MNL-OSA-PNH-RGN-SEL-SGN-SIN-TPE-TYO	16	194,773	1,973,672
1965	1 Electra, 2 CV880	HKG-BKK-BTN-CCU-FUK-JES-KUL-MNL-OSA-PNH-RGN-SEL-SGN-SIN-TPE-TYO-VTE	17	237,601	2,411,297
1966	3 CV880, 1 Electra	HKG-BKK-BTN-CCU-FUK-JES-KUL-MNL-NGO-OSA-PNH-SEL-SGN-SIN-TPE-TYO-VTE	17	296,827	2,984,570
1967	5 CV880	HKG-BKK-CCU-FUK-JES-BKI-KUL-MNL-NGO-OKA-OSA-PNH-SEL-SGN-SIN-TPE-TYO	16	324,297	3,521,235
1968	5 CV880	HKG-BKI-BKK-CCU-FUK-KUL-MNL-NGO-OKA-OSA-PNH-SEL-SGN-SIN-TPE-TYO	16	417,849	4,654,264
1969	6 CV880	HKG-BKI-BKK-CCU-FUK-JKT-KUL-MNL-OKA-OSA-PNH-SEL-SGN-SIN-TPE-TYO	16	504,369	5,646,304
1970	8 CV880	HKG-BKI-BKK-CCU-FUK-JKT-KUL-MNL-OSA-PER-SEL-SGN-SIN-TPE-TYO	15	583,607	6,171,273
1971	8 CV880 1 B707	HKG-BKI-BKK-DPS-FUK-JKT-KUL-MNL-OSA-PER-SEL-SGN-SIN-TPE-TYO	15	653,244	7,852,056
1972	7 CV880 3 B707	HKG-BKI-BKK-DPS-FUK-JKT-KUL-MNL-OSA-PER-SEL-SGN-SIN-TPE-TYO	15	827,737	14,378,262

Year	Aircraft at end of year	Destinations	Port	Pax	Cargo (Kgs)
1973	7 CV880 4 B707	HKG-BKI-BKK-BWN-FUK-JKT-KUL-MNL-OSA-PER-SEL-SGN-SIN-TPE-TYO	15	1,100,750	24,946,323
1974	7 CV880 11 B707	HKG-BKI-BKK-BWN-FUK-JKT-KUL-MNL-OSA-PER-SEL-SGN-SIN-SYD-TPE-TYO	16	1,260,663	31,924,011
1975	2 L1011 TriStars 12 B707	HKG-BKI-BKK-BWN-FUK-JKT-KUL-MNL-OSA-PER-SEL-SGN-SIN-SYD-TPE-TYO	16	1,491,364	37,380,947
1976	3 L1011 TriStars 12 B707	HKG-BAH-BKI-BKK-BWN-FUK-JKT-KUL-MEL-MNL-OSA-PER-SEL-SIN-SYD-TPE-TYO	17	1,682,137	48,442,291
1977	6 L1011 TriStars 10 B707	HKG-BAH-BKI-BKK-BWN-DRW-DXB-FUK-JKT-KUL-MEL-MNL-OSA-PEN-PER-SEL-SIN-SYD-TPE-TYO	20	1,891,197	58,690,430
1978	8 L1011 TriStars 8 B707	HKG-BAH-BKI-BKK-BWN-DRW-DXB-FUK-JKT-KHH-KUL-MEL-MNL-NGO-OSA-PEN-PER-POM-SEL-SIN-SYD-TPE-TYO	23	2,315,080	74,244,073
1979	1 B747-200B 9 L1011 TriStars 7 B707	HKG-BAH-BKI-BKK-BWN-DRW-DXB-FUK-JKT-KHH-KUL-MEL-MNL-NGO-OSA-PEN-PER-POM-SEL-SIN-SYD-TPE-TYO	23	2,629,536	86,229,796
1980	4 B747-200B 9 L1011 TriStars 4 B707	HKG-BAH-BKI-BKK-BWN-DRW-DXB-FUK-JKT-KHH-KUL-LON-MEL-MNL-NGO-OSA-PEN-PER-SEL-SHA-SIN-SYD-TPE-TYO	24	2,879,683	92,005,411
1981	5 B747-200B 9 L1011 TriStars 4 B707	HKG-AUH-BAH-BKI-BKK-BWN-DXB-FUK-JKT-KHH-KUL-LON-MEL-MNL-OSA-PEN-PER-SEL-SHA-SIN-SYD-TPE-TYO	23	3,094,722	97,152,000
1982	6 B474-200B 1 B747 Freighter 9 L1011 TriStars 2 B707	HKG-AKL-AUH-BAH-BKI-BKK-BNE-BOM-BWN-DXB-FUK-JKT-KHH-KUL-LON-MEL-MNL-OSA-PEN-PER-POM-SEL-SHA-SIN-SYD-TPE-TYO	27	3,319,076	105,450,000

Year	Fleet	Routes			
1983	7 B747-200B 1 B747 Freighter 9 L1011 TriStars	HKG-AKL-AUH-BAH-BKI-BKK-BNE-BOM-DHA-DXB-FRA-FUK-JKT-KHH-KUL-LON-MEL-MNL-OSA-PEN-POM-SEL-SHA-SIN-SYD-TPE-TYO-YVR	29	3,224,102	130,522,000
1984	8 B747-200B 1 B747 Freighter 9 L1011 TriStars	HKG-AKL-AUH-BAH-BKI-BKK-BNE-BOM-DHA-DXB-FRA-FUK-JKT-KHH-KUL-LON-MEL-MNL-OSA-PEN-POM-SEL-SHA-SIN-SYD-TPE-TYO-YVR	29	3,550,130	148,454,000
1985	1 B747-300 8 B747-200B 1 B747 Freighter 9 L1011 TriStars	HKG-AUH-BAH-BKI-BKK-BNE-BOM-BWN-DHA-DXB-FRA-FUK-JKT-KHH-KUL-LON-MEL-MNL-OSA-PEN-PER-SEL-SHA-SIN-SYD-TPE-TYO-YVR	28	3,850,150	159,228,000
1986	3 B747-300 8 B747-200B 1 B747 Freighter 9 L1011 TriStars	HKG-AMS-AUH-AKL-BAH-BKK-BOM-BNE-BWN-DPS-DHA-DXB-FRA-FUK-JKT-KHH-BKI-KUL-LON-MNL-MEL-NGO-OSA-PEK-PAR-PEN-PER-ROM-SFO-SEL-SHA-SIN-TPE-TYO-SYD-YVR	36	4,197,771	192,627,000
1987	5 B747-300 8 B747-200B 2 B747 Freighters 10 L1011 TriStars	HKG-AMS-AUH-AKL-BAH-BKK-BOM-BNE-BWN-DPS-DHA-DXB-FRA-FUK-JKT-KHH-BKI-KUL-LON-MNL-MEL-NGO-OSA-PEK-PAR-PEN-PER-ROM-SFO-SEL-SHA-SIN-TPE-TYO-SYD-YVR	36	5,085,825	219,562,447
1988	6 B747-300 8 B747-200B 2 B747 Freighters 12 L1011 TriStars	HKG-AMS-AUH-AKL-BAH-BKK-BOM-BNE-BWN-DPS-DHA-DXB-FRA-FUK-JKT-KHH-BKI-KUL-LON-MNL-MEL-NGO-OSA-PEK-PAR-PEN-PER-ROM-SFO-SEL-SHA-SIN-TPE-TYO-SYD-YVR-ZRH	37	5,686,470	245,049,575
1989	3 B747-400 6 B747-300 8 B747-200B 2 B747 Freighters 16 L1011 TriStars	HKG-AMS-AUH-AKL-BAH-BKK-BOM-BNE-BWN-DPS-DHA-DXB-FRA-FUK-JKT-KHH-BKI-KUL-LON-MAN*-MNL-MEL-NGO-OSA-PEK-PAR-PEN-PER-ROM-SFO-SEL-SHA-SIN-TPE-TYO-SYD-YVR-ZRH	38	(7,000,000) Estimate	(270,000,000) Estimate

* From October 1989.

Code Key:

AKL – Auckland
AMS – Amsterdam
AUH – Abu Dhabi
BAH – Bahrain
BKI – Kota Kinabalu
BKK – Bangkok
BNE – Brisbane
BOM – Bombay
BTN – Brunei town
(now BWN – Bandar Seri Begawan)
CCU – Calcutta
DPS – Denpasar (Bali)
DHA – Dhahran
DRW – Darwin
DXB – Dubai
FRA – Frankfurt
HKG – Hong Kong

HNO – Hanoi
HPH – Haiphong
JES – Jesselton (now BKI – Kota Kinabalu)
JKT – Jakarta
KCH – Kuching
KHH – Kaohsiung
KUL – Kuala Lumpur
LBU – Labuan
LON – London
MCO* – Macau
MNL – Manila
MEL – Melbourne
NGO – Nagoya
PAR – Paris
PNH – Phnom Penh
PEN – Penang
POM – Port Moresby

OSA – Osaka
OKA – Okinawa
PER – Perth
RGN – Rangoon
ROM – Rome
SFO – San Francisco
SHA – Shanghai
SIN – Singapore
SGN – Saigon
SDK – Sandakan
SYD – Sydney
SEL – Seoul
TYO – Tokyo
TPE – Taipei
VTE – Vientiane
YVR – Vancouver
*(No official code)

238

Index

FOR THE BEST IN PAPERBACKS, LOOK FOR THE

In every corner of the world, on every subject under the sun, Penguin represents quality and variety – the very best in publishing today.

For complete information about books available from Penguin – including Pelicans, Puffins, Peregrines and Penguin Classics – and how to order them, write to us at the appropriate address below. Please note that for copyright reasons the selection of books varies from country to country.

In the United Kingdom: Please write to *Dept E.P., Penguin Books Ltd, Harmondsworth, Middlesex, UB7 0DA*

If you have any difficulty in obtaining a title, please send your order with the correct money, plus ten per cent for postage and packaging, to *PO Box No 11, West Drayton, Middlesex*

In the United States: Please write to *Dept BA, Penguin, 299 Murray Hill Parkway, East Rutherford, New Jersey 07073*

In Canada: Please write to *Penguin Books Canada Ltd, 2801 John Street, Markham, Ontario L3R 1B4*

In Australia: Please write to the *Marketing Department, Penguin Books Australia Ltd, P.O. Box 257, Ringwood, Victoria 3134*

In New Zealand: Please write to the *Marketing Department, Penguin Books (NZ) Ltd, Private Bag, Takapuna, Auckland 9*

In India: Please write to *Penguin Overseas Ltd, 706 Eros Apartments, 56 Nehru Place, New Delhi, 110019*

In Holland: Please write to *Penguin Books Nederland B.V., Postbus 195, NL–1380AD Weesp, Netherlands*

In Germany: Please write to *Penguin Books Ltd, Friedrichstrasse 10–12, D–6000 Frankfurt Main 1, Federal Republic of Germany*

In Spain: Please write to *Longman Penguin España, Calle San Nicolas 15, E–28013 Madrid, Spain*

In France: Please write to *Penguin Books Ltd, 39 Rue de Montmorency, F-75003, Paris, France*

In Japan: Please write to *Longman Penguin Japan Co Ltd, Yamaguchi Building, 2–12–9 Kanda Jimbocho, Chiyoda-Ku, Tokyo 101, Japan*

FOR THE BEST IN PAPERBACKS, LOOK FOR THE 🐧

A CHOICE OF PENGUINS

Trail of Havoc Patrick Marnham

In this brilliant piece of detective work, Patrick Marnham has traced the steps of Lord Lucan from the fateful night of 7 November 1974 when he murdered his children's nanny and attempted to kill his ex-wife. As well as being a fascinating investigation, the book is also a brilliant portrayal of a privileged section of society living under great stress.

Light Years Gary Kinder

Eduard Meier, an uneducated Swiss farmer, claims since 1975 to have had over 100 UFO sightings and encounters with 'beamships' from the Pleiades. His evidence is such that even the most die-hard sceptics have been unable to explain away the phenomenon.

And the Band Played On Politics, People and the AIDS Epidemic
Randy Shilts

Written after years of extensive research by the only American journalist to cover the epidemic full-time, *And the Band Played On* is a masterpiece of reportage and a tragic record of mismanaged institutions and scientific vendettas, of sexual politics and personal suffering.

The Return of a Native Reporter Robert Chesshyre

Robert Chesshyre returned to Britain in 1985 from the United States, where he had spent four years as the *Observer*'s correspondent. This is his devastating account of the country he came home to: intolerant, brutal, grasping and politically and economically divided. It is a nation, he asserts, struggling to find a role.

Women and Love Shere Hite

In this culmination of *The Hite Report* trilogy, 4,500 women provide an eloquent testimony to the disturbingly unsatisfying nature of their emotional relationships and point to what they see as the causes. *Women and Love* reveals a new cultural perspective in formation: as women change the emotional structure of their lives, they are defining a fundamental debate over the future of our society.

A CHOICE OF PENGUINS

The Russian Album   Michael Ignatieff

Michael Ignatieff movingly comes to terms with the meaning of his own family's memories and histories, in a book that is both an extraordinary account of the search for roots and a dramatic and poignant chronicle of four generations of a Russian family.

Beyond the Blue Horizon   Alexander Frater

The romance and excitement of the legendary Imperial Airways East-bound Empire service – the world's longest and most adventurous scheduled air route – relived fifty years later in one of the most original travel books of the decade. 'The find of the year' – *Today*

Getting to Know the General   Graham Greene

'In August 1981 my bag was packed for my fifth visit to Panama when the news came to me over the telephone of the death of General Omar Torrijos Herrera, my friend and host...' 'Vigorous, deeply felt, at times funny, and for Greene surprisingly frank' – *Sunday Times*

The Search for the Virus   Steve Connor and Sharon Kingman

In this gripping book, two leading *New Scientist* journalists tell the remarkable story of how researchers discovered the AIDS virus and examine the links between AIDS and lifestyles. They also look at the progress being made in isolating the virus and finding a cure.

Arabian Sands   Wilfred Thesiger

'In the tradition of Burton, Doughty, Lawrence, Philby and Thomas, it is, very likely, the book about Arabia to end all books about Arabia' – *Daily Telegraph*

Adieux: A Farewell to Sartre   Simone de Beauvoir

A devastatingly frank account of the last years of Sartre's life, and his death, by the woman who for more than half a century shared that life. 'A true labour of love, there is about it a touching sadness, a mingling of the personal with the impersonal and timeless which Sartre himself would surely have liked and understood' – *Listener*

FOR THE BEST IN PAPERBACKS, LOOK FOR THE 🐧

A CHOICE OF PENGUINS

Riding the Iron Rooster   Paul Theroux

An eye-opening and entertaining account of travels in old and new China, from the author of *The Great Railway Bazaar*. 'Mr Theroux cannot write badly ... in the course of a year there was almost no train in the vast Chinese rail network on which he did not travel' – Ludovic Kennedy

The Markets of London   Alex Forshaw and Theo Bergstrom

From Camden Lock and Columbia Road to Petticoat Lane and Portobello Road, from the world-famous to the well-kept secrets, here is the ultimate guide to London's markets: as old, as entertaining and as diverse as the capital itself.

The Chinese   David Bonavia

'I can think of no other work which so urbanely and entertainingly succeeds in introducing the general Western reader to China' – *Sunday Telegraph*. 'Strongly recommended' – *The Times Literary Supplement*

The Diary of Virginia Woolf
Five volumes edited by Quentin Bell and Anne Olivier Bell

'As an account of intellectual and cultural life of our century, Virginia Woolf's diaries are invaluable; as the record of one bruised and unquiet mind, they are unique' – Peter Ackroyd in the *Sunday Times*

Voices of the Old Sea   Norman Lewis

'I will wager that *Voices of the Old Sea* will be a classic in the literature about Spain' – *Mail on Sunday*. 'Limpidly and lovingly, Norman Lewis has caught the helpless, unwitting, often foolish, but always hopeful village in its dying summers, and saved the tragedy with sublime comedy' – *Observer*

Ninety-Two Days   Evelyn Waugh

With characteristic honesty, Evelyn Waugh here debunks the romantic notions attached to rough travelling. His journey in Guiana and Brazil is difficult, dangerous and extremely uncomfortable, and his account of it is witty and unquestionably compelling.

BY THE SAME AUTHOR

'Intrepid, reflective and gregarious ... plainly a man in a million and a writer in two' – Bernard Levin in the *Observer*

Return to the Marshes

A remarkable portrait of the remote and beautiful world of the Marsh Arabs.

'A superbly written essay which combines warmth of personal tone, a good deal of easy historical scholarship and a talent for vivid description rarely found outside good fiction' – Jonathan Raban in the *Sunday Times*

Slow Boats to China

Gavin Young's bestselling account of his extraordinary journey in small boats through the Mediterranean, the Red Sea, the Indian Ocean and the Malaya and China Seas to China.

Slow Boats Home

'I am decidedly envious of Gavin Young and his *Slow Boats Home*, successor to his highly entertaining *Slow Boats to China* ... a fascinating, memorable book' – Eric Newby in the *Guardian*

'Like *Slow Boats to China* this is likely to become a classic of travel' – Francis King in the *Spectator*

Worlds Apart

A collection of journalistic pieces that are elegant, vivid and compassionate and show Gavin Young's acute understanding of the varied worlds in which we live.

'Some have to travel dangerously and it had better be Gavin Young to tell us about it' – Anthony Blond in the *Spectator*